Cuban-American Literature and Art

SUNY series in Latin American and Iberian Thought and Culture

Jorge J. E. Gracia and Rosemary Geisdorfer Feal, editors

Cuban-American Literature and Art

NEGOTIATING IDENTITIES

Edited by
Isabel Alvarez Borland
and
Lynette M. F. Bosch

State University of New York Press

Cover art: *El Arte sín historia* (2001), by Carlos Estévez. Courtesy of the artist.

Published by State University of New York Press, Albany

Printed in the United States of America

For information, contact State University of New York Press, Albany, NY
www.sunypress.edu

Production by Dana Foote
Marketing by Michael Campochiaro

Library of Congress Cataloging-in-Publication Data

Cuban-American literature and art : negotiating identities / edited by Isabel Alvarez Borland and Lynette M. F. Bosch.
p. cm. — (SUNY series in Latin American and Iberian thought and culture)
Includes bibliographical references and index.
ISBN 978-0-7914-9373-1 (hc: alk. paper)
ISBN 978-0-7914-9374-8 (pbk.: alk.paper)
1. American literature—Cuban American authors—History and criticism. 2. Cuban American art. 3. Cuban Americans—Intellectual life. 4. Identity (Psychology) in literature. 5. Identity (Psychology) in art. I. Alvarez-Borland, Isabel. II. Bosch, Lynette M. F.
PS153.C83C83 2009
860—dc22

2008017298

10 9 8 7 6 5 4 3 2 1

In memory of
Carlos Alvarez Santalís (1920–2006)
Antonio A. Bosch y Cabezola (1924–2000)

The old ones came from the sea and the people on land, the ones who lived here, let them in. But later, the ones from the land argued with the sea people and changed their minds and tried to push them back into the ocean . . . Then the ones from the sea drove the land people out and established themselves here and planted it all with palm trees. Little by little, without them realizing it, their scales and fins began to fall off, and their children didn't want to live close to the water nor hunt shrimp, and the old ones began dying of sadness because they could no longer return to the sea even if they wanted to . . . and at the very end they lost their gills. This was the curse that had been put on them by the ones from land.

—Roberto G. Fernández, *Raining Backwards*

CONTENTS

Part Two • The Art

ACKNOWLEDGMENTS

The editors are deeply grateful to all of the scholars in art and literature who generously contributed their insightful essays to this collection. We especially thank Gustavo, Adriana, Jorge F., Willy, Iraida, Eliana, Mark, Carol, Jorge G., and Andrea. We thank Carlos Estévez for his permission to use one of his works for the cover. Roberto Fernández was generous with his sensitive wit and we thank him for giving us our origins in epigraphic form. Carlos Eire's prose and Laura Imayo Tartakoff's poem provided a moving portrait of divided lives. We are indebted to Jorge Gracia whose NEH idea and enthusiasm about this topic made our collaboration and this volume possible.

This manuscript could have never been a book without the invaluable help of Mary Morrisard-Larkin and Danielle Bacon, of the Holy Cross Educational Technology Group; as well as Larin McLaughlin, acquisitions editor, Dana Foote, production editor, and Kay Butler, copyeditor, at State University of New York Press. Finally, our special thanks to Kermit Borland and Charles Burroughs who read and commented on parts of this book at various stages in its composition. We appreciate their patience with the tribe of *Cubanos* who have paraded through their lives as a result of our work.

Introduction

Isabel Alvarez Borland and Lynette M. F. Bosch

> *The Chinese horn within Cuban carnival music entails a complex historical mystery: the arrival of the Chinese in Cuba, the cruel exploitation of this ethnic group, the acculturation of the group to the criollo ways of life, its desire for emancipation, and the contributions of the Chinese during the years of the Cuban Republic.*
>
> —Antonio Benítez Rojo, "Carnaval de Ideas"

For Antonio Benítez Rojo, the presence of the Chinese horn in Cuban carnival music represents a cultural encounter that offers unique and invaluable information not only about the evolution of Cuban music, but also about the stages of the formation of the Cuban nation. The author of *The Repeating Island* observes that the anomalous presence of the *corneta china* in Cuban music of the nineteenth century speaks at once of the history, economy, and sociology of the Chinese as an ethnic group within the island of Cuba: "What had to occur in order to incorporate the rough and out of tune sound of the Chinese horn into a rhythm which was basically African was the closeness of the Chinese and the African men in the sugar plantations of the last century" (Interview by Stavans 22). The cultural juxtapositions that Antonio Benítez Rojo mentions in his commentary on the *corneta china* are not only applicable to the Cuban nation, but also permeate the sensibility of today's Cuban-American cultural production wherein diverse ethnic and racial groups (European, African, Asian, Jewish) blend to form a fluid identity traceable to Cuban cultural and societal patterns.

Much like the dissonant sounds of the Chinese horn in the music of Cuban carnival, the narratives and visual representations of U.S. artists and writers of Cuban heritage analyzed in this volume contain within themselves the sometimes disharmonious experience of a divided identity. In fact, the work of the writers and visual artists we analyze here exhibits a sensibility that is highly creative, but which is at times tragic and fractured because it is born from the precarious balance caused by the mixing of two very different cultural traditions that have coexisted in U.S. territory since the 1959 revolution. Most significantly, these Cuban-American fictions and works of art internalize crucial moments in the history of Cuba's last forty years: dictatorship, exile, and multiple migratory waves.

Because of the ethnic, racial, and cultural diversity of the groups who came or were brought to the island, cultural pluralism is a marker of Cuban and Cuban-American identity. Afro-Cubans and Chinese Cubans were two groups that influenced Cuban culture, alongside the immigrants from Spain and other European countries. Cuba also had a significant Jewish population. As these groups met and mixed to differing degrees, their individual and group contributions to Cuban culture were brought to the United States by exiles and immigrants from the island. Since the nineteenth century new arrivals from Cuba continue to change the tenor and meaning of the cultural synthesis that defines *lo cubano-americano*, an ever-shifting concept of identity defined by time, place, class, race, and ethnicity within an American matrix.

Cuban-American writers, poets, and artists thus embody a microcosmic portrait of Cuban and American society in which individual artists choose their expository territory. Within this microcosm, a shift in emphasis provides a shift in meaning in the process of defining or designing that which is Cuban or that which is Cuban-American, or for that matter, that which is American. Recording the meaning of these transformations has been the purview of the writers, poets, and artists studied in this volume. Together, they have given voice to the reality of the thresholds they occupy as Cubans and Americans living within the continuum created by their bicultural identities. At times, the essays in this collection may reflect tension, reconciliation, or even a balance between these markers of identity.

The art and the literature of Cuban America contain the fluidity and elusiveness that characterize the Cuban national quest for identity since the second half of the nineteenth century (Ciani Forza 53). A sense of the metaphysical absence of a nation, and a need to reconceptualize it from within is evident in the intellectual history of the island not only in the nineteenth-century writings of Jose Martí ("*Nuestra América*," 1891), but also in the twentieth-century treatise of Fernando Ortiz (*Contrapunteo del tabaco y el azúcar*, 1940) and the essays of Jorge Mañach (*Historia y estilo*, 1944). Ortiz, a Cuban ethnologist, was one of the first to truly bring to the forefront the African roots of Cuban culture. His seminal study of Cuban identity coins the word *transculturación* and defines this neologism as a transmutation of cultures that is essential to understanding Cuban culture. Abandoning the more accepted theory of *aculturación*—which for the author implied an imbalance between cultures—Ortiz sees *transculturación* as a slow process that is historical and cultural at once and provides a vision of Cuban culture as a process or as an unfinished synthesis.

Contrapunteo's central thesis sets up a counterpoint between what Ortiz thinks is truly Cuban—tobacco—versus sugar, a crop marked by dependency in foreign markets, and a symbol of both Spanish and North American interventions. Ortiz's well-known metaphor of Cuban identity as an *ajiaco*, or stew—a term that aptly described the heterogeneity and mix of cultures that defined Cuban identity—became a point of departure for the conceptualization of Cuban identity in exile in the theoretical work of those who followed him. In 1989, two crucial texts informed by the premises of Ortiz's *Contrapunteo* are published in the United States: Antonio Benítez Rojo's *La isla que se repite* (trans. *The Repeating Island*, 1990) and Gustavo Pérez Firmat's *The Cuban Condition*, a work written originally in English.

In *La isla que se repite*, Benítez uncovers a way of conceiving the region that includes folklore, African religions, Caribbean music, and dance creating a multidisciplinary analysis that seeks to explore the entire Caribbean's complex and syncretic culture. For Benítez Rojo, the Caribbean was both plural and chaotic. And if Ortiz had coined the *ajiaco* as his preferred metaphor for Cuban identity, Benítez Rojo's real and metaphoric "archipelago" rounds out this author's conception of what he described as the unique identity and character of the Caribbean region:

> The culture of archipelagoes is not terrestrial, as are almost all cultures: it is fluvial and marine. We are dealing here with a culture of bearings, not of routes; of approximations, not of exactitudes. Here the world of straight lines and angles (the wedge, the inclined plane, the intersection) does not dominate; here rules the fluid world of the curving line. (93)

Also drawing from the premises of Fernando Ortiz, albeit from a different generational perspective than Benítez Rojo's, Pérez Firmat's *The Cuban Condition* transposes Ortiz's concepts of "transculturation" to his own exiled generation. In *The Cuban Condition*, Pérez Firmat stresses the imperfection and heterogeneity of Cuban culture. The book examines the period of what has been called a "nation without nationhood" allowing its author to see his own *cubanía* as involving a similar displacement. Observes Pérez Firmat:

> While I was writing this book, it often occurred to me that its underlying theme was scriptive survival. My discussions of Fernando Ortiz or Nicolas Guillén or Eugenio Florit or Carlos Loveira are, in a deep sense, inquiries into how these authors survived as writers . . . My desire to demonstrate the centrality of translation in Cuban criollist literature cannot but reflect an attempt to legitimize and place my own work . . . The fate of the Cuban writer, the feat of the Cuban writer, has always been to find himself in others' words. (15)

In his study of Ortiz's works, Pérez Firmat describes the mechanism of translation as an intertextual transculturation process and as a highly sophisticated form of parody. As the author avers, it is through textuality and not scholarship that Ortiz reached for *lo criollo* through the play with imagery. Pérez Firmat sees his own *cubanía* as involving this kind of displacement and sees Cuban—*and U.S. Cuban literature*—as essentially the product of transculturation, assimilation, and adaptation (translation).

It is thus quite relevant to our collection that *La isla que se repite* and *The Cuban Condition*, central treatises on Cuban identity, were written, not in Cuba, but in exile. More recently, intellectuals exiled from Cuba as a result of the Período Especial (1990–1995) such as Rafael Rojas (*El arte de la espera*, 1998) and Antonio José Ponte (*Por los años de Orígenes*, 2001)—the latter lived in Cuba until 2007, although his works have been published abroad—continue to analyze the elusiveness of Cuban identity and the prevailing theme of a historically absent Cuban nation, a nation promised but never delivered.

As the studies of Benitez Rojo and Pérez Firmat suggest, there is no one true marker of *lo cubano* or *lo cubano-americano*. Instead, there are varying combinations of the European, the Latin American, the African, the Indian, and the Asian identities that created Cuba and subsequently Cuban America. In transforming themselves, Cuban-Americans effect change in mainstream American culture as they become part of its life and its institutions. It is this process of mutual influence that contributes to the American "mosaic," an immigration paradigm not unlike Ortiz's Cuban *ajiaco*.

Our collection of essays forms part of a cultural panorama that is larger than any of its parts, yet finds its base in cultural studies concerned with the intersection of personal and ethnic identity. The essays presented in this volume address the idea of cultural pluralism from a variety of perspectives. In some essays, the critic is self-reflective, yet in others, he or she functions as an observer. Throughout these pieces, the goal is to explore the concept of identity or identities through the specific filter of the Cuban and Cuban-American paradigm. The editors of this collection are aware that identity is not a fixed, easily defined concept and the contributors have made the most of this freedom. From diverse perspectives, the essays gathered in this volume explore the relation between memory, exile, immigration, and identity as cultural productions in literature and art. By engaging such issues as hybrid identities, biculturation, bilingualism, immigration, adaptation, and exile, their contributions offer readers an opportunity to learn about crucial issues pertinent not only to Cuban-American cultural production, but also to other immigrant groups. While these pieces deal in depth with literary and visual texts by contemporary Cuban-American artists and writers, they also explore issues that go beyond the confines of the Cuban-American case.

All of the essays found in this volume agree that the expression of identity is a changing process, yet, there are always recurring themes and concerns. Defining these markers of identity and applying them to the larger group so that the peripheries and the center could be linked is the process that guided the scholarly work of our contributors. Although focused on Cuban and Cuban-American identity, this volume aspires to make an intervention in an area of cultural study that is interdisciplinary, cross-cultural, and reflective of diversity.

Thus, we hope that this volume can act as an indexical marker for *one* American identity that is constantly changing.

The Literature

Cuban-American literature is a field very much in the process of being delineated and discovered as is attested by the number of anthologies and creative works published in the United States in the last two decades. This fertile publishing boom leads us to ponder the relationship of Cuban-American literature in English to that of peer communities of writers publishing in the United States today; namely, that amorphous grouping constituted by other U.S. Latino/Hispanic writers. Given the separate histories and diverse experiences of Mexican Americans, Puerto Ricans, and Cuban-Americans—to name only the three major groups of writers of Spanish heritage residing in the United States today—it is not surprising to find that each represents quite a distinct literary expression. If asked about personal identity, few Cuban-American writers would identify themselves as Latino or Hispanic writers. The dilemma of labeling these writers as Latinos or Hispanics runs deeper than mere pride of origin (Oboler 1–17). When Latinos or Hispanics look at each other they see Chicanos, Puerto Ricans, Cubans, Dominicans, and so on.

How Latino or Hispanic is the Cuban-American text? Cuban-American literature seems to be less concerned with issues of political advocacy than its Chicano or Puerto Rican counterparts. These groups write a literature of political engagement, speaking of issues in their lives as minority groups within American society. Compared to the ideological dimension associated with these literatures, the Cuban-American corpus as a whole has not displayed a clearly delineated political stance. Nevertheless Cuban-American male writers have concentrated mainly on issues of self-understanding rather than political activism whereas the fictions and personal writings of Cuban-American women writers such as Cristina García and Achy Obejas, for example, consistently include issues related to minority politics, gender issues, and womens' rights.

As with all ethnic literatures in English, a key issue in the study of these English narratives of Cuban heritage has to do with the English tradition itself and with the interactions between ethnic literatures and American culture. In *A Double Exile*, West Indian scholar Gareth Griffith asserts that writers writing in a language other than their own have two traditions in their background: the poetic tradition of their native countries as well as the tradition of their language of choice. In order to achieve an individual style, the writer must balance the problems of both linguistic traditions (57). According to Griffith: "Ethnic writers can borrow from more than one tradition, and this borrowing itself renews the possibilities of English" (144). The author further points out that any writer who is totally fluent in two languages and two cultures has the potential to change the perception of the English reality while still remaining in English. Thus when a non-English culture and the English language combine, the possibility to change the perception of reality as experienced by English native speakers occurs: "although the language employed is English, the experience recorded is not, and that new experience may profoundly alter the language and the form employed" (141).

A central concern with the internal and external dimensions of identity unifies a group of literary studies that ranges from traditional treatments of the subject to innovative discussions about identity and its ramifications in U.S. literature of Cuban heritage. Some essays are concerned with the forging of a new identity as reflected thematically in the fiction. In these essays the concept of identity might depend on the relationship between a fictional character and author or between author and reader. Other essays meditate on the fluidity of identity shown in the writing of Cuban-American women and explore their struggle for recognition. Still others, search for the hidden relationships between language and cultural identity. The writers chosen for analysis range from canonical figures to emerging writers, from Cabrera Infante who was one of the first exiles to publish outside Cuba, to figures such as Ana Menéndez now gaining recognition for the significance of her contributions.

Our topics span from examining the literature of identity to exploring the identity of individual texts. The essays by Adriana Méndez Rodenas, Eliana Rivero, and Iraida H. López deal with issues of feminism, gender, and matriarchy. In their panoramic studies both Rivero and Iraida López argue for a fluidity of identity in the writing of women, an identity that is not necessarily easily defined in that it is contextual and always unstable. And while Méndez Rodenas explores the relevance of the mother-daughter bond in the formation of Cuban-American identity, López analyzes the character and essence of personal essays written by Cuban-American women and relates their rhetorical qualities to the genre of the "*manifesto*" or proclamation.

Several studies featured in our volume are devoted to explorations of the work of specific authors. In pieces such "Am I your worst nightmare?" critic Jorge Febles demonstrates how Roberto Fernández's authority as creator is challenged by his own characters and how investigating the relationship between author and character allows readers to confront or examine their own identities. In some instances authorial identity is of primary concern as when Gustavo Pérez Firmat analyzes his own poetry in "The Spell of the Hyphen" or when William Luis analyzes the photographs that appear in Pérez Firmat's *Next Year in Cuba.* Finally, Alvarez Borland's "Figures of Identity" looks at photos and engravings in Cabrera Infante and Ana Menéndez and explores how the continued presence of inner images and texts in their novels invites us to study the photograph as a trope of identity by which the Cuban-American narrative tradition seeks to define itself.

In order to engage such a diversity of topics, the studies included in this treatise adopt distinct critical approaches that range from panoramic vistas of a genre to textual analyses of a specific work. Iraida H. López's incursion into the personal essays of Cuban-American women and Eliana Rivero's overview of the most recent publications by female Cuban-American writers are examples of this approach. These panoramas study a body of writing that began in the late 1970s and due to its changing character needs to be constantly updated and revised. Another approach used by our critics is to study the continuities between authors and texts. The aim here is less to track down sources or influences than to recover the uses to which a given author or text has been put by his or her successors. While some of the critics actually link the works via specific details, others chose to place the works side by side in order to elaborate thematic continuities. For example, Gustavo Pérez Firmat's survey of the poetry of several generations of Cuban-American writers becomes an exercise that allows the author to illustrate the thematics of absence across the generational divide. Alvarez Borland, Pérez Firmat, and Méndez Rodenas juxtapose the writings of a younger generation with that of older, more established writers in order to extricate patterns of writing or the meaning of a trope. By offering such a variety of critical methodologies, these essays explore how the Cuban-American writers think and imagine their community.

Cuban-American literature presents a fascinating challenge to any scholar who would attempt to study images of a concrete "home country" in their narratives. Exile has indeed proven to be a positive experience for the members of the second (and now third) generations as the physical distance from their geography and culture has led these writers to look anew at the values and traditions of Cuban culture. Rather than the usual immigrant back-and-forth journeys to and from the country of origin, for the Cuban-American writer the idea of country is truly an imaginary construct or a country that exists, in the words of Salman Rushdie, "at a slight angle to reality" (*Shame* 22). By incorporating their Cuban selves into their English selves, the writing of these authors becomes enriched and therefore their ability to create magnified.

The Art

> *The artist is different in that the artist is always able to retain the language of their specific creative impulse, yet the same in that dislocation causes a rupture beyond that language that only repetition, reconstruction and re-examination can begin to mend.*
>
> —Marguerite Bouvard, *Landscape and Exile*

It is impossible to reduce the work of Cuban-American artists active in the United States into a uniform group, yet all are joined by their need to explain how they came to be what they are and their desire to communicate their experience through their work. For Cuban-American artists, visual art gives form to the meaning of their experience, a meaning they construct from their individual perception of exile. Thus, Cuban-American artists have had to continually and continuously redefine their identity as they have sought to uncover their essential self within their split identities as Cubans and Americans.

For each artist, leading a double life has created a need to confront the spiritual implications inherent in the process of defining their identity, reconciling themselves to their fate and present situation, and confronting and resolving the conflicts that their divided lives present. Each artist has responded to this challenge in a different manner. The works of art of Cuban-American artists represent an original, cohesive, and intentional cultural movement within contemporary art. Hence, the work of the Cuban-American artists discussed in this volume should be understood as constituting a significant visual index of the experience of exile.

The essays that follow examine the work of these artists from a variety of perspectives. It is hoped that these studies will draw attention to the contributions the group has made to Cuban and American artistic culture, to twentieth- and twenty-first-century art, and to the universal experience of exile and its aftermath. Each artist discussed in this volume's essays has his or her own memories of the events that propelled their families into exile with the residue of anxiety, fear, and loss that is the result of their experience. The youngest members of the artists discussed here lack these memories, but they remember the stories of incidents told to them by their parents. It is this context that elevates their message beyond a specific and individual statement. Thus, the work of these artists represents a momentary breach in the separation of the self from the self and from the group.

The metamorphosis of trauma into creativity expressed in an artistic medium is not, as was discussed above, unique to Cuban-American artists, as their context places them within the developing cultural production of contemporary global exiles (Bouvard 14). As contemporary artists, Cuban-American artists share in the strong autobiographical element present in the works of the majority of twentieth-century visual artists, writers, and dramatists. It is this inward vision, reflective of personal concerns and experiences, that differentiates modern and contemporary art from the art of previous epochs. Within the personalized sphere of creativity defined by this autobiographical element, artists address their public from the intimacy of their private experiences and individual concerns in order to communicate the universal through the specific. Thus, their cumulative efforts have created a mirror of modern life defined by James Olney as being "intimate and public, psychological and cultural, individual and collective" (28). For Cuban-American artists, the circumstances of their displacement have created a need to, at times, withdraw from their present so that they can commune with their past. In so doing, they live not only "on the hyphen" but in a paradox created by the juncture of the competing realities within which they find their creative space. By giving voice to that which they carry within, Cuban-American artists internalize and integrate their psychic shock and emerge as whole and functioning members of the foreign culture to which they now owe allegiance.

The essays on Cuban and Cuban-American art included in this volume analyze the work of the selected Cuban-American artists from a variety of perspectives. Lynette Bosch's "From the Vanguardia to the United States: Cuban and Cuban-American Identity in the Visual Arts" traces the path taken by three distinct groups of artists: the Vanguardia, the post-Vanguardia, and those who arrived from Cuba as a result of the 1959 revolution, including those who arrived as adolescents in the 1960s. Her chapter considers how each group represents diverse ways of negotiating their identity through their visual compositions and the reasons for these changes in artistic expression. Through her exploration, Bosch establishes a paradigm of continuity and difference as a method for understanding the fluidly defined issue of identity and transformation found in Cuban and in Cuban-American art.

Carol Damian's "Cuban Artists and the Irony of Exile" explores the manner in which irony is used by some Cuban-American artists as a vehicle to express the irrationality and existential paradox of the exile condition and the bicultural experience. Damian selected a diverse group of artists, some who came to the United States as children or adolescents and those who came as adults in the 1990s in the aftermath of the collapse of the Soviet Union. Through anecdote, symbol, metaphor, and tongue-in-cheek visual play, each artist chosen by Damian explores the paradox of irony as a statement of resolution toward the establishment of a venue for negotiating identity.

Mark Denaci's essay "Challenging Orthodoxies: Cuban-American Art and Postmodernist Criticism" explores the manner in which Cuban-American artists negotiate their interaction in reaction against or acceptance of the American artistic mainstream. Denaci draws from Cuban-born artists who came to this country in the 1960s and 1970s as children and adolescents and from the group which came in the 1990s as adult, mature artists. As Denaci critiques the work of the individual artists he chose from each group, he explores how the definition of identity and its negotiation permeates another type of interaction with artistic identity—that of the modernist or postmodernist artist. The self-reflective attitude of the contemporary artist is taken into consideration by Denaci who seeks to understand the nature of the exchange between the Cuban-American identity and the identities of modernism and postmodernism in the context of the American art market. As Denaci addresses the work of each artist within this structure, he finds that some artists resist the absorption into the mainstream represented by each movement as an act of defiance of assimilation.

Jorge Gracia's chapter touches upon the relationship between philosophy and identity. His consideration of identity addresses the uneasy balance between essentialism and exceptionalism as he considers how each concept affects the selection and development of individual, group, and national identity. His consideration of how identity is developed through the consumption of food, the study of memory, and the collection of objects, photographs, or works of art, addresses the fundamental question of how to define "lo cubano."

Andrea O'Reilly Herrera's "Cuban Art in the Diaspora" concentrates on a particular group of artists, those who initiated *Café: The Journeys of Cuban Artists*, a multimedia, changing, and traveling exhibition meant to record the experiences of exiled Cuban artists. The goal of this exhibition is the establishment of a mosaic of impressions and artistic statements on how identity is defined, retained, negotiated, and altered in tension and balance. Because the exhibition travels, it forms and reforms itself in a physical manifestation of the geography of multiple identities. In her essay O'Reilly Herrera traces the development of an artistic phenomenon that articulates in visual form the complexity and transformative nature of identity.

Historian Louise Tilly argues for a two-stage process in the study of minority groups: an initial stage with the aim of identifying the contribution to history made by such groups; and, a second stage where their contribution is placed within a larger context of "analytical problem-solving that connects (this microhistory) to general questions already on the intellectual agenda" (441). Scholars who are Cuban-American engaged in the critical study of Cuban-American history, literature, philosophy, theater, art, music, and other aspects of Cuban and Cuban-American culture simultaneously become the examiner and the examined. Thus, the scholarly enterprise becomes a personal exercise in self-knowledge that transmutes the scholarly process into a personal search for information about the past that assists in reconciling that past with the present.

Because the editors—and a majority of the contributors to our collection—belong to the same generation as the Cuban-American artists and writers being studied, this book can be considered part of today's emergent field of ethnic American self-study. This enterprise in self-study challenges the critical distance that usually exists between the scholar and the subject under study. This paradoxical and sometimes even contradictory positioning is not, however, either new or unique to the study of Cuban and Cuban-American subjects by Cuban-American scholars. Yet, there is a difference in the manner in which this process occurs for Cuban-Americans (and others similarly exiled) whose scholarly work is also an attempt to reconstruct and to bridge the gap that is the result of exile. When this process is embarked upon for the purpose of discovering meaning in individual identity, it becomes endowed with an analytical subjectivity that transforms the essence of the scholarly process into a personalized odyssey meant to bring the scholar "home."

Negotiating identity—national, artistic, and ideological—is a fluid process of ever changing details. The following studies on Cuban-American art and literature point toward a production rich with allusion and recontextualization that signals the protean nature of the work of these artists who take on or off a variety of cultural garbs. Drawn from a variety of sources and reunited in a unique combination affected by their referent identities, the work of Cuban and Cuban-American writers and artists analyzed in this volume defies both total absorption and total separation from the American mainstream and its didactic modernity. As was the case with our original NEH project, a central goal of this volume is to encourage a dialogue with other current research in Cuban-American art and in literature. Viewed collectively, these scholarly pieces endeavor to create a context for further discussion of the links between Cuban-American contemporary art and Cuban-American literary expression.

WORKS CITED

Benítez Rojo, Antonio. *La isla que se repite*. Barcelona: Casiopea, 1998. *The Repeating Island*, trans. J. Maraniss, 1990.

Bouvard, Marguerite. *Landscape and Exile*. London: Rowan Tree, 1985.

Ciani Forza, Daniela M. "American-Cuban and Cuban-American: Hyphens of Identity." Ed. Susanna Regazzoni. *Alma cubana: Transculturación, mestizaje e hibridismo*. Frankfurt: Vervuert, 2006. 53–79.

Griffith, Gareth. *A Double Exile*. London: Marin Boyars, 1978.

Le Riverend, Julio. "Fernando Ortiz y su obra cubana." *Union* (1972): 119–49.

———. Fernando Ortiz en la historiografía cubana." *Anales del Caribe* 2 (1982): 45–60.

Mañach, Jorge. "El estilo en Cuba y su sentido histórico." *Historia y estilo*. Edición facsimilar. Miami: Editorial Cubana, 1944. 104–206.

Martí, José. "*Nuestra America*." In *José Martí: Selected Writings*. New York: Penguin Classics, 2002.

Oboler, Suzanne. *Ethnic Labels, Latino Lives: Identity and the Politics of Representation in the United States*. Minneapolis: University of Minnesota Press, 1995.

Olney, James. *Tell Me Africa*. Princeton: Princeton University Press, 1973.

Ortiz, Fernando. *Contrapunteo cubano del tabaco y el azúcar*. La Habana: Editorial de Ciencias Sociales, 1940.

Pérez Firmat, Gustavo. *The Cuban Condition: Translation and Identity in Modern Cuban Literature*. Cambridge: Cambridge University Press, 1989.

Rushdie, Salman. *Shame*. New York: Knopf, 1983.

Stavans, Ilan. "Carnaval de ideas: Una conversación con Antonio Benítez Rojo." *Apuntes Postmodernos* (Primavera/otoño 1996): 16–23. Translated by Isabel Alvarez Borland.

Tilly, Louise A. "Gender, Women's History, and Social History." *Social Science History* 13 (Winter 1989): 439–62.

PART ONE

THE LITERATURE

Eventually, I acquired English. It's mine. All mine. I bought it word by word, on credit, the American way. And English owns me, too. I think in English; I even dream in English . . . Spanish stopped growing and is now a homely misshapen dwarf. An all-wise and almost mystical dwarf, keeper of the keys to my soul . . .

—Carlos Eire, *Waiting for Snow in Havana*

1

The Spell of the Hyphen

Gustavo Pérez Firmat

The hyphen can play tricks on the unwary, as it did in Chattanooga when two newspapers merged—the News *and the* Free Press. *Someone introduced a hyphen into the merger, and the paper became* The Chattanooga News-Free Press, *which sounds as though the paper were news-free, or devoid of news. Obviously we ask too much of a hyphen when we ask it to cast its spell over words it does not adjoin.*

—Strunk and White, *The Elements of Style*

Years ago, in a book called *Life on the Hyphen* (1994), I attempted to do what Strunk and White warn against: I adjoined "Cuban" and "American." Ever since, I have not managed to dispel the spell of the hyphen. Unwary by nature and nationality, by temperament and tradition, I have continued to succumb to the hyphen's tricks, foremost among them the mirage of connectedness. For if the compound title of the Chattanooga daily turned it into a newspaper without news, in other situations a delinquent hyphen can manufacture the semblance of continuity between people or entities that, in reality, have little in common. Is there such a thing as a "Cuban-American Way," as the subtitle of my book proclaimed? Have American-born or American-raised Cubans created a culture, that is, a distinctive mix of style and substance equally distant from the Cuban condition and the American way? And what about the relation of Cuban America to the other Hispanic ethnicities in this country?

These are large, familiar questions, which I will address by discussing some examples of the literature that this culture, if it exists, has produced. Since its emergence in the 1980s, Cuban-American literature has occupied an ambiguous place within the canon of imaginative writing by U.S. Latinos. As the only segment of this canon produced by political exiles and their children, this literature exhibits a nostalgic streak not shared—at least, not in the same degree—by Chicano, Dominican American, or U.S. Puerto Rican writers. Instead of focusing on how the García girls lost their accents, Cuban-Americans seem more intent on explaining how the García girls, or the Pérez family, managed to keep theirs. The title of Isabel Alvarez Borland's book, *Cuban-American Literature of Exile* (1998), captures this ambiguity. Although hyphenated literatures tend not to be created by political exiles, with Cuban-Americans the two poles seem to merge: The chronic exile meets the unmeltable ethnic.

Along with remembered or received memories of Cuba comes ideological baggage—this too is an inheritance. Although the politics of the Cuban-American community are more complex than is usually recognized, it's nonetheless true that sympathy for the Cuban Revolution among Cuban-Americans is—understandably, I hope—as rare as snow in Little Havana. *Gusanos*, worms, has been the label applied by the Castro regime to its opponents inside and outside the island. For the most part, Cuban-American literature has been, and continues to be, a can, a canon, of worms. Whatever their genus or genres, whatever their species or specialties, these novelists, poets, playwrights, and essayists rarely blink their worm's-eye view: *gusano* rhymes with *cubano*. This too makes Cuban-American literature drift on the margins of the Latino mainstream, whose sources in the social movements of the 1960s have shaped its ideological commitments.[1] The fashion of "loving Che" did not begin, nor will it end, with Ana Menéndez's recent novel.

And then there is language. In "The Task of the Translator," Walter Benjamin makes the striking remark that languages are not strangers to each other.[2] Although his context is unrelated to mine, his statement certainly applies to Cuban-American writing, a body of work deeply marked—some might say, scarred—by the intimate acquaintance of its two tongues, Spanish and English. Like Latino literature, which has become the monolingual expression of a bilingual community, Cuban-American literature exists predominantly in English. Unlike Latino literature, in which the Spanish language tends to be used ornamentally, as a dash of Latin spice or a dab of exotic color, Cuban-American literature has not abandoned the Spanish language. In fact, one of the challenges facing the student of this body of writing is its linguistic variety, which runs the gamut from English-only to Spanish-always. The canon of worms contains many writers—such as Cristina García, Virgil Suárez, Ricardo Pau-Llosa, or Ana Menéndez—who write only in English; but it also includes some who write only in Spanish: Lourdes Gil, José Kozer, Amando Fernández, or Orlando González Esteva; and still others who travel back and forth between their mother and their other tongue: Roberto Fernández, Elías Miguel Muñoz, Eliana Rivero, Pablo Medina.

It's important to realize that these linguistic positionings do not result from generational differences alone. With the exception of Ana Menéndez, all of the writers I have just mentioned were born in Cuba and arrived in the United States as children or adolescents. González Esteva, who writes only in Spanish, is younger than some of those who write only in English, and he has lived in the

United States as long as they have or longer. At least in some instances, the choice of language arises from an existential appraisal, from an assessment of who one is as a person and a writer, rather than from generational imperatives or limitations. And here too the heritage of exile plays a determining role, for the mother tongue is the most precarious, but also the most prized, of an exile's possessions. Difficult as it is to hold on to one's mother tongue after decades of exile, dreaming in Cuban is easier when one's dreams continue to speak Spanish.

The first writer I want to discuss, Orlando González Esteva, is one of those who has not allowed a prolonged exile to stop him from dreaming in Spanish. Indeed, he has said that his writing bears no trace of his life in the United States: "El que busque en mis versos la presencia de mi larga vida en los Estados Unidos, la huella de la literatura anglosajona, no la encontrará, a pesar de que me eduqué en ese país y vivo en él. Encontrará sólo a Cuba" (Interview by Asiaín). Born in Cuba in 1952, González Esteva arrived in the United States when he was twelve years old. Since then he has lived in Miami, where he divides his time between writing and staging variety shows with Cuban performers, including himself. Although his work is not well known to scholars of Cuban-American literature, he has published a dozen fine books of poetry and prose, among them *Mañas de la poesía* (1981), a volume of *décimas; Escrito para borrar* (1997) and *Mi vida con los delfines* (1998), a collection of *redondillas* and an ingenious explanation of his passion for this metrical form; *Elogio del garabato* (1994), an autobiographical meditation on writing; and *La noche y los suyos* (2003) and *Casa de todos* (2005), his two most recent books, both collections of haikus.[3]

As this list suggests, González Esteva has always shown a predilection for minimalist forms: the *redondilla*, the *décima*, the haiku. Another of his books, *Tallar en nubes* (1999), gathers jottings culled from José Martí's notebooks. His characterization of Martí's *apuntes* as "un puñado de textos germinales, vivos, acabaditos de garrapatear" (XII) describes González Esteva's own work, which also consists of the condensed notation, in verse or prose, of sensations, impressions, theories, memories, fantasies—anything from fanciful *disparates* to provocative flashes of insight. As González Esteva points out in *Elogio del garabato*, for him writing is *garrapateo*, doodling, creative and recreative play. It is not surprising, then, that he likes to fix his gaze on the small and insignificant: fireflies, crickets, snails, a drop of water or of ink, the dot over the *jota*. A true virtuoso of the miniature, he has even written a little (of course) book about ants in *Fosa común* (1996).

One of my favorite poems by González Esteva is not about ants, but about their winged cousins, the mosquitoes.

> Hola, mosquito.
> ¿Te da miedo la noche?
> Zumba un poquito. *(La noche y los suyos 32)*

Everything here is small: the poem, the mosquito, and—most charmingly—the diminutive that clinches the rhyme: *poquito.* Much more than a quaint mannerism, González Esteva's aesthetics of the diminutive, his practice of *garrapateo*, reflects his predicament as a hispanophone writer in the United States. Detached from his homeland, estranged from this natural audience, the writer is reduced to scribbling, to biding his time with embryonic *apuntes*. González Esteva does not cultivate major genres; he does not write novels, plays, long poems, or essays. He is, in the best sense, an occasional writer, partly because writing is not how he makes a living, but, more fundamentally, because he works at the edges, on the boundaries of Cuban and Cuban-American literature. The occasion for all of González Esteva's work is the unacknowledged but deep-seated sense that he writes in a void. This is what is suggested by his choice of the *garabato* as a metaphor for writing, for however meaningful a *garabato* may be to its creator, its hermeticism and ephemeralness distinguish it from public discourse. As "graffiti scrawled on the wailing wall" (*Elogio del garabato*, 8), the *garabato* gives voice to private laments always susceptible to erasure. (The title of another of his books is *Escrito para borrar*). Like the mosquito perhaps, González Esteva fears extinction; his defensive reaction is *zumbar*, a verb that means "to buzz," but that in Cuban Spanish also connotes exceptionality or unexpectedness: *Le zumba el mango.* Typically, however, he generates a buzz without making a ruckus: "zumba"—but only "un poquito."

Among the dozens of haikus that González Esteva has written, only a few refer explicitly to Cuba. One of these appears in *Casa de todos* (2005):

> Aun en Cuba,
> si los pájaros cantan
> añoro Cuba. (17)

As González Esteva mentions, this poem follows a famous haiku by the Bashō, one of the Japanese masters of the genre. In English—and it's worth noting that González Esteva's Spanish version is based on English translations—the haiku has been rendered as follows:

> Even in Kyoto—
> Hearing the cuckoo's cry—
> I long for Kyoto.[4]

Since in Japanese poetry the cry of the cuckoo, the so-called bird of time, connotes temporality, the paradox of longing for Kyoto while in Kyoto is usually read as an expression of nostalgia for a bygone time. As one commentator puts it, "With the cry, today's Kyoto is instantly transformed into the Kyoto of the past."[5] Transferring this reading to González Esteva's poem, one could argue that the replacement of Kyoto with Cuba expresses a yearning for the *Cuba de ayer* that for almost half a century Cuban exiles have been pining for. In addition, González Esteva may be articulating the melancholy conviction, shared by many Cubans inside and outside the island, that Cuba has never become entirely itself, that as a national project it remains incomplete, that it continues to be, in Jorge Mañach's striking phrase, "una patria sin nación" (64).[6]

What complicates this reading, however, is that, unlike Bashō, González Esteva does not live in the place for which he longs. At its most basic, his *añoranza* is not temporal but geographical, a nostalgia not only for the Cuba that was or never has been, but for the homeland that he left as a child. That is why he replaces the name of a city with that of a country. In the mouth of an exile, the paradox of feeling homesick at home necessarily yields a counterfactual first line, "Aun en Cuba." González Esteva's most profound expression of longing, and his most radical act of translation, does not lie in feeling homesick at home, but in locating himself in a country that he hasn't seen in forty years. Written without the tilde, as here, the poem's first word—"aun"—is monosyllabic; but for the first line to scan as the required five syllables, the diphthong needs to be broken up: "Aun" must be read as "Aún."[7] Another layer of meaning then surfaces: An intensifying adverb becomes a temporal one; *aun* as "even" morphs into *aún* as "still." "Aun en Cuba" can then be construed as "Still in Cuba," a revision that underscores the denial of displacement that lies at the heart of the poem—and of González Esteva's poetics.

Another change in González Esteva's version of Bashō's haiku is substituting the cuckoo of the original with the generic "pájaros." One reason for the change is that, in Spanish (and English), the *cuco* or *cuclillo* lacks the evocative powers that it has in Japanese. But if we look at another of the poems in *Casa de todos*, we may find a further motive for the revision:

> Toda la noche
> oyeron pasar pájaros . . .
> Tú aún los oyes. (31)

The first two lines quote a well-known sentence from Christopher Columbus's *Diario de a bordo* (Colón 87). It appears in the entry for October 9, 1492, three days before Columbus and his crew make landfall on the island of Guahaní. González Esteva's use of this sentence is as revealing as it is surprising. In the diary, the cry of the birds betokens the proximity of land. Five hundred years later, a poet living in exile puts himself in the place of Columbus, as if he too were about to discover a new world. Yet for González Esteva the new world evoked through the quotation is in reality an old world, the world of his childhood—not a *terra incognita* but the land of his birth. The quotation reveals, however, that for the long-term exile, the homeland becomes foreign, a destination as strange and exotic as the Orient that Columbus believed he had reached. Bette Midler has a song entitled, "Only in Miami is Cuba so far away." This phrase could also serve as the title of González Esteva's haiku.

Notice that he not only hears the birds—he hears them still, *aún:* "Tú aún los oyes." There is no ambiguity here in the adverb's meaning. *Aún* denotes continuity—between Cuba's discoverer and the poet, and between the boy who spent the first twelve years of his life in Palma Soriano and the man who has spent the last forty in Miami. No matter how much time has passed, the child remains the father of the man. In spite of decades of exile, the feeling of imminence, of proximity persists. (The haiku could also have been titled, *Next Year in Cuba.*)

Although González Esteva is usually grouped with first-generation exile writers, this copresence of the motifs of imminence and strangeness, of memory and expectation, brands him as Cuban-American.[8] Tainted by absence, his invocation of Cuba blends the nostalgia of the exile with the discoverer's sense of wonder. Contrary to what he has asserted, permanent residence in the Spanish language fails to protect him from the spell of the hyphen. For exiles who left Cuba as adults, return is *regreso;* for the so-called ABCs or American-born Cubans, return is impossible, since one cannot return to a place one has never been. Only for González Esteva's generational cohort is traveling to Cuba, in fact or fiction, a voyage of discovery as well as recovery. If it's true that only in Miami is Cuba so far away, it's no less true that only in Miami is Cuba so tantalizingly close, like those birds that he hears flying by. And all because of that miniature of a word, *aún*, which adjoins past and present, Cuba and America, the speech of the homeland with the buzz of exile. *Aún aúna.* The spell of the hyphen spells *aún.*

I will now move on to two poems that I know well, or perhaps that I don't know at all, since I wrote them. The first one, "Bilingual Blues," dates from the mid-1980s and appeared originally in *Carolina Cuban* (1987).

Bilingual Blues

Soy un ajiaco de contradicciones.
I have mixed feelings about everything.
Name your *tema*, I'll hedge.
Name your *cerca*, I'll straddle it
Like a *cubano.*

I have mixed feelings about everything.
Soy un ajiaco de contradicciones.
Vexed, hexed, complexed,
hyphenated, oxygenated, illegally alienated,
psycho soy, cantando voy:

You say tomato,
I say *tu madre;*
You say potato,
I say *Pototo.*
Let's call the hole,
un hueco, the thing a *cosa,*
and if the *cosa* goes into the *hueco,*
consider yourself *en casa,*
consider yourself part of the family.

Soy un ajiaco de contradicciones,
un puré de impurezas:
a little square from Rubik's Cuba
que nadie nunca acoplará.
(*Cha-cha-chá.*) (164)

We are a long way here from González Esteva's composed, meditative tone. If haikus are brief illuminations, "Bilingual Blues" resembles a sequence of short circuits that makes the lights go out. Evidently, the hyphen also has cast its spell over the speaker of this poem, who tries to join words that do not adjoin, among them *tomato* and *tu madre, potato* and *Pototo*, purée and *pureza*, cube and Cuba, blues and *cha-cha-chá.* As he mentions at the start, the poem consists of a free exercise in hedging or fence sitting, a talent that—incongruously—he attributes to his Cubanness: "Name your *tema*, I'll hedge. / Name your *cerca*, I'll straddle it / Like a *cubano.*" The implicit authority for this view is none other than Fernando Ortiz, once dubbed Mr. Cuba, who famously described Cuban culture as an *ajiaco*, an indigenous stew concocted from the nonsynthetic combination of heterogeneous ingredients.[9] Exploiting, perhaps spoiling, Ortiz's metaphor, the speaker postulates that since Cubans have always been hyphenated Americans, there exists no discontinuity between the Cuban condition and the Cuban-American way. Linking Cuba and America is but another manifestation of the Cuban appetite for hyphenation.

The poem's opening lines signal, however, that this junction is not without risk. As the vocabulary modulates from the logical—*contradicciones*—to the affective—"mixed feelings"—cultural contradictions translate into psychic conflict. In González Esteva's haikus, the speaker is melancholy but he is not torn. Exile may have displaced him, but it has not disfigured him. Like that barber in Miami who advertises himself as "el mismo de Cuba," González Esteva portrays himself as resistant to change. To Neruda's line, "Nosotros, los de entonces, ya no somos los mismos," he would reply: "Nosotros, los de ahora, nunca fuimos distintos." But the speaker of "Bilingual Blues" is nothing if not changeable: "vexed, hexed, complexed, / hyphenated, oxigenated, illegally alienated."

To verify this, it is enough to listen to the dissonant literary and musical echoes in the second stanza. Its fifth line, "Psycho soy, cantando voy," rewords another poem about hybridity, though of a different kind, Nicolás Guillén's "*Son número* 6":

> Yoruba soy,
> cantando voy,
> llorando estoy,
> y cuando no soy yoruba,
> soy congo, mandinga, carabalí. (*Obra poética* 231)

In his *son*, Guillén makes a plea for racial harmony and cultural integration. As he puts it in the prologue to *Sóngoro cosongo* (1931), his poems try to bring about the day when all Cubans will be of one color: *color cubano* (114). Although integration is also the issue in "Bilingual Blues," there is no indication here that the speaker sees himself as part of a collectivity. Instead of a "yoruba de Cuba," like Guillén, he is a psycho from somewhere between Cuba and the United States, or between La loma del Chaple and Chapel Hill. Which is why no sooner has Nicolás Guillén been evoked that he gives way to to Fred Astaire and Ginger Rogers singing a Gershwin tune in the musical *Shall We Dance?*

> You say eether and I say eyether,
> You say neether and I say nyther;
> Eether, eyether, neether, nyther—
> Let's call the whole thing off.
> You like potato and I like Po-tah-to;
> You like tomato and I like to-mah-to;
> Potato, potahto, tomato, tomahto—
> Let's call the whole thing off. (Gottlieb and Kimball, 296)

In my poem, the flirtatious repartée between Fred and Ginger degenerates into interlingual invective when "tomato" is answered by "*tu madre.*" And then "potato" becomes "*Pototo,*" one of the stage names of the Cuban comedian Leopoldo Fernández, who was also part of a comedy team, Pototo y Filomeno. After mentioning Pototo, the speaker reprises the Gershwin tune, but only to poke a hole in it. Instead of repeating the song's refrain, "Let's call the whole thing off," he uses it as the springboard for another exercise in misprision:

> Let's call the hole
> *un hueco*, the thing a *cosa*,
> and if the *cosa* goes into the *hueco*,
> consider yourself *en casa*,
> consider yourself part of the family.

The last two lines sample another Hollywood musical, *Oliver* (1968), an adaptation of Dickens's *Oliver Twist*, where one of the orphans welcomes Oliver to Fagin's house by singing: "Consider yourself at home. / Consider yourself part of the family" (Bart). As the riff that began in Guillén's Cuba ends in Dickens's London, the lyric from *Oliver* serves as a pretext for an aggressive double entendre based on the homonymy of "whole" and "hole" and the near homonymy of "*cosa*" and "*casa.*" (But it cannot be said that double entendres are out of place in a poem built entirely on equivocations). More importantly, the reference to *Oliver* reveals the speaker's cultural orphanhood, his desire to find a home, to consider himself *en casa.* If a language is a place, as Elias Canetti once noted, the speaker of "Bilingual Blues" tries to be in two places at once—and fails. That's why his wordplay has an angry edge. You hum a Gershwin tune, and he cusses at you—or at himself. You want to call the whole thing off, and he sticks it to you—or to himself. Every pun is a punch, a jab, an instrument for tongue lashing. As an illustration of what Einar Haugen has termed "schizoglossia," this poem portrays a bilingual's inability to integrate his two languages, which is to say, his two worlds (86).

Fast-forward twenty years. "The Tongue Surgeon" appears in *Scar Tissue* (2005), a memoir that narrates my recovery from prostate cancer. When my son looked through *Scar Tissue*, his comment was, "This is a distasteful little book, Pop." And he's right, because in *Scar Tissue* I write about prostate cancer, a common but unliterary disease, with the same candor and even ardor with which others have written about breast cancer or AIDS:

The Tongue Surgeon

> Illness in a foreign language: There's more to this than having to discuss the diagnosis and treatment with physicians named Johnson or Sandler who cannot reassure you in the only language in which reassurance is truly possible.
>
> There's something to this about the imbrication of body and language, organ and word. A tongue is both organ and word. When I was thirteen, a couple of years after arriving in the States, I began to get mouth sores, *aftas.* I still get them, mostly on my tongue. That's what I'm talking about.
>
> Prostate is a tough word: tough on my tongue, tough on my eyes. Talking to myself, I say *próstata, próstata*, but it's not my *próstata* but my prostate that was removed. Surgeons cannot cut out what they cannot pronounce.
>
> I am a tongue surgeon. I operate on my tongue, with my tongue. This is not my tongue. (42)

Other than age, what are the differences between the bilingual bluesman and the tongue surgeon? Gone is the frenzied tone of the earlier poem, replaced by sobriety, perhaps somberness. Gone also is the unpredictable back-and-forth between English and Spanish, as well as inveterate punning. What remains, however, is the underlying obsession with language, an obsession that here too triggers a bout of tongue lashing.

Like other sections of *Scar Tissue*, this vignette uses autobiography as a springboard for a meditation on the connection between illness and language. To the diseased body corresponds a diseased tongue. The analogy is underscored by the similarity of the words "cancer" and "canker," slightly different derivations of the same Latin root. In English, an *afta* is a canker—as if the cankerous tongue, like the cancerous prostate, had been invaded by foreign bodies. And in a way it has: It has been invaded by the bodies of foreign words. The difference between the two organs is that whereas the diseased body is put in the care of medical specialists, responsibility for the ailing tongue, for *la mala lengua*, rests with the speaker alone. The only treatment available to him is homeopathic: for a talking disease, a talking cure. Yet talking, writing, languaging is the source of the illness. The more the speaker uses his tongue, the more it hurts. Hence the antinomy with which the vignette concludes: "I am a tongue surgeon. I operate on my tongue, with my tongue. This is not my tongue."

"The Tongue Surgeon" is one of those texts, not uncommon in Latino literature, that lament the loss of Spanish in English, the language that provoked the loss. To compensate, the speaker dreams of a wholeness available only in his birth language. As he says, it's not his *próstata* but his prostate that was removed. But I don't believe him. Or rather, I don't believe me. "Prostate" may be a tough word, but *próstata* might be even tougher. The fantasy of intactness, his and my belief that in Spanish we would not have gotten sick, is another version of González Esteva's *aún*, a symptom of the exile's unwillingness to accept that he is no longer "el mismo de Cuba."

Like "Bilingual Blues," "The Tongue Surgeon" evinces an inclination toward self-laceration that seems an integral part of how I experience life on the hyphen. What I would like is to say to my tongue is what my doctors did to my prostate: Cut it out. But were I to do this, I would lapse into silence. And so I talk on. The next poem in *Scar Tissue*, entitled "Afterlife on the Hyphen," compares the hyphen to a scar (43). Elsewhere in the book, a scar is defined as the shortest distance between two puns (23). With the passage of time, my life on the hyphen has turned a knife on the hyphen. Once again Strunk and White's admonition comes to mind: "We ask too much of a hyphen when we ask it to cast its spell over words it does not adjoin."

Richard Blanco, whose work I would like to discuss now, is not an aging baby boomer but a member of "Generation Ñ," as young Miami Cuban-Americans sometimes label themselves. In his own words, he was made in Cuba, assembled in Spain, and imported to the United States. He means that he was conceived in Cuba, born in Spain (in 1968), and brought to the States when he was less than two months old. Raised and educated in Miami, Blanco is the author of two impressive collections of poems, *City of a Hundred Fires* (1998) and *Directions to the Beach of the Dead* (2005). Although the poem I will discuss is not representative of all of Blanco's work, it makes for an instructive contrast with the other texts I have discussed.

> Havanasis
>
> In the beginning, before God created Cuba, the earth was chaos, empty of form and without music. The spirit of God stirred over the dark tropical waters and God said, "Let there be music." And a soft conga began a one-two beat in the background of the chaos.
>
> Then God called up *Yemayá* and said, "Let the waters under heaven amass together and let dry land appear." It was done. God called the fertile red earth Cuba and the massed waters of the Caribbean. And God saw this was good, tapping his feet to the conga beat.
>
> Then God said, "Let the earth sprout *papaya* and *coco* and white *coco* flesh; *malanga* roots and mangos in all shades of gold and amber; let there be *tabaco* and *café* and sugar for the *café;* let there be rum; let there be waving plaintains and *guayabas* and everything tropical-like." God saw this was good, then fashioned palm trees—His pièce de resistance.
>
> Then God said, "Let there be a moon and stars to light the nights over the Club Tropicana, and a sun for the 365 days of the year." God saw that this was good, he called the night nightlife, the day he called paradise.
>
> Then God said, "Let there be fish and fowl of every kind." And there was spicy shrimp *enchilado*, chicken *fricasé*, codfish *bacalao* and fritters. But He wanted something more exciting and said, "Enough. Let there be pork." And there was pork—deep fried, whole roasted, pork rinds, and sausage. He fashioned goats, used their skins for bongos and *batús;* he made *claves* and *maracas* and every kind of percussion instrument known to man.
>
> Then out of a red lump of clay, God made the Taino and set him in a city He called *Habana.* Then He said, "It is not good that Taino be alone. Let me make him helpmates." And so God created the *mulata* to dance *guaguancó* and *son* with the Taino; the *guajiro* to cultivate his land and his folklore, *Cachita* the sorceress to strike the rhythm of his music, and a poet to work the verses of their paradise.
>
> God gave them dominion over all the creatures and musical instruments and said unto them, "Be fruitful and multiply, eat pork, drink rum, make music and dance." On the seventh day, God rested from the labors of his creation. He smiled upon the celebration and listened to their music. (*City of a Hundred Fires* 37–38)

Although I like this poem very much—it is imaginative, witty, irreverent —I also find it unsettling. Ever since Columbus remarked that Cuba was the most beautiful land that human eyes had ever seen, the paradisal trope has shaped external—and to some extent, internal—perceptions of Cuba. A typical case is the Boston journalist William Henry Hurlbert, who in 1854 published an account of his Cuban journey under the title, *Gan-Eden*, Hebrew for Garden of Eden or Garden of Delight. Describing the bay of Mariel, a place that would irrupt into American political discourse a century later, he states that it resembles "those outer realms of Paradise over which the eyes of Adam ranged" (131). That Hulbert would use this kind of language is not surprising; then and now, travel writing about Cuba is full of paradisal imagery. What is surprising is that a contemporary Cuban-American writer would resurrect these clichés and stereotypes.

Blanco's exoticizing view of Cuba grows out of his relation to the country where he was conceived. In his Cuban Genesis, God's labors culminate in the creation of the poet, whose mission is to "work the verses" of paradise (incidentally, of all the characters in the poem, only two are working: God and the poet). By placing the poet in the Garden of Eden, Blanco fosters a fiction of belonging not unlike González Esteva's, for "Havanasis" was not written by a resident of paradise but by someone who has been expelled from it. In fact, *City of a Hundred Fires* opens with an epigraph from Ovid's letters from exile, the *Tristia*, where the Roman poet evokes Rome in his mind's eye (2). Contrary to appearances, Blanco's narrative does not belong to the book of Genesis, but to the one that follows it in the Hebrew Bible: the book of Exodus. No less than God, the poet creates ex nihilo, out of the void of absence, which means that the initial description of the earth as a "chaos, empty of form and devoid of music" also depicts the world of the exile. Like González Esteva's chiseled miniatures, Blanco's expansive prose presupposes an *aún* that establishes an imaginary continuity between the "here and now" and the "there and then," between the worlds *from* which and *about* which he writes. Before God said, "Let there be music," the poet had to say, "Let there be Cuba." If González Esteva imagines himself as a Columbus poised to discover a marvelous new world, Blanco writes out Columbus's vision as if it were a pre-Castro publicity poster for American tourists.[10]

I say *American* tourists because, in "Havanasis," the divine and the human authors speak and write in English. By adopting the English spelling of Havana in the title, Blanco already discloses that his will be an anglocentric—one might say, anglogenetic—recreation of Cuba. Had the Tongue Surgeon written "Havanasis," the poem's English would have served as the basis for another episode of tongue lashing. How is it that God put the poet in this tropical paradise to praise his creation in English? Aren't all those italicized words blemishes on the page, eye sores? Maybe even mouth sores? In *The Last Puritan*, George Santayana remarks that language is "one of those human troubles in which the curse of original sin, and of Babel, most surely appeared" (126).[11] But in "Havanasis" language is not troubling. Either things translate—I say *bacalao*, you say "codfish"—or they stand without translation, as if it didn't matter whether the reader knows the identity of Yemayá or Cachita. Exempt from the curse of original sin and untroubled by Babel, Blanco's English and Spanish do not afflict each other. They know and keep their place, which is why the poem refrains from code switching and interlingual play.

What we might call Blanco's "Edenic bilingualism" is also consistent with his generational location. Like most Latino writers, young Cuban-Americans write almost exclusively in English. To them the Spanish language, like Cuba, is familiar but foreign. Even when Blanco uses Spanish in his poems, which he often does, English remains his linguistic home. Not because he doesn't handle Spanish well, but because fundamentally it is not his language. In *Directions to the Beach of the Dead*, he includes a moving bilingual poem, "Translation for Mamá," which begins:

> What I've written for you, I have always written in
> English, my language of silent vowel endings never
> translated into your language of silent h's.
>
> *Lo que he escrito para ti, siempre lo he escrito*
> *en inglés, en mi lengua llena de vocales mudas*
> *nunca traducida a tu idioma de haches mudas.* (24–25)

Spanish is Blanco's mother's tongue rather than his own. To write in Spanish, he must translate himself in both the linguistic and top senses, and he does so not for his own benefit but for hers, "for Mamá." Since Blanco's investment in Spanish is vicarious, once-removed, English and Spanish abide side by side in peaceful coexistence. They are not strangers to each other, as Benjamin would say, but neither do they harass each other, a lack of contact signified by the spacing as well as by Blanco's word choices: While English is the son's *lengua*, Spanish is the mother's *idioma*. The differing names suggest that the two languages are not equivalent, and hence that they are not in competition.[12] Once again, each language keeps to itself. You say, "tomato," and he says, "Mamá."

Let me conclude by looking briefly at one more poem, the initial haiku in González Esteva's *La noche y los suyos*. The book's epigraph cites the most famous question in Cuban literature: "Dos patrias tengo yo, Cuba y la noche: / ¿O son una las dos?" To José Martí's question, the haiku answers in the affirmative:

> La noche suma
> demasiadas ausencias.
> Es, toda, Cuba. (15)

For once, in this poem González Esteva forsakes minimalism in favor of hyperbole: The night is a sum, a summa, of "too many" absences, "demasiadas ausencias." Prolonging the hyperbole, the next sentence makes the whole of the night coextensive with Cuba: "Es, toda, Cuba." The underlying poetic syllogism goes something like this: Night signifies absence; Cuba is absent; therefore, Cuba is one with the night—*son una las dos*. The emotional impact of this conclusion falls on the adjective *toda*, which bears the full stress of the speaker's insight. (Release the adjective from the encircling commas, and all of Cuba joins the equation). It is hardly a coincidence that the first line of the very next haiku is, "La noche pesa." Freighted with too much absence, González Esteva's night, like Martí's, is heavy with longing. That is why the book is entitled *La noche y los suyos* —the poet belongs to the night, because the night belongs to Cuba.

In spite of the large differences in tone, theme, and idiom, all of the poems I have discussed share a hyperbolic investment in absence. At times, it's the island as a geographical entity that is missing; at other times, it's some component of its culture—its language, its poetry, its music, its birds. Under the spell of the hyphen, Cuba appears as a lavish void, a bountiful empty set, the X that marks the spot of plenty. Cuban-American literature may originate in exile but it is not exile literature, because it is not sufficiently grounded in the facticity, in the raw reality of the island. In a well-known passage from *Dreaming in Cuban*, Cristina García's protagonist says, "Every day Cuba fades a little more inside me [. . .] And there is only my imagination where our history should be" (138). Cuban-American literature begins at the point where collective experience—"our history"—gives way to personal fabulation—"my imagination." It is immaterial whether these fabulations are rendered in English or Spanish, or whether their author was conceived in Cuba or made in the U.S.A. What matters is the specific weight of absence—the "here" of the "not there"—with its sequela of nighttime visions and tongues.

NOTES

1. In *The Last Generation*, Cherríe Moraga writes: "The generation of Chicano literature being read today sprang forth from a grassroots social and political movement of the sixties and seventies that was definitively antiassimilationist. It responded to a stated mandate: "*art is political*" (57). On the political roots of Latino Caribbean literature, see William Luis, *Dance Between Two Cultures*, 43–46.

2. Benjamin's remark is prompted by his belief that all languages strive for reconciliation and unity in a pure or perfect language; translation gestures, however incompletely, toward this end (17–21).

3. For an overview of González Esteva's career, see Carlos Espinosa Domínguez, *El peregrino en comarca ajena: Panorama crítico de la literatura cubana del exilio*, 42–43, 160–65.

4. Robert Hass, ed. and trans, *The Essential Haiku*, 11.

5. Yamamoto Kenkichi, as quoted in Makoto Ueda, trans., *Bashō and His Interpreters*, 294. See also David Landis Barnhill, trans., *Bashō's Haiku*, 235.

6. See also Rafael Rojas, *El arte de la espera*, 177–79; and Gustavo Pérez Firmat, *The Cuban Condition*, 2–7. González Esteva dedicates this haiku to Antonio José Ponte, the author of *Las comidas profundas* (Angers, France: Éditions Deleatur, 1997), a meditation on lack prompted by the rationing of food under the Castro regime. As Ponte points out, when one writes "from scarcity," one is compelled to replace the real with the imagined: plenty for empty, the Cuba that isn't for the Cuba that is (33).

7. Following the conventions of the genre, González Esteva's haikus consist of three lines of five, seven, and five syllables. He strays from convention, however, by rhyming the first and third lines, even though there is no rhyme in the Japanese originals. In *La noche y los suyos*, he explains his use of rhyme as a result of his "afición a ciertos recursos de la poesía tradicional española," which he believes have the power to generate poetic content (8). Already in *El pájaro tras la flecha*, González Esteva includes several rhymed haiku, among them "Marsyas," "La poesía," "Nanas del niño de ayer," "Haikú," "Canción de cuna." On the haiku in Spanish American literature, see Araceli Tinajero, "Haiku in Twentieth-century Latin America."

8. According to Rafael Rojas, "Dos de los poetas más importantes del exilio cubano, José Kozer y Orlando González Esteva, que siempre han escrito en español, difícilmente podrían enmarcarse en el *Cuban-American way* . . . El segundo, quien siempre ha vivido en Miami, aunque ha publicado casi toda su obra en México, está muy cerca de ese patriotismo literario del primer exilio que se empeña en recobrar, a través de la imagen, el paraíso perdido de la cubanidad: un edén que, en su caso, está siempre asociado a la infancia" (*Tumbas sin sosiego*, 417). For Kozer's relation to the "Cuban-American way," see Gustavo Pérez Firmat, *Life on the Hyphen*, chap. 6.

9. See Pérez Firmat, *The Cuban Condition*, chap 1.

10. Blanco's poems are not usually as ahistorical as "Havanasis," which opens a section that also includes "Partial List: Guantánamo Detainees," a poem that gives the names of Cubans detained in Guantánamo after the Mariel exodus; and "Found Letters from 1965: El año de la agricultura," which comments on the family strife created by the Cuban Revolution.

11. For a discussion of Santayana's relation to Spanish, see Gustavo Pérez Firmat, *Tongue Ties*, 23–43.

12. On the distinction between *lengua* and *idioma*, see Pérez Firmat, *Tongue Ties*, 14–20.

WORKS CITED

Alvarez Borland, Isabel. *Cuban-American Literature of Exile: From Person to Persona.* Charlottesville: University of Virginia Press, 1998.

Asiaín, Aurelio. "Jardín estricto: Entrevista de Orlando González Esteva con Aurelio Asiaín." *Vuelta* 149 (April 1989): 53–57.

Barnhill, David Landis, trans. *Bashō's Haiku.* Albany: State University of New York Press, 2004.

Bart, Lionel. "Consider yourself." 1963. http://www.lyricsondemand.com/soundtracks/o/oliverlyrics/.

Benjamin, Walter. "The Task of the Translator." *The Translation Studies Reader.* Ed. Lawrence Venuti. London: Routledge, 2000. 15–25.

Blanco, Richard. *City of a Hundred Fires.* Pittsburgh: University of Pittsburgh Press, 1998.

———. *Directions to the Beach of the Dead.* Tucson: University of Arizona Press, 2005.

Colón, Cristóbal. *Diario de a bordo*. Ed. Luis Arranz. Madrid: Historia 16, 1985.

Espinosa Domínguez, Carlos. *El peregrino en comarca ajena: Panorama crítico de la literatura cubana del exilio*. Boulder, CO: Society of Spanish and Spanish American Studies, 2001.

García, Cristina. *Dreaming in Cuban*. New York: Knopf, 1992.

González Esteva, Orlando. *El pájaro tras la flecha*. México: Editorial Vuelta, 1988.

———. *Elogio del garabato*. México: Editorial Vuelta, 1994.

———. *Fosa común*. México: Editorial Vuelta, 1996.

———. *Cuerpos en bandeja*. México: Libros de la Espiral, 1998.

———. *Tallar en nubes*. México: Editorial Aldus, 1999.

———. *Casa de todos*. Madrid: Editorial Pre-Textos, 2005.

———. *La noche y los suyos*. México: Ediciones del Ermitaño, 2005.

Gottlieb, Robert, and Robert Kimball, eds. *Reading Lyrics*. New York: Pantheon, 2000.

Guillén, Nicolás. *Obra poética, 1920–1972*. Vol 1. La Habana: Editorial de Arte y Literatura, 1974.

Hass, Robert, ed. and trans. *The Essential Haiku. Versions of Basho, Buson, and Issa*. Hopewell, NJ: Ecco, 1994.

Haugen, Einar. *Blessings of Babel: Bilingualism and Language Planning*. Berlin: Mouton de Gruyter, 1987.

Hurlbert, William Henry. *Gan-Eden; or, Pictures of Cuba*. Boston: Jewett, 1854.

Luis, William. *Dance Between Two Cultures*. Nashville: Vanderbilt University Press, 1997.

Mañach, Jorge. *Historia y estilo*. La Habana: Editorial Minerva, 1944.

Moraga, Cherríe. *The Last Generation*. Boston: South End, 1993.

Pérez Firmat, Gustavo. *Carolina Cuban*. Tempe: Bilingual Press, 1987.

———. *The Cuban Condition: Translation and Identity in Modern Cuban Literature*. New York: Cambridge University Press, 1989.

———. *Life on the Hyphen: The Cuban-American Way*. Austin: University of Texas Press, 1994.

———. *Tongue Ties: Logo-Eroticism in Anglo-Hispanic Literature*. New York: Palgrave, 2003.

———. *Scar Tissue*. Tempe: Bilingual Press, 2005.

Ponte, Antonio José. *Las comidas profundas*. Angers, France: Éditions Deleatur, 1997.

Rojas, Rafael. *El arte de la espera*. Madrid: Colibrí, 1998.

———. *Tumbas sin sosiego: Revolución, disidencia y exilio del intelectual cubano*. Barcelona: Editorial Anagrama, 2006.

Santayana, George. *The Last Puritan*. 1935. Ed. William G. Holzberger and Herman J. Saatkamp, Jr. Cambridge, MA: MIT Press, 1995.

Strunk Jr., William, and E. B. White. *The Elements of Style*. 3rd ed. Boston: Allyn and Bacon, 1979.

Tinajero, Araceli. "Haiku in Twentieth-century Latin America." *World Haiku Review* 2.3 (November 2002). http://www.worldhaikureview.org/2–3/index.html.

Ueda, Makoto, trans. *Bashō and His Interpreters: Selected Hokku with Commentary*. Stanford: Stanford University Press, 1991.

2

Figures of Identity

Ana Menéndez's and Guillermo Cabrera Infante's Photographs

Isabel Alvarez Borland

> *Traté de imitar esa condición de la fotografía como sueño y verdad de un arte estático.*
>
> —Guillermo Cabrera Infante, "Viaje verbal a La Habana, Ah Vana!"

An April 2006 issue of *New York* magazine sought to disprove the wisdom of the old cliché that "a picture is worth a thousand words" by offering its readers images of Brad Pitt and Angelina Jolie with their newborn baby weeks *before* the real birth actually took place. The faux pictures—which looked most credible—were created in the computer lab and even if the reader was told up front that they were false, the pictures appeared as truth in the glossy pages of the popular magazine. Below the cover image, and in very small print, the following disclaimer was made: "If the blessed event occurs by the time of publication, let's just pretend this cover never happened." The pictures in *New York* magazine "invented" a story around the impending and real birth of the famous couple's child by playing with the readers' imagination, and by giving them exactly what they wanted to see before it happened. The article and its images of look-alike models, both deconstructed celebrity coverage while also indulging in it.[1]

If computer wizardry and look-alike models have made images become as unreliable as language by providing new story possibilities for the journalists and photographers involved in the entertainment industry, contemporary writers such as Ana Menéndez have also been involved in a different process of image manipulation by imagining or inventing new contexts to preexisting photographs. In *Loving Che* (2003), Ana Menéndez takes advantage of Che Guevara's status as a pop icon and uses the published photographs of this overly recognized public figure as "props" within the story of her novel.[2] *Loving Che* presents us with Teresa, a protagonist that imagines for herself a love affair with Che inspired by the photographs of the comandante available in newspapers and magazines. Reconstructing the modern and postmodern argument about how contexts can affect our perception of visual images, Menéndez invents a story around Guevara's public photographs and invites the reader to consider the effects of truth and illusion in the construction of Teresa's personal story. Similar to the photographer from *New York* magazine who sought to give her readers the fantasy of a birth that had not yet taken place, the photos of Guevara provide a place for fantasy in Teresa's barren life.

Since the publication of G. Cabrera Infante's *Vista del amanecer en el trópico*, 1974 (*View of Dawn in The tropics* 1978), Cuban and Cuban-American writers have explored the possibilities of embedded images and texts—in particular the photograph and the diary—as rich metaphores or figures that present an enactment of the story of exile. Cuban-American novels published during the 1990s, such as Cristina García's *Dreaming in Cuban* and *The Agüero Sisters*, Pablo Medina's *The Marks of Birth*, and Margarita Engle's *Fallen Angels Sing*, among others, featured within their fictional worlds documents or photographs that allowed the central protagonists to gain access to a buried or forgotten past. Here the writers looked on an image or text that had to be interpreted in order to better understand itself.[3] More recently, for U.S. writers of Cuban heritage such as Ana Menéndez, the embedded photograph has become a repository of the "history" and the "story" of exile, a figure that is at once a site of affiliation and rupture.

In her exploration of the artistic possibilities of the visual image, Menéndez's *Loving Che* dialogues with her predecessors in the Cuban and Cuban-American tradition, in particular with Guillermo Cabrera Infante's *Vista del amanecer en el trópico*. While it is easy to accept why an older exile such as Cabrera Infante would use the photograph in order to extract meaning from a history of personal experience surrounding the Cuban Revolution, it is not so clear why an American writer of Cuban heritage such as Ana Menéndez would be interested in preserving a dialogue with the history of the Cuban Revolution. It is my contention that the visual and verbal images embedded in Menéndez's book function as primal figures that provide both a metaphor for a lost history and a code to that history's make up. Both *View of Dawn* and *Loving Che* explore the nature of historical contexts and in different ways debunk the idea that historical and fictional writing are all that different. However, it is precisely in these authors's handling of the photograph as an interpretive device that the differences between the two writers emerge. An exploration of Cabrera Infante's and Menéndez's use of the photograph in their narratives serves to illuminate the Cuban-American *imaginario's* own vision of itself as well as its evolution in the intervening half century. Moreover, the continued presence of inner images and texts in this body of writing invites us to study the photograph as a figure or trope of identity by which Cuban-American narrative fiction seeks to define itself.

Cabrera Infante's "Pura nostalgia detenida"

One of the most significant features of *View of Dawn in the Tropics* is Cabrera Infante's dialogue with the very nature of perception and the problems that arise when the artist—writer or photographer—attempts to reproduce reality. In an interview completed soon after *Vista del amanecer* had been published, I asked Cabrera Infante about his artistic use of the photograph in this book. Cabrera Infante's answer, reproduced below, is significant because it reveals how the author felt about the creative possibilities of photography:

> La fotografía . . . es una evidencia y una forma de arte en sí misma. Traté todo lo que pude de imitar esa calidad fantásmatica que parece tan real y es al mismo tiempo pura nostalgia detenida, que tiene toda fotografía, aun las instantáneas, sobretodo las instántaneas caseras. No rechazo sin embargo la imputación de truco del todo. Todo arte es un truco, un leger de main, un acto de magia a veces simpático. La misma fotografía que parece captar la realidad verazmente crea por medio de luces y sombras una apariencia, una irrealidad, una imago. Traté de imitar esa condición de la fotografía como sueño y verdad de un arte estático. Por medio de la continuidad temporal, imprescindible a la lectura, quise animarlas en el espacio verbal al tiempo que las fijaba en el tiempo de la lectura. (Interview by Alvarez Borland 59)

For Cabrera Infante, the photo could create a separate verbal reality which in turn served the author as a further example of the historical subjectivity he was trying to convey in his vignettes. The photo for this author was both real and unreal since through its own visual possibilities, such as light and shadow, it could create an irreality of its own. According to Cabrera Infante, the black and white photo could also provide an instance of "untruth" because its own properties could suggest appearances that were not there. In *View of Dawn*, the photograph becomes simultaneously "art and reality" because as an art form it could lead the reader to meditate on how we perceive the reality we call history.

Through the description of photographs and engravings, Cabrera Infante considered the importance of recovering the personal and individual versions of historical events in order to reclaim his own.[4] *View of Dawn in the Tropics* is a collage of 101 vignettes, a chronological account of Cuba's history from its physical emergence as a volcanic island to the writer's present in 1972. This is a book that portrays Unamuno's concept of *intrahistoria*, a book about the small, anonymous incidents and specific conflicts of unknown characters. From the choice of the vignettes as well as from their placement within the text, the reader gets a sense of disjunction that is reflected also by the content of each piece. Time periods are not explicit, the markers are not there, although clues do exist. The chronological order of this text would make its reading resemble the reading of a history book as the vignettes are based on a variety of epochs of Cuban history: colonial times, independence, and the bloody tyrannies of the twentieth century: Machado, Batista, and Fidel Castro. As a result, the reader—unable to judge by conventional methods of names, places, and dates—is forced to relinquish conventional ways of reading history. Ironically, Cabrera Infante uses these techniques and strategies not to maneuver an escape from history but rather to engage the central theme of the unfair recording of history.[5]

The different uses of the photograph exhibited in *Vista del amanecer* are used to probe the historical truth of an event. Some images or engravings are rooted in the historical, as they relate the occurrences the narrator presents. Other photographs are part of stories within stories in which one character relates a tale to a listener within the piece, thus adding a dramatic, oral sense to the living history the author seeks to present. Yet the most important feature in the author's use of the photograph as an aesthetic device is that Cabrera Infante exposes the tensions of the recording of history precisely by *withholding* the images he describes. In this manner, the author increases the dependency and skepticism of his readers regarding the veracity of the events narrated.

A group of vignettes—the most poetic in the collection—appear to describe photographs or "freeze frames" and seem directly related to Cabrera Infante's conception of the unreality of the photograph and of his stated intention of "animating" the images that he describes in his book. In a vignette that begins with the phrase "The Only Thing Alive is the Hand," the description centers on a dead body although the reader is only allowed to "see" parts of it:

> In any case, the hand seems alive leaning on the wall. One can't see the arm and perhaps the hand is dead too. Perhaps it's the hand of an eyewitness and the spot on the wall is its shadow and other shadows as well . . . A nearby object—a grenade, the shell of a high caliber cannon, a movie camera?—looks black like a hole in the photograph. (73)

Vignettes like this one are still-frames in which the language evokes vividly the moment itself. Words are repeated, tones of gray and black accented. The hand, "lo único vivo," is reflective of all the other hands of those who will also fall to their deaths in obscurity. This vignette attempts to figuratively illustrate the way in which, due to destruction and loss, it is most difficult to decipher whether what we perceive actually exists.

As we have noted, the vignette proceeds to describe the scene of death with living words such as "beckoning," journeying," and "awaiting" thereby causing the reader to wonder about the division between life and death: "One of the boxes is half opened and there's a corpse in it and in the nearest box there is another corpse, its arm hanging out, as if beckoning the lid." By attributing living qualities to the dead in order to create ambiguity, this vignette deliberately makes a parallel between truth and perception. At the same time, the author introduces a combination of sunlight and shadow, greenery and dirt, grass and cement. The ambiguity about what is being described, the questions from the narrator, the blurriness of the objects described, as well as the possibility of a "movie camera" within this description, present strong evidence that Cabrera's explicit task was that of evaluating visual perception and its relation to the recording of historical facts.

A second vignette that plays with the idea of "frozen frames" or *pura nostalgia detenida* serves to explore the reader's perspective of history. The vignette begins in *media res* with the character in the act of falling. The passage elaborates upon a single action. It is described in the progressive tense, as though in slow motion, illustrating and bringing to life the image of a dying man, who "hasn't yet fallen but is falling." Once again Cabrera Infante uses only black and white, allowing the existing light to help him describe the image: "the black-gray pants . . . leaning toward the black earth and death forever" (115). The recurrence of a single moment leaves the reader with a sense of disorientation. It is likely that the idea of reiteration that the author wished to create through the frozen action of falling is a reference to history's own recurrences and repetitions. This photograph or frame requires the involvement of the reader to bear witness to a single moment and captures the essence of Cabrera Infante's attempt to promote an understanding of the violence of history through literature.

In his incursion on the aesthetic possibilities of the visual image, Cabrera Infante explores the many possibilities of descriptions of real and imagined photographs. For example, in a vignette that tells about the rebel triumph in 1959, the author illustrates the importance of the photographer as editor of the reality he seeks to capture:

> In the photograph you can see the head *comandante* entering the capital in a jeep. Next to him is another *comandante* and you can see the driver and another member of the escort . . . But the photographer had a touch of foresight. As he didn't know the third *comandante*, he cut him out of the picture when cropping it. A few months later, the third *comandante* was in jail accused of treason and sentenced to thirty years in prison. All who had anything to do with him were immediately branded as suspects, and the historians proceeded to erase his name from the books. Ahead of his time, the photographer did not have to look for his photograph to cut it accordingly. That's what you call historical guesswork. (116)

While on the surface, it looks like the use of the photograph would enhance the authenticity of the historian's perspective, what matters here is the cropping decision of the photographer and his own role in the recording of history. The eye of the camera becomes an analogue of the written historical account for it makes evident how every view on reality is really interpretative and thus vulnerable to the perceiver's subjectivity. Just as the historian in the vignette "proceeded to erase his name from the books" the photographer consciously excluded the *comandante* from his picture and literally deleted him from the annals of official history. By capturing in his picture only that part of reality which he deemed important, the photographer becomes the ultimate interpreter of the reality described.

Other vignettes in *View of Dawn* use the photograph to point out to readers the incompleteness of the image and to stress that there is no recording of history that is not distorted by interpretation. In the vignette entitled "The Photograph Is an Image," Cabrera Infante creates a connection between objective and subjective realities. The irony in this vignette rests on the difference between what can be seen physically in the picture (objective) and that truth that cannot be seen. The objective photograph soon becomes a description of the moral character of the patriot being described. The anonymous historian concludes with an explanation for the reader: "Because after all, this is not a photograph, rather that *rara avis:* the image of the dead hero when alive" (118).

Clearly, for Cabrera Infante, the most important aspect of history is what society remembers. For instance, in the vignette about the Haitian and Jamaican workers' request for a salary increase, the act of picture taking becomes the main subject of the piece. Here the camera that would have taken the group's picture becomes a "false prop" that serves to tell a tale of violence since it was instead a machine gun:

> All seemed to be going perfectly well and the owner suggested that they take a picture of the group to commemorate the agreement. The Haitian and Jamaican delegates posed in a row in front of the machine, which was covered by a black cloth . . . The foreman uncovered the machine and calmly machine-gunned the group of delegates . . . The story could be real or false. But the times made it believable. (51)

Because this sad story could have happened, it becomes more important than any "official" account of such incidents. On one level, Cabrera Infante makes the readers question how history is recorded. However, the vignette's conclusion also serves to bring the readers to another point of understanding since "the times made it believable." Thus the narrator in *View of Dawn* becomes at once a reader and interpreter of the visual events he describes.

Cabrera Infante's pioneering exploration of the photograph in *View of Dawn* created a special role for the image as inner text in Cuban exile fiction. By inventing, describing, and *witholding* his photographs from his readers, Cabrera Infante's *View of Dawn* exposed the tensions of the unfair recording of history and increased the skepticism of the reader. As the author observed in the aforementioned interview, some of the photographs described in his book never really existed:

> Muchas de las fotografías de *Vista* son imaginarias. Es decir nunca han existido, nunca pudieron existir porque, simplemente, en ese tiempo histórico la fotografía no había sido inventada todavía o nunca habían sido hechas en el tiempo literario, como dos o tres *composites* contemporáneos que fabriqué yo solo. (Interview by Alvarez Borland 59)

Not having access to what the narrator/historian sees, the reader must rely on his interpretations of the unseen pictures in trying to grasp what occurred in the past. By *withholding* the images from his readers, Cabrera Infante creates our increased dependency on the fictional historian's description of his *vistas* of Cuban history. This sense of dependency parallels or mimics the reliance that individuals experience in the reading of historical documents.

The Photographs of Strangers

Ana Menéndez's aesthetic exploration of visuals in *Loving Che* takes up where Cabrera Infante leaves off as the younger author seems to turn her back on the lies of "official" history in order to explore the possibilities of the personal story. While both writers want to expose the unreliability of recorded history through their manipulation of the image, in *Loving Che*, Menéndez grasps the personalization of history and shapes a story that exposes this process, made more effective through her meditation on the power of the visual image. Unlike Cabrera Infante, Ana Menéndez believes that history is not what a society chooses to remember, but rather what an individual chooses to invent. A cursory reading of *Loving Che* would find its treatment of the inner image or text similar to the novels of her predecessors in the Cuban-American narrative tradition. Yet there is more to Menéndez's novel as her use of the image allows the author to create an allegorical tale about the task of writing a memoir, and about the centrality of the genre in the recording of the personal stories of her parents' generation.

The novel opens with an anonymous narrator who is searching unsuccessfully for details about her birth mother. She knows that she was brought as an infant to Miami from Havana by her grandfather wearing a Neruda poem pinned to her baby gown as her only link to the past. When a mysterious package arrives containing writings and photographs from her mother, Teresa, the novel shifts to the mother's account of her affair with Che Guevara. Three separate segments present us with a fantasy love story that plays with the idea of frames, embedded narrators, readers, and texts within the world of the novel:

the central segment of the book recreates the mother's construction of her memoir, while the first and last sections of the novel are narrated in the daughter's voice and concentrate on her "reading" or deciphering of the box of mementoes [vignettes, photos, and paintings] contained in the mother's package. The fragmentary writings of Teresa, combined with Menéndez's use of photographs, are significant because they present the reader with the intersection of the private versus the public realms of living. Teresa writes to her nameless daughter and explains her need to "create" a past for the daughter through her imagined affair with Che: "You and I are past forgiveness or understanding. I took a past from you and you returned carrying his memory in your dark eyes" (5).

Through the character of Teresa, Menéndez is able to put forth her theory about the personal imprint as it reaches both the creation of a story—the mother's imagined affair with Che Guevara—as well as the crafting of a work of art through Teresa's career as a visual artist. While the mother's tale as a frustrated artist provides autobiographical parallels with the story of writer Ana Menéndez, Teresa's affair with Guevara concentrates on the importance of the individual's story over the collective official record we call history. Both the love story and the artist's tale coalesce in Menéndez's exploration of the relationship between images, memory, and the act of writing a memoir.

"In the absence of a past we invent history" writes the mother figure in *Loving Che.* There is no pretense of factuality in Teresa's love story as she herself offers us an instance of how she came to forge her imagined affair. When Teresa finds a picture of Che Guevara in a magazine, she tears it out and places it in a box with other pictures; in this way, she literally *removes* the historical figure of Guevara from his official context and places him in the realm of the "personal" or private story. Teresa's imagined affair with Guevara allegorizes the construction of a memoir or personal story which for Menendez could be more real than the official account preserved in the historical annals:

> When the new *Bohemia* came, I sat on the couch, turning the pages quickly, until I came to his photo. I searched the papers, the foreign magazines. Each time I came across his image, I lay there looking at his face for a long time; then I carefully tore out the page. Over the next weeks, I did the same with other photos I found. I trimmed them and stacked them carefully in a box in my closet with these recollections. (84)

Teresa's provision of photos in her work supports the story she has created. Self-reflexivity as theme and technique serve Menéndez well as the story of the artist mother is also the story of how images [the pictures of Guevara inserted throughout the mother's diary] affect the reader when contextualized by writing. By creating new contexts to Guevara's photographs, Ana Menéndez is clearly reinventing Ernesto Guevara for the reader. Teresa's love affair through the pictures she found of Guevara would be "an idea" of herself that would have little to do with factual or recorded history. Teresa reminds her daughter of this important fact:

> I began to wonder if perhaps the outer world was no more real than our imagination and all its thrashings but a mirror of our own thoughts. And I wonder now if our recorded history isn't like this, if our idea of history isn't another way of saying an idea of ourselves. (17)

Menéndez's ideas on how the visual image affects writing, memory, and personal experience are further illustrated through the story of Teresa's career as a visual artist. Throughout the novel, Teresa struggles with the creation of a commissioned painting depicting a Miami landscape and complains about her impossible situation: "But I had never been to Miami and was forced to work from photographs and postcards, other people's interpretations. The strain of it would hurt me deeply. It was a hideous way to make art" (63). When Teresa decides to "add" to her picture fictional characters, the addition of the "invented" couple—Mina and Sami—allows Teresa to add an aspect of herself to a task that she felt was devoid of personal meaning: "Already Mina's face is a little rounder, a little echo of my own mother's . . . and Sami is himself, but someone else too, someone who is living inside me" (108). In order to inhabit the memories of others, Teresa needs to add to them a part of her own self.

Teresa's construction of her love affair with Guevara from the pictures she clipped from *Bohemia*, and her recreation of the Miami canvas from the postcards of that city, are instances of an invented personal story. And yet, the vision of the memoir presented by this mother figure is a peculiar one. As Teresa claims: "Memory is the first story teller. Anyone can simulate history, it is easy enough" (47). For Teresa, memory is a self-centered version of history since, in her words, "our idea of history is another way of saying an idea of ourselves" (17).

The Lies of Memory

An earlier short story by Menéndez by the title of "Her Mother's House" served as a building block for the themes developed in *Loving Che*. In this story, a daughter named Lisette soon finds out that not only has her mother misremembered the physical description of their house in Cuba, but also the memories of their time there. For Lisette, her mother's house in Cuba was "The house of someone else's imagining, a different story" (*Her Mother's House*, 219). In both *Loving Che* and in the earlier story, the daughters are willing to put aside the reality they encountered in Cuba, choosing instead to go along with their mothers' versions of the past. In the process of looking for the official details of their mothers' stories, each of these daughters also uncovers a truth they did not mean to find and instead choose to let illusion survive over truth. And yet, neither one of Menendez's fictional daughters has the capability for the kind of self-deception that had provided their mothers a way to survive their life in exile. In this manner, *Loving Che* recreates Menéndez's effort to examine the process through which her parents forged their own personal stories, which in turn became Menéndez's "borrowed" memories.

The act of writing a memoir is both an act of "copying" history, and an opportunity for the memoirist to define events as if they were her own. In "Memory and Imagination," Patricia Hampl meditates on the relationship between our memories and the images that trigger them exploring why we are able to recall some images from our past and not others. Hampl asserts that having access to an image from our past is only the beginning of a process that allows the writer to let that image speak to him or her, to let him or her know why it has been stored in our memories in the first place. This author maintains that there is "invention" in the act of recalling and that this inventiveness on the part of the writer is what makes a specific memory meaningful. This is why Hampl advices beginning writers of the genre of memoir to let the images speak to them, to let them know why this image was stored in their memories in the first place: "Memory itself is not a warehouse of finished stories, not a static gallery of framed pictures" . . . "Stalking the relationship, seeking the congruence between stored image and hidden emotion—that is the real job of memoir" (311).

As Teresa constructs her personal story, she listens—as Hampl would have adviced her—to the images around her.[6] The memories of Menéndez's parents and those of their generation are indeed part feeling, part fact, part invention. In her failed painting of Miami, and in her clipping of pictures of Che Guevara from *Bohemia*, Teresa dramatizes the task of a writer who, in Hampl's words, "seeks congruence between image and feeling" and who needs to create the right context to the images remembered.

Menéndez's character conceives memory as a description of how history impacted us personally, how we view the world and formulate history through our senses, and finally how this impact contributes in turn to the experience we call history. For Teresa, it is memory that recalls the important aspects of history, for memory highlights what an individual internalizes, that which is remembered because it was experienced: "These scraps of memory that become untethered from the rest, flapping disconsolately in the wind, these memories are the most important of all" (48). It is through the nameless daughter in *Loving Che* that Menéndez presents a critique of the genre of the memoir that at the end, becomes a defense of the "inventive" aspect of the genre. In the opening scene of the novel, the daughter had appeared in a junk store looking at strangers' pictures and imagining her connection to them. Not being able to grasp her actual history she becomes a wanderer that indulges in the unfamiliar, "but I know that I am playing a game with history" (1).

In *Loving Che*, the daughter's search, analytical in its beginnings, becomes an inescapable door to discerning her own past: "I found myself drawn deeper and deeper until I feared I might lose myself among the pages, might drown in a drop of my own blood (12). Eventually, Teresa's "scraps of memory" also become her daughter's. And when a former professor claims that her mother's story is "an impossible reinvention of history, a beautiful fraud" (174–75), the daughter is not shattered because for some reason she too had been seduced by Teresa's lies. The daughter's acceptance of the "beautiful lies" in the mother's diary becomes an essential step in the young woman's conception of self. What began as the daughter's search for verifiable facts about her mother soon turns into an emotional quest for her own identity.

The Cuban-American yearning to create an alternate history—even if that history never existed in the first place—seems to be one of the main goals of *Loving Che*. The irony, however, is that Menéndez's anonymous daughter cannot possess a personal story that relates to Cuba. The identity found through the mother's invented stories reveals that the daughter cannot establish an identity that is tied to one place, and that her history as an exile's daughter does not allow her a singular identity. At first, Teresa's daughter attempts to reconstruct her mother's and her own history by viewing it as one of her journalistic assignments but ultimately finding it impossible to keep the distance she wished for. Moreover, the daughter's obsessions with the images of others further illustrates Menéndez's idea that history is something the individuals create themselves.

The nature of Menéndez's writing as exile literature can help us understand the position of a writer whose fiction manifests a tension between the desire to uncover the truth and the need to preserve memories of her Cuban ancestors even if they could be false. After all, until Menéndez visited Cuba in 1997, all that she had were the stories of her parents' Cuban experiences (interview by Birnbaum). It is then not surprising that the daughter's personal story is left out of *Loving Che* because, if and when it is told, it will be a tale rooted in the images and feelings of her American experience. The photographs of strangers in Menéndez's novel are there to encourage the reader to individualize history, to further play with context, and to engage in the process of the writing our own personal stories.

By incorporating real and invented photographs in their books, Cabrera Infante and Ana Menéndez are able to bring in differing perspectives further emphasizing the idea of "scraps of history" articulated by Teresa in *Loving Che*. Moreover, in spite of their different approaches, the two writers manifest a need to tell a story that begins with the personal and accepts the necessary "lies" of memory and of history. In a recent interview with Ana Menéndez, the author confirmed my question regarding how Cabrera Infante's *Vista del amanecer en el trópico* had affected her own exploration of the image in *Loving Che*:

> *View of Dawn in the Tropics* was my main model as I was writing *Loving Che* . . . When I was living in India, I came across it in a bookstore and read it again . . . I know that people complain that it was just a bunch of outtakes. For me, it was a revelation—literature stripped down to its emotional essence. I have so much admiration for that book . . . At first I only described the photos, in the manner of GCI. Then, after reading Sontag and Barthes on the death inherent in the photograph, I realized I had to include them also. (Interview by Alvarez Borland)

The imprint of Susan Sontag's *On Photography* on Menéndez's book—in particular Sontag's essay "In Plato's Cave"—is evident in the way Teresa appropriates the public pictures of Che Guevara for herself, a fact that illustrates the predatory relationship between the photographer and his subject, a relationship that Sontag discussed at length in her writings. Yet it is Roland Barthes's theories on photography, expounded in *Camera Lucida*, that most reflect Menéndez's treatment of Che Guevara's photographs since Menéndez explicitly mentions *Camera Lucida* in the last pages of her novel (123).

According to Barthes, the subject of a photograph derives his existence from the photographer. Moreover, when the subject knows he is being photographed, Barthes reminds us, he poses and thus transforms himself in the hopes of presenting a particular image he wishes to convey (Barthes 10–14). At the end of *Loving Che*, the nomadic and nameless daughter is left in a Paris bookstore in a scene reminiscent of the way she had been introduced to the reader in the first pages of the novel. This time the daughter is looking at pictures of Che Guevara, wishing to be part of a story that could only belong to her parents (228). While in the bookstore, she encounters and buys one last photo of Guevara in which he appears holding a camera "ready to record the world that lies before him"(227). As Barthes would have observed, the image of Che as photographer in this last picture is also an example of someone trying to create a particular image of himself, just as the mother's tale had been an attempt to create an image of herself that she wanted her daughter to accept and remember.

Cabrera Infante's fictional experiments with the image in *Vista del amanecer en el trópico*, published in Spanish in 1974, explored the interpretive space between image and photograph, a site of meditation that would suggest to the reader new ways of thinking and seeing. In fact, Infante's fictional meditation on the photographic image dialogues with the theories expounded in Susan Sontag's *On Photography* (1973) and later with Roland Barthes's *Camera Lucida* (1980). These treatises on the photographic image—Barthes's in particular—were published at the cusp of today's technological advances, at a time when radical changes occurred to our conception and construction of images that the young writer Ana Menéndez could not ignore.

It is, in fact, Menéndez's irreverence toward the photograph that allows her to transcend the visual experiments of her *maestro*, Guillermo Cabrera Infante. Not unlike *New York* magazine's false pictures of a celebrity birth that had not yet taken place, Menéndez's manipulation of the public photographs of Che Guevara significantly turn away from the details and facts of official history in order to validate her very unique version of her parents' story of exile. Moreover, Menéndez's ironic, tongue-in-cheek stance toward the visual image permits the younger writer to confront and to move beyond the borrowed family memories that she unwillingly carries within herself.

NOTES

1. The cover picture of *New York* is one of a series of shots for the magazine by photographer Alison Jackson, who gives her reasons for doing the photo series: "We only know celebrities through photography . . . I'm showing how that can be manipulated in such easy fashion" ("Famous, Photogenic and Unborn," 2). For the original article in which her pictures appeared, see "Not Since Jesus" by Jason Zengerle.

2. Much has been written about Che Guevara's current status as a pop icon. For a historical account of the image of Che in Cuban media, see José Quiroga ("A Cuban Affair with the Image," in *Cuban Palimpsests* 81–115). For a different perspective, see Zoé Valdés, "Le pazze e il Che."

3. These books and their inner texts are analyzed in Alvarez Borland, *Cuban-American Literature of Exile*, 123–49.

4. *View of Dawn* has been studied from a variety of perspectives. See Peavler, "Cabrera Infante's Undertow," 125–45. See also Souza, *Guillermo Cabrera Infante: Two Islands Many Worlds;* Alvarez Borland, "Challenging History from Exile: Guillermo Cabrera Infante," in *Cuban-American Literature*, 28–38; Montenegro, "Que dise/ mi /nación"; and Pérez Firmat, "Remembering Things Past in Translation," in *Tongue Ties*, 107–23.

5. During the 1980s and 1990s the modern and postmodern concern with the subjectivity of history had much resonance with Latin America's well-known writers such as Vargas Llosa's *Historia de Mayta*, or García Márquez's *El General en su laberinto* as these writers explored the blunders committed by their governments in the name of official history. Cabrera Infante's *Vista del amanecer* also falls under this category of novels that challenge the official historical record. Can official history claim more truth than the private histories of the individuals that collectively make up such a history? From Unamuno's earlier meditations on "intrahistoria" to the volumes published by theorists such as Linda Hutcheon and Hayden White, writers, historians, and literary critics have meditated on this subject from the perspectives of their disciplines. See Hutcheon's *A Poetics of Postmodernism* and White's *Tropics of Discourse.*

6. Hampl's essay on memory seems imbued by Freud and Proust's ideas on memory and recollection. As Frauke Berndt reminds us, for Aristotle an image was always relative to something else. Imaginary identification was a way to repossess that which was forever lost, and recollection a way to supplement desire. The image is in fact our way to memory since our manner of remembering is always visual. Bernt places Aristotle' s seminal text at the beginning of a poetics of memory that took off in the twentieth cen-

tury first in the psychological field through Freud's *Interpretations of Dreams* (1900) and soon after in literature through the writings of Proust's *A la recherche du temps perdu* written between 1913 and 1920 (Berndt 24–25).

WORKS CITED

Alvarez Borland, Isabel. *Cuban-American Literature of Exile: From Person to Persona.* Charlottesville: University of Virginia Press, 1998.

———. Interview by Isabel Alvarez Borland. "Crossing the Crest of Forgetting: Interview with Ana Menéndez." In *Identity, Memory and Diaspora: Voices of Cuban-American Artists, Writers, and Philosophers.* Ed. Jorge Gracia, Lynette Bosch, and Isabel Alvarez Borland. New York: State University of New York Press, 2008. 173–81.

Barthes, Roland. *Camera Lucida: Reflections on Photography.* New York: Hill and Wang, 1981.

Berndt, Frauke. "*Aristotle Towards a Poetics of Memory.*" In Thomas Wagenbaur, ed., *The Poetics of Memory.* Tubingen: Stauffengburg-Verlag, 1998. 23–45.

Cabrera Infante, Guillermo. *View of Dawn in the Tropics* (translation of *Vista del amanecer en el trópico*, 1974). Trans. Suzanne Jill Levine, with the author. Berkeley: Creative Arts, 1978. Reprint, London: Faber and Faber, 1990.

———. Interview by Isabel Alvarez Borland. "*Viaje verbal a la Habana, Ah Vana!* Entrevista con Guillermo Cabrera Infante." *Hispamérica* 31 (1982): 51–68.

Hampl, Patricia. "Memory and Imagination." In *The Fourth Genre*, ed. Robert L. Root and Michael Steinberg. New York: Pearson Longman, 2005. 305–15.

Hutcheon, Linda. *A Poetics of Postmodernism: History, Theory, Fiction.* New York: Routledge, 1988.

Lang, Daryl. "Famous, Photogenic and Unborn." PDNEWSWIRE (April 11,2006). http://login.vnuemedia.com/pdn/newswire/article_display.jsp?vnu_content_id=1002315478.

Menéndez Ana. "Her Mother's House." *In Cuba I Was a German Shepherd.* New York: Grove, 2001. 203–29.

———. *Loving Che.* New York: Atlantic Monthly Press, 2003.

———. Interview by Robert Birnbaum. *The Morning News.* 18 February 2004. Online. http://www.themorningnews.org/archives/personalities/birnbaum_v_ana_menend

Montenegro, Nivia. "Qué dise/mi/nación? Island Vision in Guillermo Cabrera Infante's Vista del amanecer en el trópico." *Cuban Studies* 28 (1998): 125–33.

Peavler, Terry. "Cabrera Infante's Undertow." In *Structures of Power: Essays on Twentieth-century Spanish-American Fiction.* Ed. Terry Peavler and Peter Standish. Albany: State University of New York Press, 1996. 125–45.

Pérez Firmat, Gustavo. *Tongue Ties: Logo-Eroticism in Anglo-Hispanic Literature.* New York: Palgrave, 2003. 107–23.

Quiroga, José. *Cuban Palimpsests.* Minneapolis: University of Minnesota Press, 2005.

Sontag, Susan. *On Photography.* New York: Farrar, Straus & Giroux, 1973.
Souza, Raymond. *Guillermo Cabrera Infante: Two Islands, Many Worlds.* Austin: University of Texas Press, 1996.
Valdés, Zoé. "Le pazze e il Che." http://www.cubaitalia.org/n302005.htm.
White, Hayden. *Tropics of Discourse: Essays in Cultural Criticism.* Baltimore: Johns Hopkins University Press, 1973.
Zengerle, Jason. "Not Since Jesus." *NewYork* (April, 2006). Online. http://www.newyorkmetro.com/news/features/16652/.

3

Engendering the Nation

The Mother/Daughter Plot in Cuban American Fiction

Adriana Méndez Rodenas

nous sommes toujours mères dès lors que nous sommes femmes.
—Luce Irigaray, *Le corps-à-corps avec la mère*

By far the most pressing question in Cuban studies is: How has the nation been imagined across the gender divide? Whereas post-1959 Cuban fiction depicts the "heroic" exploits that led to the revolutionary takeover, Cuban American literature explores the fissures in identity irrupting during the 1960s and 1970s, with the 1980 Mariel mass exodus as a threshold in the definition of nation. While the symbolic status of the *cubana* has regressed on the territorial shore of the Cuban nation (*jineterismo* and its many variants), women's import in Cuban history—and the problematics of gender—has been addressed by anthropologists, historians, social commentators, literary and art critics of the one-and-a-half generation.[1] Despite their role as cultural "spokesmen" forced to far-flung diasporic flows from Barcelona to Mexico City, essayists and historians from the disenfranchised 1980s generation have been noticeably silent regarding the role of women, even while conjuring "la isla posible" that would bridge two halves of a lost whole.[2]

Male-authored memoirs—such as Pablo Medina's *Exiled Memories*, Gustavo Pérez Firmat's *Next Year in Cuba*, and Carlos Eire's *Waiting for Snow in Havana* —uphold the dominant gender as emblematic subject of exile. These by now canonical authors share a divided self, a backward glance to an idyllic childhood in Cuba, yet their narrators remain poised in a precarious present after acceptance (implying neither adaptation nor assimilation) of their American masculinities.

Second-generation Cuban American women authors such as Cristina García and Ana Menéndez center on that most pivotal of narrative plots—the story of female development and identity—"engendering the nation" by means of individual characters whose coming to womanhood coincides with crucial turning points in the island's history. Women's writing disturbs the linear plotting both of the canon of Cuban American autobiography and official realist novels extolling Cuban socialism. Both García and Menéndez depict the coming-of-age of its female protagonists as a repressed yet crucial factor in the refashioning of Cuban identity across the island/diaspora divide.

Adapting to our bicultural tradition Marianne Hirsch's pioneering study of the mother/daughter plot in Anglo-American literature, I want to show its crucial role in the Cuban American imagination. Though from different angles, both *Dreaming in Cuban* and *The Agüero Sisters* by Cristína García explore the intergenerational conflicts resulting from the mother/daughter bond, tensions that inflect the female characters' subjectivity, their historical experience, and, ultimately, our collective sense of destiny. While both novels span the course of modern Cuban history—the Cuban Republic viewed through Celia's letters in *Dreaming in Cuban* and emblematized in the fated marriage of Ignacio and Marta Agüero in *The Agüero Sisters*—these historical settings refract, in both fictions, the intricacies of the mother/daughter bond. Seen in terms of "A Matrix Light"—to echo García's poetic evocation in *Dreaming in Cuban* (167–81)—her novels reflect the "underside" of the Cuban nation, opening ways to imaginatively reconstruct both the psychic structure at the core of female identity and an as yet unrealized "isla posible" infused by female creativity and energy.

Ana Menéndez's *Loving Che* (2003), a haunting evocation of an orphaned daughter's search for her lost mother (of whom she has no living sign except for a few cryptic verses from Pablo Neruda), debunks the myth of the revolutionary hero while laying bare the psychological scars of a divided history. As the unnamed protagonist enters the labyrinth of her own past, she winds through a maze of torn photographs and tattered manuscripts in an ever elusive quest for her own identity. In contrast to Cristina García, *Loving Che* evokes the fragile allure of memory to trace the mother-daughter bond as an invisible pull, a bond that can no longer sustain female psychic identity. The failure of the mother-daughter bond depicted in this novel, with the daughter's permanent loss of moorings, attests to the radical inversion of insular history—the revolution not as forward teleological progress, but as negation; the island as a place of the imagination.

My analysis of the mother/daughter plot in Cuban American fiction combines two interrelated models. The first is derived from French feminist theory and its revision of psychoanalysis. By focusing on the maternal body, its recurrence as language, archetype, and symbol, this branch of feminist inquiry is most closely allied to the Cuban "family romance" and, consequently, to the Cuban American experience.[3] The second model adapts Hirsch's notion of the mother/daughter plots as part of the postmodern reshuffling of traditional gender paradigms and their respective roles in fiction.

Both approaches converge, however, in the model of female development Hirsch provides as basis for this most universal of gendered plots, which I will briefly recapitulate here. In essence, psychoanalytic theory posits the pre-oedipal bond between mother and daughter as the determining factor shaping female psychic identity (Hirsch 20). From this basic bond evolves a self-in-the-making who must strike a delicate balance between acquiring an individuated sense of identity while sustaining the vital link to the mother figure in her double role as sustenance and support and originary model for her own femininity. Female development is thus riddled "by the fluctuations of symbiosis and separation" (20). This abstract psychoanalytic model (whose claims to universality lie outside the scope of this chapter) reverberates in fiction as a writerly paradox: From the nineteenth century to the modern period, the mother/daughter plot has focused primarily on the daughter, whose subject position is *gained*—psychically and literally won—at the cost of objectifying (negating, eliding, surpassing) her mother. This "repression of the mother" relegates the maternal to "the position of silenced other," a muted space broken by the intermittent text of a daughter attempting to articulate her own budding subjectivity.[4]

The daughter's need to come to her own deepest self, separate from the mother, is exemplified in Pilar's story, the protagonist of *Dreaming in Cuban* who clearly masks Cristina García's position as a second-generation writer.[5] The rejection of the mother surfaces early in the novel; Lourdes's pro-American stance, a caricature of first-generation exiles, reveals the point of view of a rebellious daughter (170–71).[6] Pilar's rebellion is signaled not merely by her actions—as in her bungled escape to Miami (27–29; 57–64)—but also, more poignantly, by her artistic vocation. Like the artist Lily in Virginia Woolf's *To the Lighthouse*, who rejects Mrs. Ramsay's near-perfect staging of the ideal of domesticity (Hirsch 112–13), Pilar's rebuke of maternal values is transmitted via her art. Her painting mocking the State of Liberty is the antithesis of the adopted values that helped Lourdes carve out a new existence in exile with a successful commercial venture (141).[7] The Cuban "family romance" is cast here in terms of a unique female genealogy that skips one generation, hence eroding the middle position occupied by the mother.

In an effort to upstage Lourdes, Pilar seeks solace in her grandmother. When, on the brink of the Mariel crisis, mother and daughter embark on their fateful trip to Cuba, Lourdes is, despite her protests, effectively "erased" from the plot. This recalls Freud's essay on "Family Romances": The mother needs to fall so that she [the daughter] can be redeemed; she needs to err so that she can be saved" (Hirsch 55; 54–56). Pilar's connection to Abuela Celia effectively casts out the mother figure, showing not only how "maternal repression actually engenders the female fiction" (Hirsch 57), but also a "disturbance at the origin" of the Cuban family romance.[8] Pilar's portrait of her grandmother, what seals their intimate pact in subtle shades of blue (233), shows that "[t]he mother herself does not speak as subject and the woman artist writes or paints as a daughter" (Hirsch 118).

Pilar's initial sympathy for the ideals of the revolution compensates for her grandmother's solitary existence. Yet, by tacitly approving her mother's gesture to let Ivanito escape among the throngs gathered at the Peruvian embassy, Pilar ultimately betrays Celia, thus revealing her own daughterly ambivalence (238–40, 242). When she decides to return to New York (236), Pilar resolves not only her own identity crisis, but comes to acknowledge a repressed allegiance to her mother.

Pilar's coming-of-age story unfolds within an intricate web of female relationships. The "female subplot" represented by Felicia's, Celia's second daughter, unravels as a palimpsest revealing both the "role of women in an economy of male desire" and the underside of pre-oedipal bonding (Hirsch 21). In classic psychoanalytic theory, a woman gains full sexual maturity only after successfully negotiating the pull toward the maternal with the more compelling drive for individuation. Freud's essay on "Femininity" charts a "story of female development [. . .] [in which] the mother-daughter bond must be abandoned in favor of a strong attachment to the father, which, in turn, must be superseded by the adult love of another man and the conception of a child, preferably male" (Hirsch 99). Felicia's story dramatizes the failure of this model, as well as the dilemma facing a daughter who needs to compensate for a lack of maternal love by a chain of erotic entanglements. The violence riddling Felicia's two marriages—to Hugo Villaverde, who fathered her twins, Luz and Milagros, and the doted-on male child; then to the rough Ernesto Brito (148–49)—stems, in this reading, from the trauma of maternal abandonment (whose many ramifications are explored in Menéndez's *Loving Che*).

For Luce Irigaray, the primal event in the daughter's psyche is the need to break off the connection to the mother—a separation anticipated at birth with the cutting of the umbilical cord: "La blessure imparable, et irreparable, est celle de la coupure du cordon" (*Le corps* 23). Whereas in the Freudian model entry into the symbolic is marked by the daughter's rejection of the mother and adoption of her father's language, French feminist theory reverses this paradigm. In this alternative model, "the father functions as obstacle, as the antagonist who makes the continued connection between child and mother impossible, whose law decrees the maternal body off-limits to her child" (Hirsch 134). The "name-of-the-father," posited in Lacanian theory as dominant psychic structure ordering separation from the mother, is the cipher of paternal authority. Irigaray's rewriting invokes the name-of-the-father as glossing over that "irreducible trace of identity" left by the originary birth scar (*Le corps* 20).

In *Dreaming in Cuban*, the character of Felicia illustrates the effects of this daughterly dilemma—how to guard the desire for the mother while at the same time fulfilling the irrepressible mandate to cut herself off from the source. In her letters to Gustavo, her Spanish lover, Celia reveals the emotional circumstances determining the birth of her daughters—while Lourdes, the eldest, was an unwanted child ("A fat wax grows inside me. It's looting my veins . . . The baby is porous. She has no shadow," 50), the youngest, Felicia, came to compensate for a loveless marriage and her lover's abandonment ("I've named my new baby Felicia . . . She's beautiful and fat and with green eyes that fix on me disarmingly. I'll be a good mother this time," 52). Named after Celia's companion at the asylum, baby Felicia is destined to repeat the negative object-choice of her tragic namesake. As an adult woman, Felicia attempts to kill Hugo Villaverde with the same method as her precursor, only she does not succeed ("I've made a friend here, Felicia Gutiérrez. She killed her husband. Doused him with gasoline. Lit a match" 51)—what signals not only the failure of heterosexual desire (the fiery element is deployed for destruction instead of passion) but also the *cause* of this failure, an over-attachment to the maternal body.

Felicia's story aligns itself with a feminist revision of female development, in which "the connection to the mother . . . carries emotional weight, not the shift from father to husband" (Hirsch 133). Yet *Dreaming in Cuban* also reveals the shadow side of that "passionate connection to the mother" (Hirsch 134). The *santera* Herminia's recollection of Felicia, her fascination with her father's "divining coconut," prefigures the characters' obsession with coconuts as a fetish for maternal milk (184). A prelude to the deeper plunge into melancholy after her initiation, Felicia's crazed "summer of coconuts" (77, 188) culminates in a culinary frenzy sparked by the fear of separation. Ivanito, the oedipal son still tied to mother, echoes Felicia's belief that "the coconuts will pacify them, that the sweet white milk will heal them" (85), in reparation for the infant's primal need, when anxiously suckling at the breast, *to receive all* from the mother. Irigaray has beautifully evoked this primal moment in the developmental process: "Ce que l'enfant demande au sein, dès lors, n'est-ce pas *de recevoir tout?* Le tout qu'il recevait dans le ventre de la mere: la vie, la maison, celle où il habite et celle de son corps, la nourriture, l'air, le chaleur, le mouvement" (*Le corps*, 23, my emphasis).

A parallel scene occurs in Ana Menéndez's short story "The Perfect Fruit" when Matilde, the mother, throws a banana cooking spree in order to ward off the threat of separation represented by the visit of her soon-to-be-married son and his fiancée. By exorcising the phallus through ritual proliferations of the anatomically correct shaped fruit, Matilde avenges, as well, her husband Raúl's infidelity with the dark-haired stranger she had glimpsed in her wedding photograph (Menéndez 51–74).

The "longing to reexperience symbiotic union with the mother" (Hirsch 133) thrusts Felicia into madness, the *folie* theorized by Irigaray in her inscription of that most primal of affections: "Et quand le nom propre est donné à l'enfant,il vient déjà à la place de la marque la plus irréductible de sa naissance, le nombril. Le nom propre [est. . . .] toujours en décalage par rapport à cette trace d'identité la plus irréductible: la cicatrice la couture du cordon" (*Le corps* 20).

Felicia's initiation as a daughter of Obbatalá prefigures this repressed wish for the archaic: "Sixteen days before the *asiento*, Felicia went to live with La Madrina." Giving her "seven white dresses, seven sets of underwear and nightclothes, seven sets of bedding, seven towels . . . all white," *la Madrina's* lavish care and comfort—promised too by the saint's Catholic avatar, la Virgen de las Mercedes—scenifies the desire for pre-oedipal bliss (*Dreaming* 186–87). In order to reach that embryonic, *in uterus* stage, "Felicia changed every day to stay pure" (187). The flight toward a mother-surrogate evokes what Irigaray calls "le rapport au placenta, cette première maison qui nous entoure et dont nous transportons partout le halo" (*Le corps* 22).

Proof that "one does not move without the other," Irigaray's dictum for the power and perpetuity of the mother-daughter bond (*Et l'une* 22), is that Felicia's demise seals her mother Celia's ultimate erasure from the text. Grandmother Celia's final surrender to the marine matrix reenacts the negative paradigm of female development set forth in Kate Chopin's *The Awakening*, in which an unattached woman without a place in the prevailing gender system sees no choice but to swim out to sea. Before taking her final plunge, Celia had gone adrift but her bond to Pilar had made her come back to life (215)—what can be interpreted as an attempt at self-fashioning after experiencing daughterly abandonment: "Women who outlive their daughters are orphans, Abuela tells me" (222). This repeats a cycle begun years ago, when Celia's own mother had banished her. As revealed in a letter to Gustavo (100), Celia's most painful and repressed memory is of the day when her mother put her on a train to Havana and voluntarily "orphaned" her, leaving her forever stranded. "This pattern, evoked through one solitary orphan in García's novel, proves that "the mothers, themselves motherless, can only perpetuate a cycle of abandonment" (Hirsch 48).

When, at the end of the novel, Celia releases herself onto "the darkened seas" (244), this ultimate act of self-effacement repeats the trauma of a "motherless daughter" left without solace and maternal comfort (Hirsch 46). It also suggests the public repercussions of this most private of traumas. The power of the matriarch, this novel seems to imply, is weakened not only by the radical rupture between mothers and daughters, but also by the character's displacement of her archetypal power onto the *caudillo* figure. Hence maternal politics spill over into the collective destinies of the nation—despite their distance, Lourdes and Felicia resemble each other in their antipathy toward the revolution, while Celia's devotion to *el (Máximo) Líder* is marked by libidinal excess toward the "Father-of-the-Nation" (a parody of Lacan's Law-of-Father): "Felicia can't help feeling that there is something unnatural in her mother's attraction to him, something sexual" (110).[9]

In *Totem and Taboo*, Freud explained the birth of civilization in terms of the sons' primal revolt against the fathers, a compulsory sacrifice needed to insure the primacy of the social contract. Luce Irigaray claims, rather, that it is the Mother who is sacrificed in Western culture (*Le corps*, 15–16). García's second novel, *The Agüero Sisters*, opens with a scene of matricide, what forms the core of the novel and the secret that the orphaned yet estranged sisters try to unravel. The crime that Ignacio Agüero commits in secret deep in the Ciénaga de Zapata is not merely an individual act, but can be seen, from a psychoanalytic grid, as part of a collective "pattern of maternal repression" featuring only dead or absent mothers (Hirsch 48). Because Agüero's embedded story frames the entire history of the Cuban Republic, his originary matricide is necessarily linked to the violence characteristic of the period before and after the Machadato (Alvarez Borland 142, 144).

Yet the killing of Blanca Agüero has more serious implications for the imagining of nation across the gender divide. For Ignacio Agüero had gained acclaim among scientific circles for his *opus magnus* on ornithology, a book he was able to write only by taking flight outside of history (García, *Sisters* 156). Agüero's *Cuba's Dying Birds* appeared in 1933, coinciding with the turbulent year of the anti-Machado rebellion. Thus the shooting of Blanca in 1948 follows her husband's rise to the society of science, suggesting that the passage to the Symbolic or entry into the male-encoded world of knowledge is predicated on the sacrifice of the feminine and the maternal (Méndez Rodenas 405).

At first glance, Ignacio's unconscious act was allegedly motivated for the interests of science: "Agüero . . . carelessly decides to sacrifice his wife's life in order to possess a valuable specimen of a rare hummingbird" (Alvarez Borland 144). Yet the scene also shows the complicity between male dominion over nature and the equally powerful drive for mastery over women. For the body of the mother is naturalized as one of the many "dying birds" now extinct from Cuban skies, proving Irigaray's dictum that Western culture is staged as originary matricide.

In *The Agüero Sisters*, the enigmatic character of Blanca emblematizes modernity's ambivalence toward the maternal. The character's own problematic assumption of motherhood is highlighted in her recurrent obsession with milk (185–86), what parallels Felicia's insatiable thirst for coconuts; in both cases, this obsession derives from maternal lack, and the need to replenish the imaginary dyad of nursing infant and maternal breast, a pre-oedipal paradise forever lost.[10] This is an obsession skipping a generation, since Constancia's daughter Isabel devotes herself entirely to nursing her infant son Raku, exemplifying Lacan's Imaginary realm: "Isabel is here with her baby Raku. They float through the rooms together like a pair of anemic ghosts" (García, *Sisters* 287). This seamless pre-oedipal knot contrasts to her own mother, who felt a pang of desire at the tug of her baby boy's mouth (219).

Blanca's descent into madness parallels Felicia's retreat from the world as an initiate of Obbatalá, reenacting as well the gendered nature/culture split at the heart of Western logic. Despite being a scientist in her own right, Blanca's outlandish behavior depicts her as occupying the lower symbolic position attributed to woman as a being closer to Nature opposite to the Male dominion of reason (Schiebinger 144). Ignacio's seemingly involuntary act—that split second when his rifle shifted from the fluttering wings to the standing woman—is captured in a tense sentence: "I moved my sight from the hummingbird to Blanca, *as if pulled by a necessity of nature*" (García, *Sisters* 299, my emphasis). The essentializing of woman as always and already Nature, and hence paradigmatically mother before coming to her *Self* (captured in the Luce Irigaray quote with which I begin this chapter) provide a clue for Ignacio's crime. Indeed, the Male fear of engulfment by female anatomical openness could be a likely (if unconscious) cause: "Ainsi, l'ouverture de la mère, voire l'ouverture à la mère, apparaissent comme la menace (. . .) d'engouffrement dans la maladie: la folie. (. . .) La mère est devenue monstre dévorant" (Irigaray, *Le corps* 22).

What daughters Reina and Constancia inherit, on both shores of the island, is the symbolically dismembered body of the mother. The daughters' labyrinthine search back to their origins climaxes in the much-commented *Cuerpo de Cuba* sequence. With this name, Constancia markets a line of beauty products to her first-generation Miami clientele. At one level, the eroticized representation of the sisters as two racially and phenotypically distinct *cubanas* suggests a parody of the prevailing gender system during the Republic, with its rigid codes and superficial values.[11] But what Constancia ingeniously tries to sell is not so much a commercialized fetish but rather the fragmented body of the mother, sliced off and dissected by a male fantasy of possession/prohibition. Since "the figure of the mother is determined by her body more intensely than the figure of woman" (Hirsch 12), it is the *lack* of the maternal body that propels the frantic search for physical completeness that the *Cuerpo de Cuba* products intend to fill. In the last analysis, "the mothers and daughters remain alone and countryless to solve their fates" (Alvarez Borland 145).

In their role as mothers, Celia and Lourdes, Felicia and Blanca, and the next line of female progeny seem to occupy the borderline position defined by Julia Kristeva as "the abject." According to Kristeva "the abject is really the object who enables or impedes the child's development," an imposing absence who does not manifest herself as nourishing presence, but, on the contrary, as obstacle to the daughter's maturity.[12] Nowhere is this notion more compelling than in Ana Menéndez's *Loving Che*, where bondage to the mother (or to an idealized image of the mother) leads the daughter not to find herself, but, poignantly, to a state of permanent *errancia*. Rather than bolstering the daughter's emerging self, the radical absence of the mother (and the impossibility of finding her) condemns the daughter to be a perpetual nomad. The rupture of the mother/daughter bond prefigures, at the same time, the irreparable break between island and diaspora, thus symbolizing a nation bereft of itself—or, to echo Iraida Iturralde's poetic title, *La isla rota*, beyond the repair of memory.

Whereas Reina and Constancia Agüero reach the end of their journeys when they learn the secret of their mother's death in Cuba, the nameless daughter in Menéndez's *Loving Che* lacks the solace of identification with a mother figure. Cast in terms of a radical absence, the mother holds an untenable position as "neither subject nor object"; beckoning to her daughter through the mist of time. The daughter, as her life cycle advances, begins searching for a face who will reflect back her own womanly features. In the mirror of memory, the absent mother looms in the daughter's imagination as a (lost) sustenance of the self which she must irrevocably seek in order to compose those fragments dispersed by orphanhood and the after-effects of diaspora. Yet, as the daughter's story unfolds, the mother comes to occupy a role reverse from the nurturing source postulated in Hirsch's mother-daughter plot. This is because "[t]he abject has only one quality of the object—that of being opposed to I" (Kristeva 229–30).[13] Framed as fictional autobiography, the first section of the novel exposes the daughter's need of her mother, from which springs the compulsion named abjection, since "all abjection is in fact recognition of the *want* on which any being, meaning, language or desire is founded" (Kristeva 232).[14] After hearing the story of her past from her grandfather and reading the verses with which her mother endowed her as a keeper of memory (Menéndez, *Loving Che* 3–9), the protagonist undertakes a search for origins, all the while putting herself in place of that lost object. Defined from the first page of the novel as a "traveling subject" (Menéndez, *Loving Che* 1), the allure of the absent mother draws the daughter into an endless quest or wandering since "what is *abject* . . . the jettisoned object, is radically excluded and draws (the subject) to the place where meaning collapses" (Kristeva 230).[15]

That place is the island of Cuba. "When I landed and saw the capital . . . I knew I had returned to find my mother" (Menéndez, *Loving Che* 10)—the optimism of this phrase is soon tempered by a frustrated search through the streets of Havana. After returning to Miami, the daughter receives a box of photographs containing also a hidden manuscript (11–12), the inscription of the mother's desire for a daughter whom she had long ago banished from her side. The mysterious appearance of the package attests to the "massive and sudden emergence of uncanniness" associated with the abject (Kristeva 230). Like a Borgesian character, the daughter opens the labyrinth of her past, stepping into her mother's story at the same time as the reader of *Loving Che*—precisely the title of the middle section composed of Teresa's story.

As the untold in Western culture, the mother's life script is composed of short, first-person vignettes mixing erotic memories with sharp recollections of historical events. In a manner resembling Guillermo Cabrera Infante's *Vista del amanecer en el trópico*, the reconstruction of clearly identifiable episodes from the 1959 revolution compose an image of this historical process that aligns it with the notion of abject. According to Kristeva "[t]here looms, within abjection, one of those violent, dark revolts of being, directed against a threat that seems to emanate from an exorbitant outside or inside" (229).[16] Whereas the mother/daughter plot enacted in the novel represents the inner drama of abjection, the revolution (emblematized in the figure of *el Che*, an absent father) stands as its exterior threat, dominating, in the last analysis, the tenuous bond between mother and daughter.

Before reliving the memories of her dangerous liason with the Argentine, the mother recounts her fleeting (though unrecognized) encounters with her daughter, the same frustrated scenes alluded to in the latter's prologue. Since the mother-daughter bond is relived only through the machinations of memory, the uncanny quality of their relationship emerges in the sense of the strangely familiar or Kristeva's "*l'étrangeté.*" This quality will dominate, and ultimately subvert, the mother-daughter plot into a tale of abject love and submission. The first of such failed encounters—when the mother realizes the daughter is there, looking for her, but refuses to *acknowledge* her—triggers the recollection of a past episode of "loving" Che: "Memory, he'd said, is a way of reliving the past, the dead" (15). As Teresa had also experienced her mother's death (25–27), her orphaned condition transforms her into an "interior traveler," roaming Havana in much the same way as her daughter would later wander abroad as a result of her own stateless self. Why does the mother, seeing her daughter, continually refuse her? This double banishment—one from reality, the second from memory—attests to the power of abject; by leaving her daughter only unfulfilled maternal longing, Teresa places her in the desire of the Other, for, "from its place of banishment, the abject does not cease challenging its master" (Kristeva 230).

In terms of Hirch's mother-daughter plot, the middle section of *Loving Che* unfolds a tale of *jouissance*, narrating Teresa's sexual awakening but still repressing the story of her motherhood. In a sense, the abject floats on the surface of her furtive encounters with Guevara, as erotic joy and fulfillment are predicated on the lover's abandonment, or lack: "He said that the love lives inside the leaving" (Menéndez, *Loving Che* 110). Anticipation of Che's imminent sacrifice in Bolivia is present even in the most sublime of moments—"his first desire is to wear furrows into the earth; uncover mountains and forests until he finds beautiful death waiting faithfully for him" (113). Sensing the outcome of their forbidden passion, Teresa's fear is what eventually propels her to abandon her daughter: "I am afraid of his going, of the black space he will leave when he vanishes from my life" (111). Instead, Teresa projects this void unto her daughter as unfulfilled maternal longing, while seemingly denying maternal desire.

Mother and daughter are caught, in this novel, in "a deep well of memory that is unapproachable and intimate: the abject" (Kristeva 234). The daughter's estranged memories of her mother (which are rather the shreds of memory—fragments of verses, faded photographs, a scripted fiction) illustrates how "abjection is elaborated through a failure to recognize its kin; nothing is familiar, not even a shadow of a memory" (Kristeva 233). The daughter's struggle to recover her origins—her search in the final section of the book to legitimize Teresa's story, to find "the untouchable, impossible, absent body of the mother" against all odds—in that final journey to Cuba, is a poignant testament to what Kristeva had defined as the power of "the abject" (233).[17]

The same sense of uncanniness surfaces here, particularly in the eerie encounters narrated in the last section of the novel, when, going up the flight of stairs to one of the rickety houses where she knocks incessantly, the protagonist is greeted by an older woman, Caridad, who later entices her to a family dinner in that strange familiarity of postsocialist Cuba (*Loving Che* 191–94; 197–202). The daughter's missed opportunity with Manny, Caridad's son (202), is a parody of Teresa's ardent love for Che, almost as if maternal abandonment had precluded the daughter's sexual maturity. When the daughter finally steps into Teresa's studio, the mystery of her origin once again eludes her: "This woman who had put herself always beyond my grasp. Had her notes really been a fiction? An elaborate fable of her own life and death?" (215). By questioning the validity of the mother's story (as a young woman), the daughter's script remains open-ended, the secret of her paternity still haunting her.

Unlike the Miami Cuban in Pérez Firmat's *Next Year in Cuba* who frantically wants to know "Billita, *Who* am I?" (171), in *Loving Che* the daughter asks the only pertinent question for "a deject" or excluded one: "*Where* am I?" (Kristeva 235). Like the lost self of Kristeva's fashioning, "a deject . . . strays instead of getting [her] bearings, desiring, belonging, or refusing" (235).[18] When, at the end of the novel, the protagonist finds an image of *el Che* among old photographs in an antiquarian bookstore in Paris (an ironic resolution to the tale of female development), this image ciphers a transference of affect that attenuates (but does not alleviate) the pain of maternal rejection. The photo of *el Che* is "[t]he sublime object [that] dissolves in the raptures of a bottomless memory" (Kristeva 238).[19] At the end of "Letter on the Road," the forsaken daughter in *Loving Che* has no choice but to accept the fate of exile (228).

Beyond the psychological, Cuban American fiction shows that there is a major obstacle to full female development other than the failure of motherhood: the tortured course of Cuban politics, what mirrors the twisted destinies of the mother/daughter plot, effectively framing García's and Menéndez's novels beyond island and exile.[20] Recent Cuban American fiction reveals, then, the "underside" of the nation, the antiheroic (and mostly silent and *silenced*) story of mothers and daughters, who, at every stage of Cuban history, have been present, yet as continued and symbolic absence.[21] García and Menéndez seem to urge their readers to renegotiate the terms of Cuban identity by reverting their invisibility. As feminist critics, it is our task to gather these stories into the texture of a yet-to-be-born nation.

NOTES

1. Ruth Behar's *Translated Woman;* Marifeli Pérez Stable's, *The Cuban Revolution;* Ileana Fuentes's *Cuba sin caudillos;* Eliana Rivero's *Discursos de la diaspora;* Madeline Cámara's *La letra rebelde;* Isabel Alvarez Borland's *Cuban-American Literature of*

Exile, and Andrea O'Reilly Herrera, *Re(membering) Cuba*—a list not meant to be exhaustive but rather indicative of the revisionist efforts of this transitional generation.

2. Very few women are mentioned in either one of these works. See Rafael Rojas, *La isla posible;* Ivan de la Nuez, *La balsa perpetua.*

3. Hirsch shows how African American women's writing alters dominant paradigms for motherly-daughterly connection (15–16). Because of similar histories of uprooting and collective traumas, I suggest that Cuban American authors follow a similar path.

4. See Hirsch's description of mother/daughter plot in her introduction (12–14). She adds: "The work of women writers . . . participates in the process of placing the maternal in the position of silenced other" (20).

5. Alvarez Borland considers that "García's skillful use of point of view provides the reader with a variety of perspectives from members of the various generations and migratory waves and produces a panorama of Cuban history that transcends the story of 1959" (137–38).

6. "A representative of the first exile generation that left Cuba in the 1960s, Pilar's mother is ridiculed in the text" (Alvarez Borland 139).

7. Luis sees in the painting a critique of U.S. emigration policy, while Pilar's radical politics echoes the anti–Vietnam War perspective of Latino groups in New York (217–18).

8. Luis coincides in his appreciation that "[t]he hatred for the mother, expressed in generational terms," infuses García's novel. He then examines the characters' electra and oedipal complexes in relation to the paternal figure (225).

9. It is interesting to note that García refers to Fidel Castro only as "El Líder," without the superlative Cubans in and outside the island have attached to him (110). This may be a sign of the author's second-generation perspective, as are the intrusions of Mexican customs and idioms—the use of "*mi reina*," and the description of a Mexican-style *piñata*, rather than the ribbon-pulled type normally used in Cuba.

10. I show the link to the Linnaean classification of the mammalian gland as the primary identifying feature of mammals in the animal kingdom (Méndez 411–12). For Hélène Cixous, maternal milk becomes the metaphorical equivalent of the mother's speech (Hirsch 132).

11. "Reina y Constancia son dos cuerpos de Cuba—el mulato, oloroso al trauma de su quemada, y el blanco, oloroso a fragancias florales (. . .)—dos dimensiones físicas concretas en las que la corporeidad de la hembra se asume de manera consciente para replicar y mimetizar, así ironizándolo, el discurso tradicional sobre la mujer cubana" (Rivero 96). On how the sisters are diametrically opposed in terms of body type and libidinal energy, see Rivero 98.

12. Julia Kristeva, *Studies in Classic American Literaturers of Horror: An Essay on Abjection* (1982) cited in Hirsch, 171.

13. "De l'objet, l'abject n'a qu'une qualité—celle de s'opposer à je." (*Pouvoirs* 9).

14. "[T]oute abjection est en fait reconnaissance du manque fundateur de tout être, sens, langage, désir" (*Pouvoirs* 13).

15. Kristeva describes the abject in terms of a subject-object relationship in which the banished object "teases" or dominates the subject by creating an incessant (and unattainable) pull toward it, resulting in a "brutish suffering" ("une souffrance brutale") that won't let go of its victim ("Powers" 230).

16. "Il y a, dans l'abjection, une de ces violentes et obscures révoltes de l'être contre ce que le menace et qui lui paraît venire d'un dehors ou d'un dedans exorbitant" (Pouvoirs, 9).

17. "Essentiellement différente de 'l'inquietante étrangeté,' . . . l'abjection se construit de ne pas reconnaître ses proches . . ."; "fond de mémoire inaccessible et intime: l'abject."

18. "Celui par lequel l'abject existe est donc un jeté qui (se) place, (se) sépare, (se) situe et donc erre, au lieu de se reconnaître, de désirer, d'appartenir ou de refuser" (Pouvoirs 15). The original emphasizes the cutting off of a vital part of the self.

19. "L'objet' sublime se dissout dans les transports d'une mémoire sans fond" (Pouvoirs 19).

20. Luis details the historical subtext of *Dreaming in Cuban*, 219–22.

21. Lourdes Gil conjures the symbolic weight of two generations of women forced to remain outside the borders of nation in a stunning essay, "*Tierra sin nosotras.*"

WORKS CITED

Alvarez Borland, Isabel. *Cuban-American Literature of Exile: From Person to Persona*. Charlottesville: University of Virginia Press, 1998.

García, Cristina. *Dreaming in Cuban*. New York: Knopf, 1992.

———. *The Agüero Sisters*. New York: Knopf, 1997.

Gil, Lourdes. "Tierra sin nosotras." *Encuentro*, vols. 8–9 (1998): 166–71.

Hirsch, Marianne. *The Mother/Daughter Plot: Narrative, Psychoanalysis, Feminism*. Bloomington: Indiana University Press, 1989.

Irigaray, Luce. *Et l'une ne bouge pas sans l'autre*. Paris: Les Editions de Minuit, 1979.

———. *Le corps-à-corps avec la mère*. Montréal: Les editions de la pleine lune, 1981.

Kristeva, Julia. "Powers of Horror." *The Portable Kristeva*. Ed. Kelly Oliver. New York: Columbia University Press, 2002. 229–63.

———. *Pouvoirs de l'horreur. Essai sur l'abjection*. Paris: Éditions du Seuil, 1980.

Iturralde, Iraida. *La isla rota*. Madrid: Editorial Verbum, 2002.

Luis, William. *Dance Between Two Cultures. Latino Caribbean Literature Written in the United States*. Nashville: Vanderbilt University Press, 1997.

Méndez Rodenas, Adriana. "En búsqueda del paraíso perdido: La historia natural como imaginación diaspórica en Cristina García," *MLN* 116 (2001): 392–418.

Menéndez, Ana. *In Cuba I Was a German Shepherd*. New York: Grove, 2001.

———. *Loving Che*. New York: Atlantic Monthly Press, 2003.

Montenegro, Nivia. "The Agüero Sisters: Dismembering a Cuban Past." *Revista Hispánica Moderna*, vol. 57 (2004): 267–85.

Pérez Firmat, Gustavo. *Next Year in Cuba: A Cubano's Coming-of-Age in America*. 2nd ed. Houston: Scrivenery, 1995.

Rivero, Eliana. *Discursos desde la diáspora*. Sevilla: La Aduana Vieja, 2005.

Schiebinger, Londa. *The Mind Has No Sex? Women in the Origins of Modern Science*. Boston: Harvard University Press, 1989.

Trigo, Benigno. *Remembering Maternal Bodies: Melancholy in Latina and Latin American Women's Writing*. New York: Palgrave MacMillan, 2006.

4

Reading Lives in Installments

Autobiographical Essays of Women from the Cuban Diaspora

Iraida H. López

It took me a year's groping to discover what I call my tunneling process, by which I tell the past by installments as I have need of it.
—Virginia Woolf, *Moments of Being*

Animating this essay is the notion that narratives of selfhood have a bearing on the making of memory—even if they involve some renegotiating and reworking of the past—and that each one of these narratives can potentially help shape the outline of our collective consciousness. Furthermore, although every one of these narratives should be recognized as legitimate, backed by the corresponding life experience—however it is recalled and recounted—not all of them manage to survive the ravages of time and the zealousness of canonical selection. So we may ask: In weighing these texts, which memory ends up being discarded and which preserved? Whose memory is likely to be passed on as representative of a period? How can we avoid the seemingly inevitable fact that, in the words of a Chilean critic, "for every activated memory there are others that are repressed, inactivated, silenced, [and] for every legitimized memory plenty of memories wind up being excluded"? (Martín-Barbero). I shall come back to these questions later on in this chapter.[1]

My focus herein is directed at a number of autobiographical essays written by Cuban American women who have carved out a tradition that, although largely unacknowledged, should not be consigned to oblivion. I am referring to essays written by women in such collections as *Bridges to Cuba/Puentes a Cuba* (1995), edited by Ruth Behar and Juan León; *ReMembering Cuba: Legacy of a Diaspora* (2001), that we owe to Andrea O'Reilly Herrera; and *By Heart/De memoria: Cuban Women's Journeys In and Out of Exile* (2003), compiled by

María de los Angeles Torres; as well as other relevant pieces published independently or in collections whose principal theme is not the Cuban experience in itself, such as *Telling to Live: Latina Feminist Testimonios*. These are all essays by highly accomplished women, well known as academics, writers, and artists. Their essays signal the existence of a tradition since, as Jerome Bruner recognizes, "narratives do accrue, and, as anthropologists insist, the accruals create something variously called a 'culture' or a 'history' or, more loosely, a 'tradition'" (18). While the titles of these compilations, especially the first, *Bridges to Cuba*, come up once and again in studies of Cuban American literature because of the alternatives and originality they embody as editorial projects, the essays themselves have hardly been discussed. Although quite diverse, all are centered on a fragment of life—hence the title of this essay, "Reading Lives in Installments." Even those women writers who have published more works of this type, Eliana Rivero and Ruth Behar, reveal moments that define a female, bicultural self over the stretch of several essays. Instead of offering a sustained account of life's vicissitudes, trying to impose an order and presenting a rounded, polished life through a full-blown autobiography in which the subject feels authorized to represent herself as whole, these essays offer nonsequential episodes of a life lived in another language and other latitudes. This random, chopped approach to writing a life is far from being awkward; after all, one is more likely to recall the past in bits and pieces, in no predetermined, linear fashion. Moreover, the personal essay falls within a feminine tradition that has cultivated marginal subgenres, such as diaries, letters, and other noncanonical modalities within the autobiographical genre, a marginal one to begin with (Meyer Spacks 112). It would seem that many women feel comfortable with segmented structures such as the essay—judging by statements made by feminist critics (Jelinek 17).[2] My aim is to draw generalizations on these texts by looking at a small sampling that meets certain conditions, and from a particular vantage point. I propose to read them as manifestos sharing a number of noteworthy features—namely, their community-building efforts, in some instances transnational; their implicit questioning of a naturalized, archetypal (Cuban American) subject; the assertive tone corresponding to proclamation documents; and, last but not least, their impulse toward the future. What I hope to gain is recognition for this essayistic tradition in Cuban American letters.

First, however, a quick summary of the broader Cuban American autobiographical tradition will help identify the place women's texts occupy within this corpus. The few studies on Cuban autobiographies that exist have noted that only after the coming to power of the socialist regime in 1959 was there an increase in the publication of self-referential texts (Clark 9). Although not immediately in the wake of the revolution, the memoirs of renowned writers such as Heberto Padilla (*La mala memoria*), Reinaldo Arenas (*Antes que anochezca*), and Eliseo Alberto (*Informe contra mí mismo*), as well as by Carlos Franqui (*Retrato de familia con Fidel*) and Húber Matos (*Cómo llegó la noche*),[3] did not take long to be written, appearing between 1981 and 2004. All of these writers identify with Cuban culture, which, in spite of its notorious Caribbean extroversion, shows little proclivity to airing private matters, at least in writing. There is, in fact, a marked shortage of memoirs or autobiographies from the prerevolutionary period. Yet the Cuban Revolution had an effect similar to Mexico's in 1910, which also generated much interest in autobiographical writing. In fact, according to R. Woods, the Mexican Revolution paved the way for that type of literature in Mexico (13–22). The authobiographical boom during periods of revolution may be due, as Stephen Clark states, to the break with the past implicit in any substantive sociopolitical change. "A revolution as radical as the one in Cuba," Clark writes, "encourages self-reflection in terms of before and after, urging the individual to examine his or her own evolution within the context of national history" (9, my translation). Revolutions may also intensify the struggle for the control of memory. In such juncture, it may be vital for writers antagonized or marginalized by the revolutionary process, as the aforementioned certainly were, to want to settle accounts with dominant discourses by ministering their own "truth" or interpretation of the events in question.

Besides the radical change that took place on the island, there is the equally unsettling, far-reaching transformation brought about by exile and migration. This transformation gives rise to personal experiences placed at the outer limits of the memoirs by Padilla and the others, since these focus solely on events lived on the island during the Cuban Revolution. Events occurring elsewhere are, for the most part, of no consequence. Other writers, however, call attention to the hardships encountered within the new environment. There is no doubt that the uprooting and the subsequent adaptation to new surroundings bring about ruptures just as serious, if not more traumatic, that set off the need to recall and remember. Chicano writer Richard Rodríguez, himself the author of two autobiographical books, as well as postcolonial writers who have analyzed the figuration of the self have stated that the autobiographical genre allows minority writers to provide an appearance of continuity and cohesion to events perceived as disconnected, inconsequential, and anomalous. Although giving meaning to disjointed experiences is quite possibly the raison d'être of more than one autobiographical project, the necessity of this type of reflection for exiles and migrants cannot be understated. At the same time it is true, as Gustavo Pérez Firmat suggests, that the causes for the surge of autobiographies, from all quarters, within the United States may include the cult of individualism (and the democratic ideals, we may add, that make a potential autobiographer out of every citizen) that is symbolically ingrained in the common use of the first-person-singular pronoun, the essential subject of predication in the literary genre at hand and, as we know, one that is preferably omitted in Spanish: "When the language itself makes the writer's I grammatically redundant, autobiography verges on barbarism, and self-disclosure risks becoming a slip of the tongue" (*Facts of Life*, 175). As language instructors like to remind us, language does aim at transmitting culture and values. Also an outcome of the Cuban Revolution, the move to the once unfamiliar United States has inspired a good number of memoirs, some of them quite well known, such as *Next Year in Cuba: A Cubano's Coming-of-Age in America* (1995), by Pérez Firmat; *Waiting for Snow in Habana: Confessions of a Cuban Boy* (2003), by Carlos Eire; and *Exiled Memories: A Cuban Childhood* (1990), by Pablo Medina. Others include *The Write Way Home: A Cuban American Story* (2003), by Emilio Bejel,[4] and *Cuba on My Mind: Journeys to a Severed Nation* (2000), by Román de la Campa, whose differences with respect to the former I have examined elsewhere.[5] Since these authors left Cuba as children or adolescents—in most cases because of their parents' decision—they are located on the threshold of what Marianne Hirsch wisely calls "postmemory," which manifests itself when the traumas and crises of a generation have an impact on the identity of subsequent generations (cited by Reyes 848). This liminal location is also shared by the women autobiographers and essayists.

While the nearly twenty-five single-authored works in the bibliography of Cuban American memoirs attest to the vitality of the genre in this community, only recently have women begun to publish book-length first-person narratives—as if there remained shards of memory only in their midst. To date, only four of these have been published, all within the last eight years. Of uneven literary quality and comprising diverse approaches to subjectivity, María del Carmen Boza's *Scattering the Ashes* (1998), Flor Fernández-Barrios's *Blessed by Thunder: Memoir of a Cuban Girlhood* (1999), Mirta Ojito's *Finding Mañana: A Memoir of a Cuban Exodus* (2005), and Gigi Anders's *Jubana! The Awkwardly True and Dazzling Adventures of a Jewish Cubana Goddess* (2005) are all texts that betray feminine points of view, marked by the double articulation of ideologies of cultural difference and patriarchy. As such, they should not be overlooked in any gendered approach to the literature. Boza and Anders emphasize family relations; Fernández-Barrios, the legacy of spirituality; and Ojito, the Mariel exodus, about which she offers a poignant chronicle rather than a memoir. While these make up an incipient corpus of women's full-blown memoirs, I would argue that it is in the personal essay where Cuban American women, as memory keepers, are leaving a mark.

Indeed, the most remarkable contribution by women to the autobiographical literature of the diaspora to date is found in personal essays, rather innovative in comparison to previously used rhetorical forms. These testimonies serve to underscore the differences among autobiographical narratives, since, as Bruner points out, "[t]he perpetual construction and reconstruction of the past provide precisely the forms of canonicity that permit us to recognize when a breach has occurred and how it might be interpreted" (20). The frame of mind behind some of these essays, as Isabel Alvarez Borland has observed, differs from that conveyed by the memoirs of male writers. In reviewing the autobiographical essays by the two women writers included in the chapter on self-referential narratives of *Cuban-American Literature of Exile: From Person to Persona*, she states:

> Whereas the rhetorical task of the memoirs of [Virgil] Suárez, [Pablo] Medina, and [Gustavo] Pérez Firmat seeks to give homogeneity to a social group's awareness of itself socially and culturally, Eliana Rivero's and Ruth Behar's essays emphasize issues of definition and affirmation of identity. For the male writers this experience leads toward an unsettled view of the self and its relation to language; for the women authors the very separation from one's language and culture of origin becomes a step toward redefinition (62).

This redefinition hinges on the exploration of discourses on identity. Equally important are Alvarez Borland's comments about the inherent temporal dimension in texts written by these women, a temporal framework spanning the future: "Cuban-American women writers such as Eliana Rivero and Ruth Behar look mainly to the future in order to assert issues pertaining to identity and minority politics" (80).

This turn toward the future identified by the critic is one of my motivations for reading these texts as manifestos, in line with Sidonie Smith's definition.[6] The manifesto, as defined by Smith, is "a proof, a piece of evidence, a public declaration or proclamation . . . for the purpose of announcing past actions and explaining the reasons or motives for actions announced as forthcoming" (157). To be sure, those who pen any manifesto express, tacitly or explicitly, their discontent with what has prevailed to date, trying to replace it with another modus operandi (as an example, one need only remember André Breton's surrealist manifesto of 1924 going after Realism in favor of that other movement). Similarly, in order to modify the status quo, the authors of these Cuban/Cuban American manifestos set forth propositions that deviate from prior figurative practices.

What are the elements that make up these essays-manifestos? To begin, most of the essays are the result of a collective effort or common project around which Cubans and Cuban Americans, especially women, are grouped. Essays by women abound in the collections quoted above. Two of these collections, *Bridges to Cuba* and *By Heart/De memoria*, lay a bridge between the diaspora and the island, combining contributions from each side, thus reaffirming a legacy of dialogue and interaction that has prevailed throughout the years and against all odds. In the preface of *By Heart/De memoria*, María de los Angeles Torres refers to the cutting-edge role that women have played in this effort: "It had been women from many different perspectives, after all, who had played important roles in forging a paradigm of politics and identity that was inclusive of both home and host countries, mindful of multiple points of reference. Surely, men have been involved, but women have been most critical to the endeavor and have seldom been recognized publicly" (x). Notably, the editors of these anthologies have all been women (academics), and at least one woman, Lourdes Casal, was a force behind a previous collection, *Contra viento y marea* (1978), which ushered in the tradition of these encompassing projects.[7] They would appear committed to the forging of communities so as to ward off the adverse effects of exile, since, as Laura Alonso Gallo and Fabio Murrieta have pointed out, ". . . the perspective of the exile . . . tends to be personal, not collective, due to the impact of separation. It is hard to understand oneself as part of an exodus and see oneself as belonging to a larger group that includes the individual self. That is why one of the major efforts in exile entails seeking the unity or integration of its parts" (13, my translation). For whatever reason, there is every indication that many women have successfully met this challenge—and not because of any innate attribute. It is likely that women's lesser position in the host society as well as in their own subgroup prods them to understand the need for solidarity and alliance, just as, similarly, other Latina writers come to appreciate the value of coalitions when they gain consciousness of some kind of oppression that makes them vicariously experience other types of injustices (Lourdes Torres 275). It is easier to empathize when one's experience runs parallel with that of others. Therefore, their interest in inclusive projects would come about as a response to their subordinate position within a social fabric still infused with patriarchal values rather than to a natural, inborn trait that leads them to support collective projects. Be that as it may, Cuban women living on the island have also done their part in this collaboration, as can be culled from the essays by Josefina de Diego or Teresa de Jesús Fernández in *By Heart/De memoria*. These essays compassionately portray, as has seldom been done publicly, the sense of absence and loss caused by migration among those who stayed behind. They suggest that it is now imperative to gather experiences lived on both sides of the Florida Straits in order to underline their inextricable bonds.

According to Sidonie Smith, another characteristic of manifestos is the questioning of a universal subject and of a fixed identity corresponding to cultural models seemingly natural and neutral. This critical questioning—not exclusively women's (let it be clear), although stressed in their writing—has a dual target: The identity explored in many of the texts undermines theories about the impending assimilation to U.S. society as well as the predicted dissolution of ties to the native homeland. Perhaps as a result of lives lived in contact or border zones, the most successful essays reveal a resistance to paradigms sanctioned by hegemony. It would seem there is an awareness of ethnic labeling as a minefield because of its reductionist constrictions, and, consequently, of the strategic value of constructing a personal identity. Thus, the national identity of some of the essay writers is rehashed—mixed or adjoined with other identities, such as that of Latina, in María de los Angeles Torres, Ruth Behar, and Eliana Rivero; *cubacana* (a combination of Cuban and Chicana), *fronterisleña* (an amalgamation of border and island identity) or cubana plus, in Rivero; *Cubanḋ* or *cubanita pasada por agua*, in Andrea O'Reilly Herrera; *judía* or *jubana* (a mixture of Jewish and Cuban), in Behar and Kenya Dworkin y Méndez; *mulata*, in Lourdes Casal. These mixed identities ultimately transgress the pigeonholing, be it Cuban, Cuban American, or the American black/white script. For understandable and sometimes not so understandable reasons some of these labels (*latina, judía, cubacana, fronterisleña*) are considered out of place within the Cuban American rubric. A leitmotiv in these texts is the urgency to coin new, individually tailored categories, since the authors are aware of other components and other "voices" (the term used by Rivero in her essay, "I Can Fly") that do not always coexist in harmony yet do not necessarily cause confusion or distress. The result is an intricate ambivalent sense of identity. María de los Angeles Torres sums up the process as follows: "While for years I felt that I had neatly put away pieces of my identity in different parts of the world, I now understand that I do not have to accept categories which split who I am. Instead I must construct new categories, new political and emotional spaces in which my multiple identities can be joined" ("Beyond the Rupture" 36).

Eliana Rivero refers to her myriad identities in the introduction to her book of essays *Discursos desde la diáspora:*

> . . . upon settling in the western United States, near the border with Mexico . . . I let go of many of the notions I then considered narrow concepts of nationalism and of its subsequent labeling and limitations, and sailed in a changing sea of fluid identities that eventually included my strong adherence to a U.S. Latino identity, with Cuban roots but with many other modifying factors. (19, my translation)

This, of course, has always been the paradox of identities—its multiple components. The difference lies in bringing to the fore those other "modifying factors," which Rivero goes on to explore in her book, thus rendering more complex the apparent essentialism and strict confinement of national identity. This calls for making up a sense of self not attached to culturally prescribed criteria. Carlota Caulfield personalizes the dilemma in the following way:

> Since 1981, I have been "jumpy" and suffer through continual metamorphosis. Years later, in the late 1980s and 1990s in California, people didn't know how to pigeonhole me, due to my "complex" origins; thus, I created confusion for the lovers of order. I am labeled Cuban American, Hispanic, Latina, Cuban Irish American, Caribbean American, Cuban Irish Catalán Jewish American, and a woman of color. I remember somebody saying that my combination of blood made me a Molotov cocktail. (240)

For Kenya Carmen Dworkin y Méndez, her name in and of itself contains a similar dilemma:

> Even my name evokes an identity crisis. Kenya (African) + Carmen (Hispanic) + Dworkin (Russian/Polish) + Méndez (Hispanic) is not only a mouthful. It is a challenge that defies national or cultural identification. I have been persistently called Carmen by an Africana studies professor at Berkeley, who couldn't bring himself to call me Kenya; I have responded to my name, Kenya, being called on the first day of class and had the teacher stare right through me and mark me absent; and Dworkin—well, I give up. (204)

It is no wonder that new terms are needed in order to capture the diversity these women embody. As an element of that diversity, race adds its own quandaries to the topic. Lourdes Casal reflects on a childhood lived amid dynamic processes of religious, ethnic, and racial syncretism in "Memories of a Black Cuban Childhood," published in *Nuestro* magazine in 1978, three years before her untimely death. With a truly mixed ethnic makeup, Casal had all the markings of a syncretic Cuban identity that she absorbed through family portraits—one of a Chinese man with a "very stern look in his small, black eyes"; the other one of a mulata "with a somewhat sad expression"—and her own initiation into *santería.* Still, she gains full awareness of that mixed-race identity only upon discovering, as an immigrant, that racial categories current in other societies do not take her own into account:

> In the U.S. during the 60s, I was forced to look at my Blackness with different eyes. I had become accustomed to considering myself una mulata in a mulatto country, in a quintessentially mulatto culture. The U.S. was a shock. Here I had to assert my Blackness somehow—even of particularly as a Hispanic Black—in a country where Black and White were defined in opposition to one another. (62)

Though she is classified as black in the United States (at a time when static racial categories determined by genealogy still ruled), in Africa, during a trip in search of her ancestors' culture, her relative whiteness is thrown in her face. Casal refuses to accept these classifications of exclusion and, at the top of her voice, claims her mulata identity.

Casal's text represents the qualities of a manifesto, a proclamation document that publicly states, at the top of its voice, the matter at hand. It is in this third aspect that the manifesto differs from other Latin American autobiographical texts written by women that have been studied by Sylvia Molloy: "Women's autobiographical accounts have generally opted for the intimist mode, which is unusual in male Hispanic American literature" (14, my translation).

Many of the essays examined touch on personal subjects such as family loss and separation, sometimes viewed as dismemberment; not knowing where "home" really is; the travails of adapting to a new society, even more difficult for those who came as children, by themselves, through the Peter Pan operation; and the challenge of mastering a second language, along with the flipside of this coin: refusing to lose the mother tongue as a means of expression. The essays written by Lourdes Gil, Uva de Aragón, Flora González Mandri, and Carlota Caulfield are representative and resemble, because of the personal nature of these topics, the texts studied by Molloy. These females' narratives stand in marked contrast with memoirs of male writers such as Padilla or Franqui, in which private life, family relationships, and the intimate recesses of personality are barely mentioned. This is not to say, however, that manifestos by women avoid public subjects. Quite the contrary, many have no qualms about intervening in areas involving matters of nation and state, an area which is to this day so problematic for women. Some essays stop to consider alternative political viewpoints such as the "third option," distant from both the Cuban revolutionary ideology and that sector of the Miami enclave that dances to the tune of the more recalcitrant exiles, as conveyed by Madeline Cámara and María de los Angeles Torres. They denounce authoritarian projects that repress individuality. Others are in favor of redefining the boundaries of the homeland, as reflected in the essays by Rivero and Torres. Ultimately, these essays call for uncoupling the triad of territory, culture, and identity—a political agenda if there is one. Still others condemn the torture suffered in prisons, as María Brito does by evoking one such tragic incident in one of her installations, a description of which she offers in an essay. According to Sidonie Smith, the autobiographical manifesto asserts "the politization of the private and the personalization of the public" (160). There is no space for the dichotomy between private and public affairs. Smith also points out that the manifesto "always foregrounds the relationship of subjectivity to power" and that it insists on new interpretations as tools in the struggle against power (163). When these autobiographical manifestos venture into this field, they concur with feminists who promote the "theory in the flesh" and, as Cherríe Moraga has written, the politics they thus embrace arise from a need, from experiences that leave a painful scar under the skin (23). They appeal for the adoption of more tolerant State and national policies.

Instead of wallowing in the nostalgia for the past that has marked a good part of the literature written by exiles, these personal essays are instead projected toward the future. In fact, the inevitable look at the past that is part and parcel of all autobiographical reflection, which in these manifestos often goes back one or two generations, serves as a guide for the future. For example, in María Cristína García's essay "Abui," included in *ReMembering Cuba*, the grandmother provides the role model for this attitude: "She never let her nostalgia paralyze her as it did so many of our elders; there were just too many things to do and see in *el exilio* . . ." (140). When the granddaughter is about to visit Cuba for the first time, the grandmother draws a map of Havana, by heart, for her use. Thanks to this map, the granddaughter can find her way in the reclaimed city as adeptly as "abui" learned to get around in Miami. So the map provided by the grandmother-turned-cartographer serves the narrator not only as a tool to avoid feeling physically and metaphorically lost, but also as a means for superimposing temporal planes (what existed then versus what exists now). Hence it provides a continuum of memories and a frame of reference for what is to come. A contemporary of María Cristína García's, María Martínez-Cañas, whose artistic work integrates artifacts imbued with memory such as personal documents, photographs, and maps, has said of the latter: "A map . . . is not only a representation of a territory. To me, it is a visual source for a unique language and, at the same time, a painful tool for understanding where I came from and who I am" (261). This visual space, juxtaposed to the grandmother's previous stories that lend narrative density, is the one partly reclaimed by María Cristina García with her handmade map. Her memory now contains the cumulative imagination of historical memory.

Maps are no doubt a recurring motif in the texts I have examined, surpassed only by family albums. The essay "Juban América" begins with a reflection on a photograph of Ruth Behar's grandfather. Behar recalls the itinerant history of her Jewish ancestors to advocate for the recognition of an also hybrid, itinerant Cuban identity at odds with hardened notions of cultural authenticity and racial purity. But the photograph, a substitute for referents we don't know because they belong in the past—and also a substitute for referents we do know because they exist in the present—disappears at the end of the article, which opens up to the future. Significantly, Behar's camera breaks down when she is taking pictures at the gravesite of a relative in Havana and then ends up reclaiming her place in the present Cuba: "This *Jubana* will have to taste the salt of memory and of loss, but she will also have to make a *rinconcito*, a small place, for herself in the Cuba of the present" (221). Her integration at this point makes taking photographs less necessary, since these are replaced by unbounded, unframed reality. Another role played by photographs is shown in the essay by Ester Rebeca Shapiro Rok, "Finding What Had Been Lost in Plain View," in *Bridges to Cuba*. After twenty-nine years of absence, Shapiro Rok returns to Cuba in 1990, where she recovers a part of the family that she thought she had lost. Although her family on this side of the Florida Straits initially opposes Ester's trip, the photographs she takes during her stay make up for part of the pain: "While my father continued, resentful and embattled, to insist that I was betraying the family with my communist sympathies, my mother, Tía Elsa, and Sofía poured over the photographs of our old neighborhood in El Vedado . . . surprised and delighted to see the preservation of their lost, once much-loved world" (95). In this case, the role of photographs is to reconnect what has been disjointed by time and history. It affords the women in the family—the father's self-exclusion having been established—the possibility of regaining the city and reunifying the Cuba of their memory with today's Cuba, thus giving them a sense of wholeness.

I would like to conclude by betting on a future more just and tolerant of the differences presented in these autobiographical accounts, as if they were "recollections of things to come" (to make use of Elena Garro's clever title), and at the same time to vie for their wider recognition. At this point, it makes sense to take up again and paraphrase Martín-Barbero's pertinent question: How can the repression and silencing of certain memories be prevented while others are legitimized and kept alive? I believe it behooves critics and scholars to pay more attention to these women's lives—told in installments, and full of other expectations and other poetics—as befit manifestos. Instead of silencing them, we should hold on to them as a celebrated and celebratory part of Cuban "postmemory." At stake is something I associate with a quote by Milan Kundera. In it, the Czech writer cautions that at the root of human conflict there is a struggle for the definition of the past, that is, a struggle for history as it has been passed down from generation to generation:

> People are always shouting they want to create a better future. It's not true. The future is an apathetic void of no interest to anyone. The past is full of life, eager to irritate us, provoke and insult us, tempt us to destroy or repaint it. The only reason people want to be masters of the future is to change the past. They are fighting for access to the laboratories where photographs are retouched and biographies and histories rewritten. (22)

Appreciating these manifestos means winning half the battle over forgetfulness (the other half, of course, is out of our hands, for other interpretations and reimaginings will replace ours in the future). There is at least one case in world literature of a character whose faulty memory renders him incapable of facing the rest of his life. I am referring to Septimus Warren Smith in Woolf's *Mrs. Dalloway*. According to at least one critical interpretation, Septimus loses his will to survive when he is no longer able to remember the past.[8] Surely there is something to be learned about the dangers of forgetting.

NOTES

1. An earlier version of this chapter, "La vida por entregas: textos autobiográficos femeninos," was presented at the Sixth International Conference on Cuban Studies organized by the Cuban Research Institute at Florida International University in February 2006.

2. Estelle Jelinek's still influential book is required reading in studies on women's autobiographies. For a critical balance of the observations made in this and other feminist studies, see Domna Stanton's book, *The Female Autograph*. For Stanton, what intelligibly makes autobiographical work difficult for women is not their tendency toward fragmentation or collectivity (*we* instead of the requisite *I*), as other critics claim, but the act of writing itself, which in symbolic terms (the phallic pen) is a masculine prerogative.

3. Most of these books have been translated into English. Padilla's memoirs have been published under the title *Self Portrait of the Other* (Farrar, Straus and Giroux 1990); Franqui's, as *Family Portrait with Fidel: A Memoir* (Random House, 1984); and the book by Arenas, as *Before Night Falls* (Viking, 1993).

4. The original Spanish version of this book, titled *El horizonte de mi piel*, was published by Editorial Aduana Vieja, Cádiz, Spain, in 2005. As far as I know, the others were written (and published) originally in English.

5. See "La elaboración del espacio en la última narrativa autobiográfica cubanoamericana" in *Temas: Cultura, ideología, sociedad*, 156–60. The narratives by Bejel and de la Campa place the reader in a different terrain, one that replaces the emphasis on time, that is, on a *before* and *after* typical of ethnic literature, with an emphasis on space inherent in the diasporic memoirs' back-and-forth movement between the island and the United States (I refer interested readers to Susanna Egan's distinction between the two). The memoirs by Pérez Firmat, Eire, Medina, Bejel, and de la Campa are not, by any means, the only memoirs published in recent times, which number nearly thirty in total when both single- and multiple-authored works are taken into account.

6. Sidonie Smith's book, *Subjectivity, Identity, and the Body. Women's Autobiographical Practices in the Twentieth Century*, is a study of women's autobiographies as resistance to cultural practices and meanings that naturalize the unifying, stable subject. Smith plays with the word "body" in phrases such as "cultural body" and "body politic," arguing that many women subvert the normative content of these entities through the autobiographical genre. Smith quotes the hybrid forms of the genre that Caren Kaplan calls "out-law genres" and adds the term "manifesto," whose constituting elements Kaplan derives from the work of Gloria Anzaldúa, from Cixous's essay, "The Laugh of the Medusa," and from Donna Haraway's article, "A Cyborg Manifesto: Science, Technology, and Socialist-Feminism in the Late Twentieth Century." I adopt the term because I am drawn by the convergence of some of the elements, explained below, of the manifestos with those found in the best essays I have read by Cuban American women. Of course, not all of the four elements are present in each of the essays.

7. Ruth Behar and Lucía M. Suárez have recently compiled another anthology of testimonies by Cubans from the diaspora living in various countries and by Cubans living in Cuba. It represents a follow-up to Behar's earlier *Bridges to Cuba* project, but from a global perspective. This new book, entitled *The Portable Island: Cubans at Home in the World* (2008), is published by Palgrave Macmillan.

8. See Jeanne Schulkind's introduction to the book by Woolf, *Moments of Being*.

WORKS CITED

Alberto, Eliseo. *Informe contra mí mismo*. Madrid: Santillana, 1997.

Alonso Gallo, Laura P. y Fabio Murrieta. *Guayaba Sweet: Literatura cubana en Estados Unidos*. Cádiz: Editorial Aduana Vieja, 2003.

Alvarez Borland, Isabel. "Autobiographical Writing. Negotiating an Identity." *Cuban-American Literature of Exile: From Person to Persona.* Charlottesville and London: University Press of Virginia, 1998. 61–87.

Anders, Gigi. *Jubana! The Awkwardly True and Dazzling Adventures of a Jewish Cubana Goddess.* New York: HarperCollins, 2005.

Arenas, Reinaldo. *Antes que anochezca.* Barcelona: Tusquets, 1992.

Behar, Ruth, ed. *Bridges to Cuba/Puentes a Cuba.* Ann Arbor: University of Michigan Press, 1995.

———. "Juban América." *King David's Harp: Autobiographical Essays by Jewish Latin American Writers.* Ed. Stephen A. Sadow. Albuquerque: University of New Mexico Press, 1999. 199–223.

Bejel, Emilio. *The Write Way Home: A Cuban-American Story.* Trans. Stephen J. Clark. Andover, MA: Versal, 2003.

Boza, María del Carmen. *Scattering the Ashes.* Tempe: Bilingual, 1998.

Brito, María. "Merely a Prayer." *ReMembering Cuba: Legacy of a Diaspora.* Ed. Andrea O'Reilly Herrera. Austin: University of Texas Press, 2001. 54–57.

Bruner, Jerome. "The Narrative Construction of Reality." *Critical Inquiry* 18.1 (1991): 1–21.

Cámara, Madeline. "Third Options: Beyond the Border." *Bridges to Cuba/Puentes a Cuba.* Ed. Ruth Behar. Ann Arbor: University of Michigan Press, 1995. 217–24.

Casal, Lourdes. "Memories of a Black Cuban Childhood." *Nuestro* 2.4 (1978): 61–62.

Caulfield, Carlota. "Even Names Have Their Exile." *ReMembering Cuba. Legacy of a Diaspora.* Ed. Andrea O'Reilly Herrera. Austin: University of Texas Press, 2001. 236–41.

Clark, Stephen J. *Autobiografía y revolución en Cuba.* Barquisimeto, Venezuela: Fondo Editorial Río Cenizo, 1999.

De Aragón, Uva. "Sentir en cubano, escribir en español: un testimonio generacional." *Guayaba Sweet: Literatura cubana en Estados Unidos.* Ed. Laura P. Alonso Gallo and Fabio Murrieta. Cádiz: Editorial Aduana Vieja, 2003. 351–64.

De Diego, Josefina. "Through Other Looking Glasses." *By Heart/De memoria: Cuban Women's Journeys In and Out of Exile.* Ed. María de los Angeles Torres. Philadelphia: Temple University Press, 2003. 85–102.

De la Campa, Román. *Cuba on My Mind: Journeys to a Severed Nation.* London and New York: Verso, 2000.

Dworkin y Méndez, Kenya Carmen. "Next Stop Ninety Miles." *ReMembering Cuba: Legacy of a Diaspora.* Ed. Andrea O'Reilly Herrera. Austin: University of Texas Press, 2001. 202–206.

Egan, Susanna. *Mirror Talk: Genres of Crisis in Contemporary Autobiography.* Chapel Hill: University of North Carolina Press, 1999.

Eire, Carlos. *Waiting for Snow in Havana: Confessions of a Cuban Boy.* New York: Simon & Schuster, 2003.

Fernández, Teresa de Jesús. "From This Side of the Fish Tank." *By Heart/De memoria.*

Cuban Women's Journeys In and Out of Exile. Ed. María de los Angeles Torres. Philadelphia: Temple University Press, 2003. 75–84.

Fernández-Barrios, Flor. *Blessed by Thunder: Memoir of a Cuban Girlhood.* Seattle: Seal, 1999.

Franqui, Carlos. *Retrato de familia con Fidel.* Barcelona y Caracas: Seix Barral, 1981.

García, María Cristina. "Abui." *ReMembering Cuba: Legacy of a Diaspora.* Ed. Andrea O'Reilly Herrera. Austin: University of Texas Press, 2001. 137–42.

Gil, Lourdes. "Against the Grain: Writing Spanish in the USA." *ReMembering Cuba: Legacy of a Diaspora.* Ed. Andrea O'Reilly Herrera. Austin: University of Texas Press, 2001. 179–81.

González Mandri, Flora. "A House on Shifting Sands." *Bridges to Cuba/Puentes a Cuba.* Ed. Ruth Behar. Ann Arbor: University of Michigan Press, 1995. 76–79.

Grupo Areíto. *Contra viento y marea.* La Habana: Casa de las Américas, 1978.

Jelinek, Estelle, ed. *Women's Autobiography.* Bloomington: Indiana University Press, 1980.

Kundera, Milan. *The Book of Laughter and Forgetting.* New York: Knopf, 1980.

Latina Feminist Group, ed. *Telling To Live: Latina Feminist Testimonios.* Durham & London: Duke University Press, 2001.

Lopez, Iraida H. "La elaboración del espacio en la última narrativa autobiográfica cubanoamericana." *Temas: Cultura, ideología, sociedad* 44 (2005): 156–60.

Martín-Barbero, Jesús. "Medios: olvidos y desmemorias." http://www.revistanumero.com/24medios.htm (August 7, 2005).

Martínez-Cañas, María. "Historia rota (Broken History)." *ReMembering Cuba: Legacy of a Diaspora.* Ed. Andrea O'Reilly Herrera. Austin: University of Texas Press, 2001. 260–62.

Matos, Húber. *Cómo llegó la noche.* Barcelona: Tusquets, 2004.

Medina, Pablo. *Exiled Memories: A Cuban Childhood.* Austin: University of Texas Press, 1990.

Meyer Spacks, Patricia. "Selves in Hiding." *Women's Autobiography.* Ed. E. Jelinek. Bloomington: Indiana University Press, 1980. 112–32.

Molloy, Silvia. "El teatro de la lectura: cuerpo y libro en Victoria Ocampo." *Autobiografía y escritura.* Ed. Juan Orbe. Buenos Aires: Ediciones Corregidor, 1994. 13–30.

Moraga, Cherríe, and Gloria Anzaldúa. *This Bridge Called My Back: Writings by Radical Women of Color.* San Francisco: Aunt Lute, 1981.

Ojito, Mirta. *Finding Mañana: A Memoir of a Cuban Exodus.* New York: Penguin, 2005.

O'Reilly Herrera, Andrea. *ReMembering Cuba: Legacy of a Diaspora.* Austin: University of Texas Press, 2001.

Padilla, Heberto. *La mala memoria.* Barcelona: Plaza y Janés Editores, 1989.

Pérez Firmat, Gustavo. *Next Year in Cuba: A Cubano's Coming of Age in America.* New York: Anchor, Doubleday, 1995.

———. "The Facts of Life on the Hyphen." *ReMembering Cuba: Legacy of a Diaspora.* Ed. Andrea O'Reilly Herrera. Austin: University of Texas Press, 2001. 173–76.

Reyes, Israel. "Recuerdos 'parciales' y el *closet* de la literatura: ficción y autobiografía de Judith Ortiz Cofer." *Revista Iberoamericana* 212 (2005): 847–63.

Rivero, Eliana. *Discursos desde la diáspora.* Cádiz: Editorial Aduana Vieja, 2005.

———. "'Fronteraisleña' 'Border Islander.'" *Bridges to Cuba / Puentes a Cuba.* Ann Arbor, MI: University of Michigan Press, 1995. 339–44.

———. "I Can Fly: Of Dreams and Other Nonfictions." *Telling To Live: Latina Feminist Testimonios.* Ed. Latina Feminist Group. Durham and London: Duke University Press, 2001. 156–66.

Rodríguez, Richard. "An American Writer." *The Invention of Ethnicity.* Ed. Werner Sollors. New York: Oxford University Press, 1989. 3–13.

Shapiro Rok, Ester Rebeca. "Finding What Had Been Lost in Plain View." *Bridges to Cuba/Puentes a Cuba.* Ed. Ruth Behar. Ann Arbor: University of Michigan Press, 1995. 85–95.

Smith, Sidonie. *Subjectivity, Identity, and the Body: Women's Autobiographical Practices in the Twentieth Century.* Bloomington: Indiana University Press, 1993.

Stanton, Domna. *The Female Autograph: Theory and Practice of Autobiography from the Tenth to the Twentieth Century.* Chicago and London: University of Chicago Press, 1984.

Torres, Lourdes. "The Construction of the Self in U.S. Latina Autobiographies." *Third World Women and the Politics of Feminism.* Ed. Chandra Talpade Mohanty, Ann Russo, and Lourdes Torres. Bloomington: Indiana University Press, 1991. 273–87.

Torres, María de los Angeles. "Beyond the Rupture: Reconciling with Our Enemies, Reconciling with Ourselves." *Bridges to Cuba/Puentes a Cuba.* Ed. Ruth Behar. Ann Arbor: University of Michigan Press, 1995. 25–42.

———, ed. *By Heart/De memoria: Cuban Women's Journeys In and Out of Exile.* Philadelphia: Temple University Press, 2003.

Woods, Richard D. "An Overview of Mexican Autobiography." *a/b Auto/biography* 3–4 (1988): 13–22.

Woolf, Virginia. *Moments of Being.* 2nd edition. Edited with an introduction and notes by Jeanne Schulkind. London: Hogarth, 1985.

5

Am I your worst nightmare?

Reading Roberto G. Fernández's Major Fictions

Jorge Febles

As parodist of an identifiable community, Roberto G. Fernández has assigned himself a powerful authorial voice—even if usually distant and merely implied—that invariably places itself at opposite extremes of his characters' discursive tactics. Fernández views Cuban Miami with a distorted and distorting lens, conveying at once a grotesque cacophony that overwhelms readers because of the inherent logic that tinges prevailing ideological and cultural nonsense. Bakhtin explains that "every parody is an intentional dialogized hybrid. Within it, languages and styles actively and mutually illuminate one another" (*The Dialogic* 76). He adds that these hybrid constructs entail "an argument between languages, an argument between styles of languages. But it is not a dialogue in the narrative sense, nor in the abstract sense; rather it is "a dialogue between points of view" (76). Guided at least partly by these notions, I envision in this essay a tacit dialectic between Fernández—both as real and implied author/narrator—and Mirta Vergara, a recurring character who undergoes a series of arbitrary metamorphoses in the writer's major fictions. A personage manipulated at will by her creator, she nonetheless establishes a recognizable *personal* voice, perhaps in spite of the aspiring ventriloquist who handles her. In that sense, she persecutes her author like a bad dream, exhibiting traits of a possessive alter ego with whom the real Fernández has developed a love-hate relationship.

Despite her irrational demeanor and bizarre speech acts, Mirta's multilayered consciouness may be counterposed critically to the implied author's omniscient persona much in the manner that Unamuno juxtaposes his authorial volition to Augusto Pérez's quest for self-liberation. As Feal Deibe avows, Unamuno's character advocates for the internal logic of any fictional being, which even his author must not contravene (113). Tied to name rather than to any particular story, Mirta's emphatic voice underscores the dialogic substratum of Fernández's works. Yet she remains a flat character, a caricature even, that never achieves roundness because the author does not permit it. Critically, therefore, it is appropriate to address her maker through her in order to inquire about his intentions (about the hidden signifieds in an apparently upside-down, meaningless world) as well as about the perplexing peculiarities of his craft.

Since Mirta is the only personage that appears in each of Fernández's major works, her myriad masks are negotiated by the reader instantaneously rather than sequentially. She performs coherent independent sketches that configure disparate impressions when gathered together. From text to text Mirta evolves like an eel, assuming contradictory faces and roles. Hence, instead of pretending to read directly through a character in search of herself, I will attempt to empathize with Mirta's ambiguous self, to juxtapose her perennial incompleteness to the omniscient narrator's own imperfections and apparent confusion, which Andrei Codrescu anathematizes all too harshly as a lack of "authoritative and original idiom" (1). In so doing, my intention is to demonstrate that Mirta, in all her ambivalent and polimorphous glory, reflects as would a prism Fernández's ideological mindset, his creative system, and his arbitrary or sadomasochistic relationship with those characters whom he struggles to control while they rebel silently as well as overtly against his failed monologic dictatorship.

The question posited in this chapter's title, "*Am I your worst nightmare?*" implies notions that mutually clarify (or obfuscate) each other. First, it reflects the character's implicit outlook toward her author. If like Augusto Pérez she had the opportunity to confront her creator, Mirta would undoubtedly ask why she evolves from book to book as if she were part of a dream sequence, acquiring divergent traits and life experiences while Fernández expands his carnivalesque environment through bizarre transfigurations of plot and story. Second, the query counterposes Mirta's passive-aggressive personality to authorial voice: She appears textually as a dynamic other that haunts the omnipotent craftsman. Mirta seems part of a quasi paranoid scheme, an object that becomes a subject almost in spite of the implied author. Third, her unavoidable reappearances transform her into a metaphoric or synecdochic entity, a figure that suggests much more than her actions or her words signify. Invariably marginal, she represents regardless the hinge that binds merely by her name and presence quite dissimilar anecdotal structures. Fourth, the question tacitly suggests an existential conundrum: The "Am I" leads to a "Who am I?" never answered completely in any of Fernández's texts. Mirta's unuttered question provokes countless others that must be asked of an entire fictional world not to seek precise responses, but rather to inquire into those discernible features that lend it some semblance of unity. She is the face we recognize, or imagine that we do, when, while meandering through Fernández's esoteric geography,[1] we encounter an amalgam of types, countless of whom make but brief appearances before vanishing into the alleyways of the author's imagined community.

Pérez Firmat, Doris Sommer, Ibieta, Vásquez, López Cruz, Deaver and Alvarez Borland, among many, describe Fernández as a debunking minstrel of Cuban Miami, whose fictions mock an exiled community that "sees itself as isolated, besieged, and misunderstood" (Quiroga 219). The habitat configured by the author is peopled, according to Alvarez Borland, by "the Cuban community of [the author's] parents" (98), whose aspirations, beliefs, and peculiarities he distorts gleefully in carnivalesque fashion. Along the way, Fernández adds to his tableau *foreign* elements reflective of hegemonic culture, but also of an increasing acculturation that promotes something different, something born wholly out of an omnipresent past, an ever-changing present, and an unforeseeable future. The writer creates from the perspective of his own one-and-a-half generation, perspicaciously dissected by Pérez Firmat in *Life on the Hyphen*. By implication, he becomes perhaps the primary literary exponent of the following Pérez Firmat decree: "Lo que esta generación tiene que acabar de comprender es que, aun cuando naciéramos en Cuba, nos formamos en Estados Unidos, y que aun cuando Cuba sea nuestra primera casa, Miami es nuestro hogar permanente. Y eso nos hace otros, distintos a los cubanos y distintos a los americanos" ("*Trascender el exilio*" 23–24). Rather than preach total assimilation, Fernández waxes enthusiastically about cultural hybridity, about the inherent virtues of a space and a society in a permanent state of crisis and transformation. Instead of feeling a pernicious nostalgia for the past that never was, the author—as orchestra director—has his multifaceted ensemble play often unwillingly to the present that is not quite what it seems and the future that never will be, while echos of the bygone era resonate in counterpoint, sounded most loudly by Fernández's "worst nightmare." Consequently, Mirta emblematizes an antispace to the one currently inhabited by the errant community that the writer perceives transforming into a unique hybrid culture linked specifically to a South Dade devoid of the geographic specificity to constitute a *real locus*.

E. M. Forster describes the verisimilitude of literary beings in precise terms. "A character in a book is real . . . when the novelist knows everything about it. He may not choose to tell us all he knows . . . But he will give us the feeling that though the character has not been explained, it is explicable, and we get from this a reality of a kind we can never get in daily life" (63). Despite this premise's questionable merit, particularly given the parodic tension between character voice and authorial voice that defines Fernández's dialogic constructs, Forster's appraisal guides me in probing through Mirta's enigmatic consciousness into her author's handiwork and awareness of his offspring's inherent nature as well as life experiences. I will argue that, like the fictional space whence she resides, this character is a palimpsest, a document that the writer erases at will to inscribe her functionally within the artifacts he fabricates.

In her analysis of *Raining Backwards*, Vásquez calls Mirta "the primary purveyor of fantasy" (76). She is that in this book without a doubt, but Mirta is protean, Medusa-like, not a figment but manic figments of authorial imagination. Mirta changes without necessarily expanding coherently from text to text, retaining but traces of an original persona defined almost exclusively by her name and by the paradoxical vigor of a voice that counterpoises itself of necessity to the parodist. Rather than convey that sense of human wholeness provided by the implied creator's omniscience, she assumes concrete metaphorical attributes. Mirta reflects more often than not that "unhealable rift between a human being and a native place, between the self and its true home" that, as Said argues, characterizes exile, promoting an "essential sadness that can never be surmounted" (*Reflections* 173). In defiance of her monstrous desires and endeavors, Mirta conveys the endless pathos associated with most first-generation Cuban emigres. Her ever-changing personal story signifies exilic schizophrenia. Additionally, as human palimpsest, Mirta substitutes for the macrocosm that surrounds her and through parts of which she ambles. By representing with her bizarre endeavors and her chameleonic nature the city's innate fragmentation, she surpasses her narrative role, portraying the "staccato quality of Miami life" identified by David Rieff (13). Mirta, like the city and like the author who constantly recreates her, is an individual in perpetual motion who symbolizes "'the Latin temperament'" that, according to David Reiff, has altered forever South Dade's urban environs. Emblematically also, Mirta has no precise personal history. In some texts, she makes up her own story, always depending upon exaggeration and distortion. In others she experiences circumstances and traumas contravened subsequently by the very writer who assigned them to her because they serve a better purpose elsewhere. Finally, she portrays alternative roles, assuming life stories and plagiarizing metatexts so that she may become other Mirtas, even if her voice retains a familiar ring.

Mirta's narrative debut transpires in the third segment of Fernández's *La vida es un special*. There she meditates on a personal ordeal: Her son Federico García (Freddy throughout the book) left Cuba before turning twelve. She stayed behind with her unnamed husband until both finally received permission to leave the country seven years later during the 1968 exodus, which is why another character, Nivaria, derisively calls her "*Milta Camarioca nomber tu*" (*La vida* 56). For a while, Freddy lived with a cousin of Mirta's husband. Since she and her spouse abused him, he left their home. After several Anglo-American juvenile delinquents beat him, Freddy joined a gang, "*Los Leones de la 17*" (*La vida* 18), beginning a life of crime that landed him in jail for drug possession. According to one of his friends, "Estaba tripeando y no se dio cuenta y pasó la jara y el policeman se lo llevó. Ahora lo acusan de haber querido reipear a la vieja de enfrente" (*La vida* 40).[2] Mirta confronts this maternal tragedy in two ways, both of which reveal psychological instability. First, she recites perplexing litanies that display her inventiveness and her odd religious faith. Second, after Freddy is arrested she denies her motherhood in a manner suggestive of incipient madness. During the episode titled "La cigüeña desorientada," Mirta explains to Domingo Zepelín that the weak stork entrusted with delivering her son encountered high winds as it approached Tierra del Fuego and became extremely tired. A stronger stork took pity on the fatigued bird and offered to transport Mirta's baby to Cuba after completing its own mission to Tierra del

Fuego. The weaker stork returned to Paris to rest, while the other one pursued a dual mission. Regretfully, the generous bird made a mistake and delivered Mirta's son to an expecting mother in Tierra del Fuego, taking Freddy to the unfortunate Cuban woman instead. Hence by disavowing her son, Mirta upholds her absolute maternal virtue.

Moreover, Mirta assumes, by implication, a prominent secondary role in *La vida es un special*. She becomes Eloy de los Reyes's tutor in the process of concocting Cuban memories in Miami. The adolescent decides to transform his bedroom into the proper site in which to hold an *areito*. Upon donning some feathers to mimic Siboney attire, he walks to Primitivo's convenience store with the intention of purchasing items required to perfect the tropical ambiance. On his way, Eloy sings Félix B. Caignet's famed *pregón* to the fruits of Oriente province, stopping himself to ponder: "¿Cómo son las frutas en el caney de Oriente? [. . .] Mirta debe saber. Paso mañana por su casa después de ir al grocery" (*La vida* 14). By identifying Mirta as his mentor, he assigns her the role of principal fool in the carnivalesque environment crafted by Fernández. Eloy's indebtedness to the enigmatic woman is enhanced when he fashions in his bathroom a replica of the quintessential Cuban beach. The teenager runs sand through a mill six times in order to make it as fine as possible before filling the tub with it. Then he places a fan at the doorway and a portable heater on top of the toilet to reproduce Cuban breezes, because "La brisa debía ser cálida pero no caliente. Esto siempre se lo afirmaba Mirta" (*La vida* 19).

Eloy's anomalous behavior, which predates Mirta's thought processes in *Raining Backwards*, highlights of necessity both characters' problematic relationship with their creator. Dialoguing in *La vida es un special* with a psychiatrist who functions as authorial alter ego, Eloy complains about his narrative mistreament, emphasizing: "A mí se me prometió que se me iba a dar la oportunidad de desarrollarme y ahora no veo cómo. Usted sabe, me calificarán de personaje poco profundo" (*La vida* 41). If we assume that like his predecessor Augusto Pérez, Eloy as character questions not only authorial objectives but the very method of assigning literary beings the necessary qualities to be perceived as human—as *real*, in the sense ascribed to the word by Forster—all of Fernández's creations, but most definitely Mirta, contest tacitly their fictional role. By confronting his *maker*, Eloy voices a collective concern, replicated almost identically by Connie Rodríguez in Fernández's *Raining Backwards* and hidden in Mirta's arbitrary discourse.

La vida es un special either summarizes or points toward defining qualities of Fernández's major work. Most significantly, the book provides rudimentary story lines, sketches, and anecdotes that serve the author well in subsequent efforts. The reader familiar with Fernández's entire production corroborates through *La vida es un special* that for him neither story nor speech belong to specific characters, but rather traverse capriciously from voice to voice, configuring a bizarre kaleidoscope of images accompanied by discordant sounds. Not surprisingly, Mirta's incipient role and personal travails change slightly at first, radically afterward, while portions of her actions as well as her speech acts become the property of subsequent characters.

Her performance in Fernández's *La montaña rusa* (1985) consists of a rather minor cameo appearance, more or less circumscribed to a few pages 53–57. If in *La vida es un special* she acted the role of tragic, albeit purposely forgetful mother, as well as consultant to the mythmaker Eloy, in Fernández's second novel she surrenders at least partly her story line to characters who debut in this text. As she reveals in her "Cantar," she is still a pathetic figure, forced by her nameless husband to send Fredito (the former Freddy) to the United States in order to save him from Cuban communism. Mirta remains an alienated and introspective individual—"siempre en las nubes" (*La montaña* 48), according to her spouse—who for two years recited a modified version of her litany, pleading that her visa would arrive so that she could see her son once again. A temporal lapse emblematic of Fernández's arbitrary chronotopes tinges her recollections. In *La vida es un special* she did not see her son for seven years (from 1961 until 1968), while now she avows: "Y mi Fredito se fue antes de cumplir los doce y se me fue solito Fredito, pero si yo hubiera sabido que no lo volveríamos a ver en diez años no hubiera rezado más" (48). Her subsequent depiction of Fredito's *American tragedy* coincides essentially with the one provided in *La vida es un special*, except for the fact that, after taking to the streets upon being mistreated at the home of Jacinto and Toto Martínez de Lamartiné, he lives with his parents for a period once they arrive in the United States. Finally, he fights with his father, leaves home, and becomes a drug trafficker. When he is arrested while putting an emerald ring on his mother's finger, Mirta lapses into denial once more, and in "Cantar del olvido," she again tells the aprocriphous stork story.

In spite of these and other anecdotal variations, the character develops intelligibly in *La vida es un special* and *La montaña rusa*. By the time she stars in the opening chapter of *Raining Backwards* (1988), however, speaking English "to reach a wider audience" ("A Surging" 47)—to paraphrase Fernández's justification for writing this book—Mirta has endured a stupefying metamorphosis. Her son Fredito as well as her nameless husband disappear from this and all subsequent narratives, so that she may be reconstructed at will in a manner befitting the fictional artifacts in which the author inscribes her. The English language, apparently, allows Fernández to alter story lines as he pleases, to *kill off* characters or to vest them with different names, to redefine a chronotope and to enhance the carnivalesque environment.

Raining Backwards is Mirta's novel at least to a point since by demeanor as well as physical appearance she represents the paradigmatic "gay monster" (*Rabelais* 197) of carnival time, the grotesque queen of the "'feast of fools'" (*Rabelais* 81) enacted in Fernández's narrative. Her rebirth is signaled by demeaning descriptive snippets as well as by her diva-like performances in scenes stolen (or maybe recovered) from Eloy de los Reyes. The reader must decipher

her age from information provided by the character. For instance, Mirta divulges to Eloy that she *met* her imaginary fiance on Varadero beach, "a week after the 1943 storm, two days before [her] fifteenth birthday" (*Raining* 16). She also writes pop psychologist Helen Kings about her arrival from Cuba on September 24, 1962, when she was thirty-five. Were one to assume, given other internal clues, that the narrative present coincides with the year that the novel came to press (1988), Mirta is approximately sixty years old. Paradoxically, her age complies with previous depictions of the character, but the date of her departure from the island clearly does not. The "*Milta Camarioca*," who came to this country in 1968, according to *La vida es un special*, and three years later in *La montaña rusa*, given the decade that she was away from her son, now arrives in Miami with that initial contingent of Cuban exiles, who fled the island between 1959 and 1962. This authorial transgression, which alters dramatically Mirta's "graph of life, the spiritual curve along which the entire movement of an individual takes place" (Adler 80), results basically from the intention of stealing essential experiences from the character in order to transfer them to another, Mima de Rodríguez, the "*cremita de leche*" entrepreneur from *La montaña rusa* who becomes a plantain chips magnate in *Raining Backwards*. When Freddy vanishes, relinquishing his plot line to Keith Rodríguez, Mirta absurdly recovers her virginity and enters the fictional world at an earlier date. The reader ponders at this stage whether a character who suffers such a violent attack upon her already incoherent "graph of life" would take kindly to such a re-evolution.

Sixty-year-old Mirta María Vergara reemerges, consequently, as an eroticized fiend endowed with grotesque feminine attributes that, nonetheless, prove appealing at least to one fictional companion. The author traces his character's portrait through diminutive particles, much like the punctilist painter would shape a human body. Readers learn that she has long, red hair, that her back is covered with blackheads, that her breasts are "two udders" that sag "with the weight of virginity" (*Raining* 16), that her pubic hairs are also red, and that she has "an adorable beauty mark on [her] left breast [. . .] which forms "a star, a lone star" (*Raining* 37). In her application to *rule* in carnivalesque fashion as "Queen Calle Ocho," she reveals that her eyes are "black," that she is five feet one inches tall, and that she weighs 135 pounds. Additionally, Mirta unwittingly emphasizes the feeblemindedness with which her creator seeks to imbue her by explaining that her goal in life is "to go back to Varadero Beach and marry [her] one and only and have three children" (*Raining* 95).

In the lengthy chapter "Who Killed C.R.? which Fernández shapes, on the basis of a pre-text, Mario Vargas Llosa's *¿Quién mató a Palomino Molero?*[3] Mirta's body, undergoes a subsequent twist. Like *La Chunga* in Vargas Llosa's novel, Mirta exercises an oddly hypnotic seduction on police captain Carter. The investigator designates her as "the most beautiful creature ever seen by human eyes" (*Raining* 177). By citing, Christopher Columbus's oft-quoted description of Cuba, Carter implicitly compares Mirta to the motherland, thus turning her into a female symbol of the island's physical appeal. Later, the captain paints even more vividly his love interest by mistranslating Vargas Llosa's depiction of La Chunga: "The most beautiful woman ever to walk on the face of the earth. Hodel, when you grow up, when you become a real man, you'll know what a real woman is. If you could only see her thighs the way I saw them when she was crossing the street. They were firm, warm, unyielding to pressure, well-distributed. Oh Hodel, a muscular woman is a dessert for kings, princes and cardinals!" (*Raining* 178). When the captain makes an effort to interrogate the narrator, quoting Jimmy Clanton's 1962 hit, ludicrously terms "his Venus in blue jeans" (*Raining* 186), he again praises her exuberant beauty: "The whole purpose was to see her rosy cheeks, to feast on her creamy cleavage, to contemplate her placid eyes" (*Raining* 187). At the chapter's end, Carter describes once more the woman that he has never met: "Maybe she's taking a bath with delicate oils, perhaps combing her reddish lock, possibly massaging her firm thighs . . . The most beautiful legs ever produced by creation, beautiful without blemish" (*Raining* 193). Acting against authorial vision, an outsider perceives Mirta in a manner that raises her to the level of the feminine ideal, much like the exiles debunked by Fernández praise hyperbolically the island whence they came. Thus, the imperfect lecherous old maid whose breasts "sag with the weight of virginity" (*Raining* 16) and whose back is replete with ugly blackheads is transformed magically, through a simple change in focalization, into a walking royal palm, an "Habana Vieja" building, Varadero Beach. By Carter's grace and the implied author's lampooning, Mirta becomes space herself, that Cuba of the mind so many inhabit on an alien territory that she also represents, due to her ambiguous physique.

Mirta's symbolic role as body complements her equally important purpose as mind. In *Raining Backwards*, as well as in *Holy Radishes* and *En la Ocho y la Doce*, the character reflects exilic neurosis. When Fernández reconstructs her personality for the third time, he adds an unexpected psychological twist. If in the first two books Mirta assumes the role of parodic victim, whose innate schizophrenia is furthered by her husband's and her son's imprisonment, in *Raining Backwards* her dreamlike inner life acquires a pragmatically erotic substratum that subverts her pathetic persona. The character confirms through her individual trauma and the manner in which she copes with it a collective exilic angst that, in Pérez Firmat's opinion, teaches but a single important lesson: "el único regreso posible es hacia adentro, no hacia atrás" (*Cincuenta* 51). As a result, she manipulates experience, time, and space in order to ensure survival. Alfred Adler explains that "[t]he characteristic of dreams is also found in our waking life. We always have a strong inclination to deceive ourselves emotionally" (12). Mirta's dream world, which she materializes through discourse so as to justify her actions or inaction while explaining individual suffering and longing to herself as well as to others, not only deceives her but also her only disciple, who thus becomes the repository of invented remembrances. This intergenerational ideologic contagion guarantees the permanence of that "old world talk" endemic to all exilic communities.

Viewed in this manner, Mirta's role as Eloy's mentor is dangerous only in the sense that it perpetuates Miami's "culture of the living dead" to cite the phrase used by Quiroga (222) to validate Reinaldo Arenas's characterization of the city. The difficulty lies in the fact that in *Raining Backwards* Mirta the naif becomes Mirta the vamp (or Mirta the perverse meta-author?), employing not only her recollections but also her capacity to embellish them or even to invent them for the purpose of securing sexual gratification. In "Retrieving Varadero," the book's first chapter, the omniscient narrator alludes to the symbiotic relationship between Mirta and her protegee:

> Eloy had been serving Mirta faithfully for the last two months in exchange for tidbits of the past. He was thirsty for information on those golden cities, those fabulous places in that enchanted island his aunt refused to mention because they were so sacred. He wanted to savor tidbits from that past he longed to relive somehow and share it in his old age with his grandchildren. (*Raining* 11)

A victim of the one-and-a-halfer neurosis lucidly explicated by Pérez Firmat in numerous essays, Eloy perceives his mentor not only as the imaginary island's collective memory but as the island itself. In this grotesque coming-of-age episode, while the youth bathes Mirta with a sponge in the same tub that, later in the novel, she transforms into Varadero Beach much like Eloy had done in *La vida es un special* (Who taught whom what? reader and characters may very well ask), he recognizes his erotic powers as the elderly woman becomes increasingly aroused. When at the moment prior to climax, he withdraws the sponge to demonstrate sexual mastery, mocking the memory provider with this provocative iteration, "Tell me more, Mirta. Tell me more, baby"[4] (*Raining* 19), Eloy possesses at least emblematically the imaginary Cuba designed and indeed portrayed by her seducer.

More importantly, Mirta's remembrances and self-identification in this chapter augment as well as distort her fictional persona. First, she evinces a creative capacity merely insinuated in the prior two books. Her exaggerated description of Varadero reaches incongrous extremes when she strives to forge disproportionately vivid images to make Eloy push the pimples on her back and, above all, sponge her body more enthusiastically. Fernández succeeds in accelerating narrative rhythm by mimicking conventional pornographic strategies, which promote a shared onanistic act. If Mirta masturbates physically through Eloy's manipulations, he masturbates mentally because of her stories. Second, the character identifies herself as "Miss Mirta María Vergara, not Mrs. Mirta Verga" (*Raining* 13). Pun aside, the "miss" that she attaches to her persona implicitly refutes her previous life as mother and spouse. Subsequently, she introduces the henceforth recurrent motif of "her one and only," whom she saw, but never met, on Varadero Beach. This enduring love affair with a stranger to whom she has remained faithful until the narrative present (1988), further substantiates her new part as a sixty-year-old neurotic virgin. Finally, Mirta reveals to Eloy that her mother was Señora Nelia's cleaning woman, who followed her mistress to Miami after the revolutionary upheaval. If this Nelia Pardo is the Nellie of *Holy Radishes!* as she logically should be, Mirta's life experiences take another odd turn, at least in light of the servants mentioned in Fernández's fourth novel. Even if Señora Nelia is not Nellie, Mirta's socioeconomic status diminishes according to her self-depiction. The prototypical bourgeois Cuban mother of *La vida es un special* and *La montaña rusa* links herself to a lower class.

No doubt Mirta would question, like Eloy and Connie, the violent upheaval she incurs as an ordeal that leads her to forge for herself an alternative life story along the lines of those imaginary tales manufactured by countless exiles. In a letter to Dr. Helen Kings, she writes that her father was president of the Cuban Senate and died in a plane crash; her mother was an aristocratic lady who remained in Cuba because she had a seizure after her properties—which included a beautiful home in Varadero Beach—were confiscated by the revolutionary government. Mirta herself left Cuba on September 24, 1962 to avoid persecution for her subversive activities. Currently, she tells Dr. Kings, she works as a gluer in a shoe factory. The culminating component of her story, which becomes a leit motif of sorts in the novel, deals with Mirta's purported rape at the hand of Eloy, the ungrateful boy whom she labels her "delivery boy" (*Raining* 37). She makes clear: "I pay him very well. I pay him with memories. It's the best way to fight forgetting. The day we forget, we are all dead" (*Raining* 37). Mirta's preposterous tale gains that fluid verisimilitude endemic to all the stories interpolated in this enigmatic text, whether they emanate from an ambivalent omniscient narrator or from the characters themselves. Within the fictional context, in fact, Mirta's invented violation is accepted as truth by her, by the community that searches for the "Little Havana Raper" (*Raining* 155) and, finally, by the implied author's own voice, who *validates* it through restatements.

In the topsy-turvy world of exile, lives are not only reinvented according to circumstances; they also parallel each other. Therefore, this character readily yields (or is forced to yield) her past experiences to Mima de Rodríguez, who even has the audacity to explain her son Keith's inexistence to Mirta herself with the very fable about the mistaken stork used by the latter to deny Freddy in *La vida es un special.* In *Raining Backwards* Mirta practices similar acts of discursive thievery. She borrows Solange Du Ville's pornographic tale "¿Por qué eres así, mami?" included in *La montaña rusa*, retitling it "You Really Drive Me Wild, Baby" and dating its composition on December 31, 1969. The virginal "Venus in blue jeans" waxes passionately on a mythical encounter with her "one and only" (112–15). Since by having an affair with Mirta's husband, Solange initiated the latter's fictional return to premarital chastity, their voices coalesce somewhat logically to fabricate identical erotic stories.

Given the multitude of changes she bears as character, particularly in *Raining Backwards*, Mirta exemplifies what Frantz Fanon terms, following Germaine Guex, an "abandonment neurosis" (74), which turns her not only into an other but into numerous others so that she may better metaphorize, albeit grotesquely, the exilic condition in its totality. More than any other of Fernández's creations, Mirta reflects that ambiguous eccentricity that Said attributes to émigrés. She, like Nellie in *Holy Radishes!* Eloy de los Reyes as well as Domingo Zepelín in *La vida es un special*, and the monstruous Ignacio Valls of *En la Ocho y la Doce* portray emphatically the paradoxical state of dislocation and ambivalent identity described by Edward Said: "For an exile, habits of life, expression, or activity in the new environment inevitably occur against the memory of these things in another environment. Thus both the new and the old environments are vivid, actual, occurring together contrapuntally" (*Reflections* 186). Rather than a mere personage, Mirta is a fluid mirror image, a microportrait of a whole that persecutes Fernández much like his worst nightmare. He even assigns her quasi-mythical attributes in "I Cultivate a White Rose," *Raining Backward's* last chapter, where the flag girl Linda Lucía depicts the *defiled* old maiden as a bag lady who lives under the 826 overpass, speaking to anyone who approaches in a codified ancient language (Spanish?), impossible to understand in the indefinite future described because the roots of the past whence Mirta emanated have been eradicated from collective memory. As the last survivor of "the old ones who came from the sea" (*Raining* 218), the bag lady retains dangerous scales that terrify the metanarrator because they may well be contagious, triggering a retrograde process of remembrance.

In *Raining Backwards*, the author lays the basis as well for Mirta's final (final?)[5] metamorphosis, which transpires in *En la Ocho y la Doce*. During a conversation with her friend Barbarita, she confesses that, given her current state of degradation, the love of her life will never marry her. She explains her only option in this manner: "I was saying that now I am truly lost, forever a fallen woman. I have no choice but to join the convent. Barbarita, I am taking my vows with Mother Teresa. I am leaving for Calcutta tomorrow morning unless something drastic happens" (103). This brief narrative segment motivates not only Mirta's reappearance in Fernández's latest book, but also that of Eloy—who resurrects under the appropriate pseudonym of Siboney. In this text, Mirta again constructs Varadero in her bathroom in order to lend credence to her continuing role within Fernández's fictional world. Nonetheless, the book focuses more on Siboney, who remains traumatized from the sexual abuse he suffered at his mentor's hands. In keeping with the author's arbitrary collage technique, that allows characters to usurp other's life stories, Siboney appropriates traits as well as experiences from Keith Rodríguez, Freddy, and Eloy.

In *En la Ocho y la Doce* Fernández employs Mirta and Siboney to create contrapuntal storylines that parody communal value systems imagined on the basis of knowledge and lack thereof. Mirta, the selfmade victim of *Raining Back-*

wards, appears as the victimizer whose exploitation of an adolescent turns him into the sufferer of a quaint psychological malady: spongeophobia. Yet, given her religious profession, Mirta is perceived by the community as a saint deserving of an apotheosic welcome upon her return from Calcutta. In addition, much like in *Raining Backwards*, she proclaims her blamelessness in an undated letter, ascribing guilt instead on Siboney. Mirta alludes indirectly to the initial chapter of Fernández's third novel: "Recuerdo que [Siboney] llegó a fines del verano y hasta lo llevé a visitar mi playa. Y ¿cómo crees que me pagó? Me pagó burlándose de mi inocencia" (*En la Ocho* 101).

As preface to the segment described, Mirta *speaks* in accordance with one of Fernández's favorite discursive estratagems. She interpolates borrowed lyrics debunked by context, misusage, or satiric alterations. Not only does the nun *cite* unconsciously segments of such well-known songs as "*El arroyo que murmura*" and "*Lágrimas negras*," but she also claims authorship of Lecuona's "Siboney," which she renders grotesquely to honor the object of her desire. Mirta's malapropistic contrivance underscores two significant notions. First, its inherently erotic tone confirms her seductive intent and documents Siboney's assertion that she is a child molester. Second, by stating that "Siboney" (the fictional being, not the mythical figure of Lecuona's song) is the "dueño de la patria," Mirta postulates that, in her private dream world, she is Cuba. Hence, due to her abandonment neurosis and to her intense loneliness, seducing Siboney becomes a salient component of the attempt to pay him with memories. In doing so, she allows him to touch at least a portion of the elusive motherland.

Mirta *dies* in *En la Ocho y la Doce*, at least according to the radio announcer who, interrupting symbolically "El Rincón del Recuerdo," describes the accident in which she supposedly perished: "El avión en que viajaba la religiosa Mirta María Vergara procedente de Calcuta, India, desapareció de las pantallas de los radares precipitándose al mar. El avión perdió altura, y según testigos oculares que pescaban cerca del lugar del suceso, voló al revés antes de precipitarse a las aguas de la Bahía de Biscayne" (*En la Ocho* 189). Such a miraculous occurrence refers readers unavoidably to *Raining Backwards.* Quite appropriately, Mirta flies backwards toward her death in an ocean that links mainland and island, that locates her in-between spaces, but staring of necessity to the place whence she migrated and to whose mythification she devoted her life. By succumbing in such a fashion, she promotes an ultimate act of the *collective catharsis* (Fanon 145) she emblematizes throughout.

In contrast with protagonic performance in *Raining Backwards* and her more or less significant cameo appearances in *La vida es un special, La montaña rusa,* and *En la Ocho y la Doce*, in *Holy Radishes!* Mirta plays a fleeting role. Nevertheless, since by happenstance she shares a space in Belle Glade, Florida, with Nellie, Mrs. James B., Nelson Guiristain, and the other perplexing characters who coincide in this town during the 1960s and early 1970s, Mirta's life story obtains another problematic twist. In this incarnation, she works in the radish packing plant along with several formerly well-to-do Cuban women. Identified merely as a "freedom fighter" (*Holy* 92) who dresses in "camouflaged, tight, army pants" (94), Mirta replicates in speech and potential actions the qualities she assigns to her "one-and-only" in "You Really Drive Me Wild, Baby." There she is the relatively passive "Lady of the Pastries," a devout patriot committed to fulfill a subservient female role, while her fictitious beau is "the universal soldier" (*Raining* 113) who ravages her in order to satisfy his male urges so that he may serve more enthusiastically the cause of Cuban freedom.

In *Holy Radishes!* however, Mirta undergoes a sea change, becoming essentially her "one-and-only's" rhetorical double, *plagiarizing* sentences from Martí's "Nuestra América" to harangue the gossipping co-workers that pay scant attention to her diatribe:

> This is the struggle between civilization and barbarity. The hour has arrived to dislodge the sanguinary tyranny that has enveloped our beloved island. We must keep the pressure on. We musn't be soft with the oppressors, for the tigers, scared by gunfire, return at night to their prey. We were that prey. The tigers approached on their velvet paws. We were relaxing, enjoying ourselves, with our guard down, asleep, and when we awoke and realized what had happened, the tigers were already upon us, devouring our flesh.[6] (94–95)

In her invective, Mirta proclaims the need to liberate the motherland, Xawa, predicating, like Martí, an inevitable, just war. She concludes her speech explaining her objectives and requesting assistance:

> I know you are ready like I am, willing to expose myself to death in order to enable our country to live. I am working in this place instead of training for the invasion because I am in need of cash to buy a machine gun. Now I want you to start your commitment to freedom by donating any amount, a quarter, a dime, a half dollar to expedite the process of freedom by helping me buy my weapon. Then you can rest assured that I will join the freedom fighters' training camp by the lake. (*Holy* 95–96)

Nobody contributes a cent to Mirta's cause because these Cuban women and her American counterparts are much too involved in the travails of daily survival.

That is the extent of Mirta's performance in *Holy Radishes!* Readers learn later that she quit her job, bought a machine gun at The Pawn Shop and went to the Everglades to train with the freedom fighters (*Holy* 171), where she promptly ascended to the rank of colonel (*Holy* 243). Yet, her brief appearance further complicates her fictional persona. By showing up in Belle Glade circa the 1960s and early '70s, she is strangely out of place, or rather, she is in two places at once. In both *La vida es un special* and *La montaña rusa* Mirta strolls the streets of Little Havana during this period. Additionally, the story "You Really Drive Me Wild, Baby" is dated December 31, 1969 and transpires, one infers, in Mirta's Miami home. Significantly as well, in *Holy Radishes!* the character develops an unusually aggressive discursive pattern. Mirta, the dreamer and/or sexually charged virginal vixen, evolves into a boisterous manly woman, not to be mistaken for Captain Carter's "Venus in blue jeans." Finally, she acquires a novel fictional role merely implied in the meta-story "You Really Drive Me Wild, Baby." The pathetic victim who suffers pangs of abandonment, later to become a sexual predator, an object of desire identifiable with Cuba itself, and a missionary who emulates Mother Teresa, transforms herself (or is transformed against her will) into another aberration: a ridiculous tin soldier ready to lead men (and only men) into battle to rescue her homeland of Xawa.

"How many faces do I have?" Mirta must ponder. "Who, in God's truth am I?" she may reasonably ask her author along with those readers equally cognizant of her chameleonic persona and ever ambivalent voice. In his "*Díptico de la identidad*," Pérez Fimat defines quite simply his own personal trauma by affirming "*Soy yos*" (*Equivocaciones* 31), multiple and often contradictory entities residing in a single conflictive and conflicted personality. Fernández may well echo the critic, responding to his character as follows: "But Mirta, you are all of them, you are yous," a fluctuating metaphor for a peculiar human condition shared by a specific collectivity. The author's worst nightmare never acts out one story because she stands for countless stories that vary invariably with each telling, since displacement entails the necessity to reinvent constantly the past, be it immediate or remote. In "A Real Durwan," Jhumpa Lahiri writes about Boori Ma, a Bengali refugee who could be Nellie, or Domingo Zepelín, or Mirta. Boori Ma, like Fernández's characters, dreams of a prior life that may or may not have been as she describes it. When questioned, she responds: "Why demand specifics? Why scrape lime from a betel leaf? Believe me, don't believe me. My life is composed of such griefs you cannot even dream them" (72). The narrator then avers: "So she garbled facts. She contradicted herself. She embellished almost everything. But her rants were so persuasive, her fretting so vivid, that it was not easy to dismiss her" (72). In a sense, Mirta's perpetual ambiguity corresponds to the sole facet that accompanies her throughout Fernández's books: the ability to live in the present as if it were a dream readily alterable by her remarkable fancy. In the imaginary community of Fernández's exilic fictions, nothing is ever permanent and no one has a fixed identity. Rather, character traits and even recollections are transferred arbitrarily from one to another to suggest a general state of carnivalesque schizophrenia. Within such a bizarre environment, Mirta looms large due to those pluridimensional figurative attributes, that intrinsic fragmentation, which precludes her from being merely one unto herself. Rather, she is a cubist painting so disjointed that even her creator blends nose and neck when trying to draw her arms. No matter the number of reincarnations, she appears condemned to function forever as a construct pointing in multiple directions. If Cuban exile identity may be understood in terms of the divided subject, Mirta's tour through Fernández's hall of mirrors exemplifies the ultimate breakdown, the shattering of the subject into pieces both infinite and diverse.

NOTES

1. In "La tríada Belle Glade, Miami, Xawa: tres nombres, tres culturas y un solo espacio novelesco en la narrativa de Roberto G. Fernández," I delve into the *place* where Mirta "locates" her peculiar extraterritorial and idiosyncratically immigrant culture, arguing that, whether or not they name Miami as site, Fernández's books lack what Anderson terms a precise "*tour d'horison*" (30), given the quasi-mythical nature of the city landscape depicted in the narratives. I may ascertain that the author invariably manufactures a walkable environment, reminiscent of Sagua la Grande, which becomes a synecdoche for Cuba. Thus, as Eliana Rivero has suggested, his books acquire a nostalgic substratum despite their parodic intention (Rivero 43).

2. Fernández uses this allusion in *Raining Backwards* and *En la Ocho y la Doce*. In those texts, "la vieja de enfrente" turns out to be Mirta, who accuses of rape both Eloy de los Reyes and, subsequently, his *double* Siboney.

3. I discuss this episode as parody in an article entitled "El pretexto de la parodia" (69–77).

4. In this instance, Eloy *quotes* the erotic song "Tell Me More," sung by Olivia Newton-John in the musical *Grease*. Elsewhere I have studied Fernández's intertextualization of songs as part of character speech for the purpose of enhancing its *alienness* and innate biculturalism.

5. Fernández is working on a new book, tentatively entitled "Angry Letters to Former Lovers," in which Mirta reappears to write bitterly about her "one and only."

6. Compare the quoted fragment with a portion of Martí's text: "El tigre, espantado del fogonazo, vuelve de noche al lugar de la presa. Muere echando llamas por los ojos y con las zarpas al aire. No se le oye venir, sino que viene con zarpas de terciopelo. Cuando la presa despierta, tiene al tigre encima" (30).

WORKS CITED

Adler, Alfred. *The Science of Living.* New York: Doubleday, 1969.

Alvarez Borland, Isabel. *Cuban-American Literature of Exile: From Person to Persona.* Charlottesville/London: University Press of Virginia, 1998.

Anderson, Benedict. *Imagined Communities.* London/New York: Verso, 1991. [Revised Edition.]

Bakhtin, Mikhail. *The Dialogic Imagination: Four essays.* Trans. Caryl Emerson and Michael Holquist. Ed. Michael Holquist. Austin: University of Texas Press, 1981.

———. *Rabelais and His World.* Trans. Helene Iswolsky. Bloomington: Indiana University Press, 1984.

Codrescu, Andrei. "A Mad, Mad, Mad, Mad Mundo." *Book Review: The New York Times* August 14, 1988.

Fanon, Frantz. *Black Skins, White Masks.* Trans. Charles Lam Markmann. New York: Grove, 1967.

Feal Deibe, Carlos. *Unamuno: "El otro" y Don Juan.* Madrid: Planeta, 1976.

Febles, Jorge. "A Character's Indictment of Authorial Subterfuge: The Parody of Texts in Roberto G. Fernández's Fiction." *Intertextuality in Literature and Film.* Ed. Elaine D. Cancalon and Antoine Spagna. Gainesville: University Press of Florida, 1994. 99–108.

———. "El pretexto de la parodia o la parodia del pre-texto: en torno a un capítulo de *Raining Backwards.*" *Hispania* 75 (1992): 69–77.

———. "La tríada Belle Glade, Miami, Xawa: tres nombres, tres culturas y un solo espacio novelesco en la narrativa de Roberto G. Fernández." *Hispanic Journal* 25 (2004): 225–41.

Fernández, Roberto G. *La vida es un special: ~~$1.50~~. 75.* Miami: Universal, 1981.

———. *La montaña rusa.* Houston: Arte Público, 1985.

———. *Raining Backwards.* Houston: Arte Público, 1988.

———. *Holy Radishes!* Houston: Arte Público, 1995.

———. *En la Ocho y la Doce.* New York: Houghton Mifflin, 2001.

Forster, E. M. *Aspects of the Novel.* New York: Harcourt, Brace and World, 1955 [1927].

Lahiri, Jhumpa. *Interpreter of Maladies.* Boston/New York: Houghton Mifflin, 1999.

Martí, José. *Nuestra América.* Selección y notas de Hugo Achúgar. Segunda edición. Caracas: Ayacucho, 1985.

Pérez Firmat, Gustavo. *Equivocaciones.* Madrid: Betania, 1989.

———. *Life on the Hyphen: The Cuban-American Way.* Austin: University of Texas Press, 1994.

———. "Trascender el exilio: la literatura cubano-americana hoy." *Memorias recobradas.* Ed. Ambrosio Fornet. Santa Clara, Cuba: Ediciones Capiro, 2000. 16–29.

———. *Cincuenta lecciones de exilio y desexilio.* Miami: Universal, 2000.

Quiroga, José. *Cuban Palimpsests.* Minneapolis: University of Minnesota Press, 2005.

Rieff, David. *Exile: Cuba in the Heart of Miami.* New York: Touchstone, 1993.

Rivero, Eliana. "Cubanos y cubanoamericanos: perfil y presencia en los Estados Unidos." *Memorias recobradas.* 30–50.

Said, Edward. *Reflections on Exile and Other Essays.* Cambridge, MA: Harvard University Press, 2000.

———. "A Surging New Spirit." *Time* 11 July 1988, 46–50.

Vargas Llosa, Mario. *Quien mató a Palomino Molero?* Toledo, Spain: RBA Editores, 1992.

Vásquez, Mary S. "The Fantastic and the Grotesque in the Fiction of Roberto Fernández: The Case of *Raining Backwards.*" *Confluencia* 6.1 (1990): 75–84.

6

Exile, Memories, and Identities in Gustavo Pérez Firmat's *Next Year in Cuba*

William Luis

Exile and migration to the United States have produced fragmented Latino or Hispanic families that, over time, develop mixed identities. The change in family structure created by the movement or displacement of people has been especially disturbing to the members of the Cuban exile community, many of whom have vowed not to return to their homeland until Fidel Castro's regime falls from power and a new and different government takes its place. Gustavo Pérez Firmat's *Next Year in Cuba: A Cubano's Coming-of-Age in America* describes, from the perspective of a Cuban exiled in Miami, the breakup of the Cuban family, a breakup that the narrative attributes to the Castro dictatorship. Prior to the Cuban Revolution, Pérez Firmat and his family lived in a virtual paradise. His father owned a store, with more than one million dollars in inventory. Shortly after Castro came to power, the protagonist was ejected from his childhood Eden; but unlike other refugees, the Pérez Firmat family was able to leave with many of its possessions.

Pérez Firmat's recollections follow closely the sensibility of the Cuban exile literature of the 1960s and 1970s Castro dictatorship, a body of writing by authors who were born, raised, and educated on the island and sought exile in the United States where they continued to write in Spanish and denounce the current dictatorship.[1] Hence the title of his memoir, *Next Year in Cuba*, which captures the popular saying that many Cuban exiles believed would become a reality, a reality that has yet to materialize. Like many exiles, Pérez Firmat's family expected to return to the island after Castro's defeat and resume life as if time had not passed. And like them, the narration is preoccupied with a yearning for a previous life in Havana. But as a member of the 1.5 generation—which includes exiles who were born in Cuba but raised in the United States—Pérez Firmat goes beyond this desire for a lost Havana and includes the narrator's childhood in the Miami enclave.[2] The character thus experiences a double exile. The first takes place when he leaves Cuba for Miami, a city he later accepts as his home. The second "exile" occurs when he departs his Miami home for Michigan, and then North Carolina and, if we extend the narration into the present, New York. Each geographic location is associated with a distinct lifestyle. As Isabel Alvarez Borland states, as a child Pérez Firmat lived an upper-class existence, and as an adolescent the family had to start anew (69).

The son of a well-to-do businessman, Pérez Firmat is uprooted from his island home at the tender age of eleven. Though Pérez Firmat cannot and will not return to Cuba, the imaginary voyage he undertakes in the book is not about the reality of the situation he and his family had to abandon, but to the memories of the past. The protagonist states: "Although my memories of Cuba may seem firm and clear, in fact I remember very little" (32). The past is not necessarily a recreation of what was, but of what should have been. The past which is remembered in accordance with the present life of the character gives meaning to and justifies his present existence. It is not so much a reconstruction of chronological time, but of memory, of things as we imagined them to be. This may be one of the reasons why the character does not want to return to Cuba, or listen to his brother's account of his recent visit to the island, home, and store. Pérez Firmat prefers to defend his recollection or recreation of the past, which he refuses to question or alter.

While Pérez Firmat is careful to provide the reader with glimpses of his mother and father, and the rest of the family, he inadvertently shows that not every Cuban in his household thinks like him, and therefore challenges the myth that Miami Cubans represent a homogeneous community. This is especially the case with his siblings, who are also Cuban Americans. He describes them as individuals trying to fulfill a different role from his: "My brother Pepe pretends to be a socialist. Mari pretends to be a banker. Carlos pretends to sell dope. I pretend to be a professor" (178). Even as Gustavo holds passionately onto his parents' past, his brothers and sister made other life choices. José is a leftist, who lived in Guatemala and supported the Sandinista government. Carlos, to whom he dedicates an entire chapter, is a hustler who steals his older brother's identity, or anything else for that matter, to make ends meet. His sister has a conventional life with a regular job and fixed schedule. If the other siblings were allowed their own individual voice, would they not claim that their experiences are also a part of the Cuban American way of life?

Though Pérez Firmat never returns to Cuba, the analogous Miami exile provides insight into how he relates the past and present. After many years of absence, the character revisits his parents' house in Coral Gables, where he was reared. "Retracing my steps thirty years later, I'm struck by how close my old haunts really are" (55). While the physical geography of any location may not change, the perspective of a child is different from that of an adult, even if he is the same person at two different stages of his life. Since this is the case with Miami, what would happen to the protagonist's memories of Havana if he were to return to the island? The character interprets everything by comparing it to his Cuban childhood memories, but the past can never be the same; and as a function of time, it always changes and evolves. This is evident when he realizes that Miami has undergone its own transformation. As later waves of Cubans arrived in Miami, the first group moved outside of Little Havana, to Coral Gables or South Miami, then to Kendall or Perrine. In recent years, other Hispanic groups have sought the same refuge enjoyed by Cubans. Miami has been transformed into a lively Hispanic community.

Next Year in Cuba, which could have been entitled *Next Year in Miami*, also reconstructs the protagonist's return to his life in Miami, thus providing a glimpse of how Cubans live in a city that has become another Havana. Pérez Firmat offers the reader a vision of how Cubans attempt to transpose and therefore reproduce their way of life, if only in a symbolic manner, in Miami:

> Nearly every time I go to Miami my father takes me to lunch or dinner at *La Habana Vieja* . . . Especially in the last few years, Old Havana has become a shared habit, a way of bringing out the moods and memories we have in common. Under the phony street signs and the kitschy murals, our disparate lives come together. La Habana Vieja opened sometime in the mid-1980s, but I had gone there several times before I noticed that my father always sits in the same section, by Paula Street. Then it dawned on me that this is where the *almacén* was located, on the corner of Paula and San Ignacio, and I realized what should have been obvious to me all along: that my father goes to Old Havana to revisit the business that he inherited from his father and that my brothers and I were supposed to inherit from him. Since he cannot take me to the *almacén* the way he did when I was a child, he takes me to its ghostly exile double. Sitting at a table for two on the corner of Paula and San Ignacio, he can imagine himself back at the helm of J. Pérez, S.A. (96)

The exile refuses to let go of the past; he relives it, and perpetuates this existence abroad. The Pérez Firmat family continued to celebrate the traditional holidays and eat the same types of food once enjoyed on the island. Continuing the traditions, the celebration of Noche Buena became a way of holding on to the Cuban past. Though Pérez Firmat is tied to his father's memories, he is also aware that Havana is not the same city he left behind. On the contrary, Havana has undergone its own transformation: "Carlos III became Salvador Allende Avenue; the Havana Hilton became the Habana Libre; the Casino Deportivo was renamed the Sierra Maestra" (85). For him, Miami is like the Havana he knew. Perhaps, recognizing the changes is what forces the exile to hold on to the paradisiacal past. Nevertheless, Pérez Firmat's communion with Miami represents a transition into mainstream society, as illustrated later by his faculty positions, first at Duke and later at Columbia University. In fact *Next Year in Cuba* attempts to portray life on both sides of the "hyphen."[3]

As with any memoir, the narration is not a chronological reconstruction of events, but an imposition of the present onto the past. The protagonist has already changed, he is no longer the person he was before, and his transformations are present from the initial moment of writing. From this perspective, Pérez Firmat's memoir is structured around his identity as a member of the 1.5 generation. This idea is evident at the outset of the work, as the boy who stays in Cuba, sees the boy departing on the ship headed for America, and vice versa, thus highlighting both sides of the Cuban and American experience, that is, both sides of the hyphen. This is also evident as Noche Buena, a Cuban celebration, is juxtaposed to Christmas; Rosa, his Cuban or Cuban American wife, to Mary Anne, his American spouse.

When Pérez Firmat says "I love Cuba with the involuntary, unshakable love that one feels for a parent," he is not referring to the Cuba of the present, but the Cuba prior to the events of 1959, that is, the Cuba of his childhood, the fatherland of his memories. He intends to preserve the past, so that as time changes him, his memories will always be the same. Pérez Firmat exhibits a fear of letting go of the past, as he moves from becoming an exile to becoming an immigrant, from marrying and divorcing his first wife Rosa, a Cuban American, to marrying Mary Anne, a divorced woman with two grown children. Similar to Ricky Ricardo's marriage to Lucy, or César Castillos's desire for Vana Vane, in Oscar Hijuelos's *The Mambo Kings Play Songs of Love*,[4] Pérez Firmat's marriage to Mary Anne is a way of finally moving from one side of the hyphen to the other, and grasping and obtaining the American Dream.

Though memory attempts to fuse the past with the present, pictures represent a synchronic moment in chronological time. Unlike memory, which continues to evolve and unfold according to events that impact our daily lives, pictures freeze the past, reducing it to a specific moment in time and place. The photograph encases and protects the instant in which the image was taken, allowing the viewer to remember the past as it actually occurred. This may be the reason why photographs become a prized possession for many immigrants and exile. Pictures provide for a momentary digression from the present; they are a road for us to find our way back and return to a previous time and place. It forces us to reconsider the past in a very different manner than what we had envisioned in the present. The image transforms the past into an immutable event that will never change and will always be the same. For the exile, pictures become an origin, a gathering place from which to start anew. Pictures become an indispensable *aide mémoire*.

As I read *Next Year In Cuba*, I ask myself how do the pictures of an earlier period help to understand life on both sides of the hyphen? Certainly, we know that the photographs in this book are an important vehicle for reconstructing the present, since the author uses them in writing his memoir. For this part of my study, I will refer to Pérez Firmat's *Next Year in Cuba: A Cubano's Coming-of-Age in America* (2000), with additional pictures and a postscript, released five years after the first edition.[5] The Second Edition reproduces three pictures on the book's cover. Two appear to have been taken in Cuba, and another in transition, perhaps on the family's voyage to exile in the United States. However, this edition contains a fourth picture that does not appear on the cover, a more recent one, embedded in the text, as we shall later see. Photographs are essential for the author's remembrance; they allow him to recollect, narrate, and relive the past. Each picture tells a story about Pérez Firmat's earlier years, which can be contextualized by the narration. Furthermore, the pictures are interspersed and can be read alongside the sections in which they are located.

When commencing the act of reading *Next Year in Cuba*, the reader encounters one of three pictures that appears on the book's cover, the one of the two Gustavos, father and son. It is located at the very beginning, before the table of contents and the prologue (x). The picture was taken in Cuba, and both, father and son, pose to commemorate the conclusion of the first grade. This picture, which could have been taken by the mother, shows a proud father standing next to his son. The son is dressed in a white suit, with matching white shoes, with a tie of a color not discernible in the black and white photograph. On his suit jacket, the narrator proudly displays what could be eight or nine medals, thus underscoring his high accomplishments. In contrast to his son, the father is dressed in a dark suit with a light colored (striped?) tie. The son stands to the father's left, that is, to the reader's right, and the father holds a cigar in his right hand, the side opposite of his son. Indeed, father and son pose for the picture: the son stands tall, with his legs pressed together; the father stands with his legs comfortably apart. I read the positions in the photograph to be significant, and will return to this idea later.

There is, however, a slight difference between this photograph and the one that appears on the cover. The one the reader sees when first observing the book is in the form of a snapshot, printed in a rectangular shape. The one inserted in the book is not rectangular, but oval, and inserted in a different frame. Unlike the one on the cover, the oval shape blocks most of the background, drawing the viewer's attention to the father and son, who figure prominently in the picture. It appears as if the reader is looking at the male members of the family up close, though a telescope or telephoto lens. There is another change which should not go unnoticed. The photograph on the cover contains a caption that has not been reproduced with the one inside the book. Written in the mother's handwriting, it highlights the following celebratory words: "Terminas el 1er Grado en La Salle y te llevastes toda clase de premios . . . Que orgulloso estaba tu padre!" She, in essence, confirms her son's success at the conclusion of the first grade and, like the picture, captures the father's proud feelings. As I mentioned, the caption does not appear in the picture reproduced at the outset of the book. Rather, the words are replaced by the book's subtitle, placed at the top of the image, by the father's head; the author's name appears in the middle of the picture, and divides it in half; and the book's title is located at the bottom, that is, nearer to the location of where the caption should have been, but in a larger font. The picture is emblematic of the memoir; the father and son have a strong relationship, and the son, clearly, has worked very hard to please his father. Certainly, the past, or the father's past, is also an integral part of the memoir. In some respects, the family's past is a concept the young child was not able to comprehend, but with the passing of time, the father conveys the memories to the son, and they also become a part of his life. This idea is present throughout the book but it is most evident in part 2, chapter 4: "On the Corner of Paula and San Ignacio," referring to a restaurant frequented by the father, which marks the streets of Havana, in particular the location of the father's warehouse, which gives title to the chapter. The father is nostalgic for the past, and the father and son commiserate together. Rather than to follow the family tradition and inherit the family business, in exile the son has become a distinguished professor, a career that the father cannot comprehend.

The second picture is located after the prologue and opens the first part of the book. Like the first one, it does not have the shape as the one seen on the cover. The square picture has now become oval shaped. Part 1 is written on the upper left-hand side of the picture, and Waving Good-Bye appears in a larger font, on the bottom right-hand side. The first part of the title moves from the white page into a corner of the picture, and the second one from the picture into the white page (15). The photograph relates to the title, or the title explains the image, since it was taken on board the ship "City of Havana," as perceived on the ship's lifesaver, which traveled from Havana Harbor to Key West. With this title, the reader assumes that the ship crosses from Cuba to the United States, as the Firmat family escapes into exile. In the picture, the father stands between his two sons, Gustavo and Pepe. The narrator is to the left of his father, between him and the boat's railing, and the brother is to the right of his father. Both narrator and brother are dressed in the same fashion: Each has rolled up jeans, an aviator jacket, and a captain's hat. In the narration, Pérez Firmat tells the reader that he and Pepe used to be close: "In Cuba my brother Pepe and I had been almost twins—we were the same height, had the same haircut, wore identical clothes. I was two years older, but you could never tell" (171). However, once in Miami, they separated and lived separate lives. The father, on the other hand, wears the same suit described in the previous photograph, and, possibly, with the same tie. All three pose for the camera, the father has his arms around Pepe and appears to be restraining him with his right hand. He is perhaps holding him still to pose for the camera. Pepe is turned sideways, with his back to the father and brother, as he tries to move in the opposite direction. The narration refers to the photograph and the trip's importance:

> In the black-and-white photo my mother took of us on the ferry to America, my brother Pepe and I are horsing around next to the railing. Pepe is doing his Jerry Lewis imitation, and I'm making monkey faces. The open sea is behind us. My brother Carlos and my sister, Mari, are hiding behind a funnel, with only a leg and two hands showing, as if their limbs had already been detached from their bodies.

> My father is standing off to one side, wearing tinted glasses in heavy black frames, a half-smoked cigar in one hand. Staring at the camera with an empty, faceless expression, he looks as if he doesn't know whether he's coming or going. Traveling to the States on a tourist visa, maybe he foresees or intuits that in a few weeks, when our visas expire, he'll have to request political asylum and begin a new life. As I look now at the photograph that my mother took thirty-four years ago, I wonder what phantom on the dock waved good-bye to him. I wonder whose neck he wanted to wring. (23)

The description provided above uncovers a discrepancy between the narration and the photograph that accompanies the text. In the one I described, Pepe makes faces and the narrator stands still, waiting for the picture to be taken. Moreover, the father is not alone, but is visibly featured with the boys. If there is a difference between the photograph and the narration, then there is more than one photograph; the one described in the text is not included with the ones reproduced in the book. The one included does not show the father staring aimlessly at the camera; rather, he concentrates on Pepe, and may even want to wring his neck. The discrepancy raises the following question: Were there other photographs taken during that momentous trip of exile? Does the one in the book mark a different period, not of exile but prior to the event that caused the family to abandon the country of origin, but of business or pleasure as the family traveled to and from the mainland, that is, before the father was lost in his gaze?

The third photograph begins part 2, and is entitled "Family Ties" (91). As with the others, the third picture is framed in an oval, thus allowing the reader to focus on or peek through a keyhole and watch the Pérez Firmat family. And like the first photograph, the one on the cover reproduces the mother's caption that reads: "Tus 5tas Navidades," which has been omitted when inserted in the book. Similar to the second one, part 2 is written on the upper left side, and crosses from the white page onto the picture; Family Ties appears on the lower right, and extends beyond the picture frame onto the page, and is written in a larger font.

In this photograph, the protagonist's family celebrates Christmas; there is a Christmas tree in the background of the picture, with traditional ornaments. The picture appears to have been taken in Havana, thus suggesting that while the family lived on the island, the parents followed U.S. customs and traditions. This may have been the case among certain sectors of the Cuban population who embraced U.S. culture on the island, and was a viable model for members of the wealthy classes. It even reflects the traditions that may have been associated with Nena, who was born in Virginia, and Gustavo, who attended school in Jacksonville, Florida. Many years later, the father traveled to the United States, and conducted business in Crowley, Louisiana, "the rice capital of America" (17). All but the mother seem to be in their pajamas or night clothing. The father wears matching top and bottoms and the mother sports a dress. As I mentioned, there is a Christmas tree in the room, erected adjacent to the fireplace, with the customary Christmas stockings. The family sits on the tiled floor, in the foreground, with visible presents to be opened.

I want to study more closely the composition of the photograph, the position of the tree and family's seating position. In this picture, which I believe captures Christmas morning, the tree divides the picture into two parts. The father and mother are seated on the opposite sides and each occupies one half of the picture, with corresponding children. In other words, they frame the outer edges of the photograph, with the children in the middle. On one side, the father sits with two of the boys, the narrator on his left and the toddler, Carlos, between his legs. On the other, the mother sits on her legs next to Pepe, who is to her right. While the mother and children look at the camera, the father does not make eye contact with the lens and, in fact, may be looking down in the direction of his right shoe. As with the description of the second picture, he may be lost in his own thoughts. Except for the children they have in common, there is no line of communication between the mother and father. As I mentioned before, the Christmas tree divides the picture in two, with the mother on one side and the father on the other. There is also a visual composition, which unites all those looking at the camera, the mother and three children, which separates them from father. Regardless of the various interpretations, the image shows disunity between mother and father. If this explanation is correct, the family discord is not due exclusively to the Castro revolution and subsequent exile conditions, as book's title indicates, but was present many years before.[6]

When narrating his genealogy, the narrator traces his family to the origin of the Republic of Cuba, and like Sarmiento's *Recuerdos de provincia*, and Cristina García's Ignacio, of *The Agüero Sisters*, among other texts, the members foretell the country's history. Gustavo junior writes that his grandfather, Pepe, emigrated from Valladolid, Spain, to Cuba, in 1903, one year after Cuba's emergence as a nation. Shortly thereafter, he opened a store, which soon became the first *almacén*, and married Constantina in 1917. After a series of good fortunes, they bought a larger warehouse, previously the British Railway Company, only one block from the docks, which would become the family business, J. Pérez S.A. (26). Moreover, the narrator explains that the mother and father married in 1942, but did not have children until 1949, the year that young Gustavo was born. Prior to having children, the mother and father negotiated their terms; the mother first wanted her home, and the father insisted on having a son. "My mother wanted her own home, but my father, in one way or another, gave her to understand that he would build her a house when she gave him a son. She had given him to understand that she would have children only if she had a house in which to raise them. The standoff lasted until 1949, when their understandings merged: My mother had me and construction began on a lot next to my grandmother's house in the Reparto Kohly" (38).

I wonder if the disunity evident in the third photograph set the stage for the early family dynamics. Could the father and mother still hold grudges for so many years after the children were born? Is the discord connected to other events? The text reveals more about the life of Gustavo senior in the section that accompanies the photograph, "On the Corner of Paula and San Ignacio." This section underscores a comraderie, a male bonding if you wish, between a father and son who share the same name. Though we are later told that Gustavo and his son hardly exchanged words, in this chapter we do hear them talk to each other; they put politics aside, have drinks, and tell stories. However, I am most interested in the part that describes a casual acquaintance with Chucho, an older man dressed to kill, waiting for his younger girlfriend. Father and son soon learn Chucho's exile story: He lived in Pennsylvania, then moved to California, and most recently to Miami. He has two older children, and does not wear a wedding ring, to which the narrator responds: "He isn't wearing a wedding band, but that's not all that unusual among Cuban men. I don't either. But my guess is that he's divorced and regrets it" (107). As the conversation develops, father, son, and bartender seize the opportunity to get Chucho's goat. The bartender and Gustavo ask Chucho if he needs a manual pump to engage in sexual intercourse. The son, then, refers to the father's own sexual exploits. He claims that the father is jealous of Chucho, since "It's been a while since Gustavo waited for a jebita at a bar. More than a few years ago, Gustavo may have been a lot like Chucho" (106). This comment allows me to return to the picture. Can the family discord have anything to do with Gustavo senior's Chucho-like habits, of having his own *jebita?* Though this was considered Cuban male habits, the women were also aware of their spouse's actions. In addition, the narrator refers to the father's impotence (108), and that he had not made love to his mother in years (109).

Gustavo senior was expelled from the Belén academy. As punishment his family sent him to Bowles, a military school in Jacksonville, to study English. Gustavo took over the *almacén* in 1937, when his older brother Pepín, who was being groomed for the job, died after an alcoholic doctor botched an operation to cure him of peritonitis. In 1942, he met his wife on a blind date and married her over Constantina's objections. The wife was the daughter of divorced parents and, worse, had no money (113). Nevertheless, the marriage was mutually convenient: The mother spoke English and the father had money. During the early part of their marriage, the parents traveled to the United States, buying merchandise for the store. Nena's English came in handy when doing business with non-Spanish-speaking sellers. In 1954, the grandfather, Pepe, passed away and Gustavo inherited the company. A rudderless man who gave no advice, on the eve of his son's wedding counseled him: "If you don't keep women in their place, they will walk all over you" (117). And, perhaps, he himself was not able to follow his own advice, and tensions in the marriage persisted. Nena tells her son "exile saved her marriage" (166). While both Nena and Gustavo blame all their economic, familial, and societal problems on exile, the marriage was far from perfect. In Cuba they quarreled, Gustavo wanted to party, and Nena did not, always then and after giving proper importance to the family. At times Gustavo went out with his cousin, Joseíto, and it was not easy to track him down.

I believe that the recreation of the family history is important for understanding the novel in general and the third picture in particular, which suggests disharmony between mother and father. Yet this tension could be attributed to Cuban macho culture, and Gustavo's actions were no different from Chucho's, at an earlier time in his life. Other members of the family seem to follow a similar pattern. The narrator refers to his three great uncles: Pepe, Manolo, and Octavio. Pepe, the syphilitic one, was a great *jodedor*, and did not let marriage change his bachelor lifestyle. After his marriage, he attempted to escape Josefina's vigilance. "A man is only as good as his secrets" (134). Manolo was a bachelor who kept two concubines, one white and the other mulatto (137). Octavio, unlike the others, was involved in politics in the Machado era.

Though the memoir is written from a male perspective, once in a while we do observe a woman's point of view. Constantina told the narrator that the day his father was born, she told Pepe that from then on "if he wanted sex he should go to see the putas (whores) because she had had enough. Another time she said that by the time Pepe was fifty 'his joints had rusted' and they didn't have to sleep together anymore. Although she wasn't prudish about sex, it was clear that she thought of it as a nuisance that distracted her from a higher calling—selling bags of rice and playing canasta" (144). In the third picture, was Nena fed up with Gustavo? Was Gustavo a Chucho type? By the time the narrator speaks to Gustavo on the corner of Paula and San Ignacio, Gustavo is not the man he used to be. The narrator associates his father's real or imagined impotence with his exile condition.

The fourth and final picture does not appear on the cover; rather, it is embedded in the text. Unlike the other ones, this one is not about his childhood past but refers to his life during the time of writing, that is, after Pérez Firmat divorced Rosa and married Mary Anne. In fact, the photograph is in the form of a modern family portrait. Like the other ones reproduced in the text, the picture is oval, thus allowing the reader to peek at Pérez Firmat's most recent stage. Located in the chapter appropriately entitled "Discovering America," the photograph brings together Pérez Firmat's two families, comprised of the children from his first marriage and the stepchildren from his second marriage.

A close reading of Pérez Firmat's U.S. family allows the reader to consider to what degree his character accepts the mainstream culture of his adopted country. Let us study the composition of the photograph. Like the Christmas photograph, the family portrait seems to be divided into two parts: Mary Anne and Gustavo and his children are on one side of the picture, and her children on the other. Pérez Firmat's children stand in front of him and Mary Anne, and Mary Anne's children are alongside her, and consequently farthest from the protagonist. Moreover, each partner has a son and daughter, and they are placed in the same position as the parents, that is, the males are to the right of the females, or the females are to the left of the males. Interestingly, of the six subjects only Pérez Firmat and his daughter appear to be posing for the camera. The other four subjects come into view as having other concerns. In Mary Anne's family, she looks at Chris, thus giving him her full attention (I find it difficult to determine if Chris has his eyes closed or if he is looking down, but I do not think that he is staring at the camera); her daughter, Jen, stands politely with her hands crossed in front of her, looking down (perhaps being well-mannered and civil, as the author describes her demeanor when her mother and father divorced). In Pérez Firmat's family, son David is looking down, and the father has his arm over David's shoulder, producing the same calming or controlling effect Mary Anne's stare has on her son. Pérez Firmat's daughter, Miriam, is facing the camera and seems to be looking into it, but may in fact be glancing to one side, wearing the same picaresque smile seen on her father's face, with the same strength and independence known to her grandmother Constantina. Of the six people in the picture, Pérez Firmat is the only one ready or willing to pose for the family portrait, whereas everyone else appears to be distracted. The family members are standing next to each other, but they are not together or in harmony with one another. While Pérez Firmat wishes to read his and Mary Anne's situation as a nineties version of the *I Love Lucy* show, what would this other picture, the one depicted in the photograph really say about this Cuban and American family?

Pérez Firmat's marriage to Mary Anne personifies his own transformation in the present, that is, from the Cuban to the American side of the hyphen. Though he is far from embracing the Women's Movement, the first person narration has accepted many aspects of U.S. culture as his own. Cuban men, belonging to a traditional Hispanic culture, generally tend to marry women with little experience, and virgins are more coveted. The idea of marrying a woman for who she is, regardless of background or previous experience, comes closer to a presumed equality associated with U.S. customs and notions about freedom of choice. That the author falls in love with a woman with grown children is even more striking. Let us remember that his father and uncle gave him sound Cuban advice when he threatened to leave Rosa and marry Mary Anne:

> The problem with me, my father began, is that I had been a faithful husband for too long, and therefore was suffering from a bad case of *atraso*, the Cuban word for long-term or protracted horniness (the literal meaning of the word is "backwardness"). According to his old-country mores, it was one thing to have a fling—everybody had them—but it was very different to leave your wife for another woman. Cuban men sometimes cheat on their wives, Pedro said, but we do not abandon them. (214–15)

When Pérez Firmat abandons Rosa, the protagonist does not follow in the footsteps of the Cuban men of his father's generation, but his actions are closer to those of his U.S. counterparts, who, in theory, are more apt to be true to their own feelings. Equally telling is Pérez Firmat's use of the memoir, the most intimate form, to express his past, to which Cuban or Hispanic culture does not subscribe with any regularity. Though the picaresque genre gave origin to the modern Spanish and Spanish American novels, the memoir is not a preferred form of narration.

Pérez Firmat is caught between the Cuban and the American hyphen. In chapter 11, appropriately entitled "Earth to Papi, Earth to Papi," Pérez Firmat provides a glimpse of his children. While the boys are expected to follow the men and the girls the women, we get a sense of how Cuban Pérez Firmat wants to make his children and how North American they really are. In fact, he claims that his children have helped him in his transition to become an American. In a similar manner, in one of the shortest sections of the book, he explores the lives of his second wife's children, proudly stating that the mother left the father for the narrator. He boasts that he "broke up their happy home (which wasn't all that happy)" (261). If he broke up a happy home that was not happy, what did he do to his own? And how happy was it? While Rosa is present in the book, Mary Anne's husband, the other male rival, is conspicuously absent. And the protagonist claims that her children will be influenced by his Cubanness.

If we were to read the description of the children with the picture mentioned above, his newly formed American family is more dynamic than serene. Jen is prepared, perhaps reluctantly, to accept her status in the family; Chris needs to be consoled; David is restless and, like Chris, needs further reassurance. Miriam, on the other hand, seems to be sure of herself and is drawn to her father, and each shares the same smile seen on the other's face.

It is puzzling to me why Pérez Firmat chose to include this photograph as his American family portrait. Would it not have been more constructive to take a second family portrait, one that would represent a more traditional setting not present in the one included in the book, and thus render my interpretation meaningless? If that were the case, the reader would not have access to the first photograph, and only the second one would project an amicable transition from the Cuban side of the hyphen to the American side. However, it is possible to conjecture that there were two or more pictures, and Pérez Firmat or someone else selected the one reproduced in the book, which shows the complex process of becoming an American.[7] There is still another interpretation. This other one suggests that after the picture was taken, the discord was such that the protagonist was not able to regroup the children, that the members of his family would not come together for a second picture. David and Chris's behavior in the portrait reinforces the latter interpretation.

Reading the photograph that opens "Discovering America" along with the other three that appear on the cover and are reproduced in the body of the memoir, reveals additional information about Pérez Firmat's hyphenated identity. In all three pictures in which the father is present, the son always stands to the father's left. This is the case when the son receives the medals at the conclusion of the first grade, when the father and two sons are on board the City of Havana, and when the family celebrates Christmas Day. In the most recent picture, the father is absent. But if the son were to represent the father, as he does by keeping the father's memory of Cuba alive, then Mary Anne is to the left of the protagonist, that is, in the same position in which the protagonist stands as a child. David, on the other hand, is to the right of the protagonist, who in the earlier picture represents Pepe, when the father appears to restrain him on board the ship, and Carlos, during the Christmas Day celebration. More accurately, in this latter picture Carlos sits between his father's legs, whom Gustavo senior restrains or comforts. Will this position foretell what would happen many years later, when Carlos stole the protagonist's identity? Did the lack of comfort or assurance created by exile force the younger brother to do what would have been unimaginable in Cuba? Did exile also change the protagonist, who turned his brother in, an act that would not have occurred on the island? For the most part, in Hispanic culture, blood is thicker than water, and the family will tend to take care of its own business. As the mother claimed, family loyalty is supreme. Perhaps the protagonist is right, exile has affected his relationship with his brothers, as they moved closer to the American side of the hyphen. However, the discord could be understood as sibling rivalry. Were not his great uncles Pepe, Manolo, and Octavio very different from each other, as narrated in the chapter "Domino Theory, Canasta Klatch"? Would that rivalry have existed in Cuba, but no one would have known since family secrets are not shared with anyone? However, we do know that Pérez Firmat turned his brother into the police and wrote about this and other family matters.

Let us return to the family portrait, and to Mary Anne's position, which is the same one the protagonist occupied when standing next to his father. I read this as a symbolic bond between Gustavo and Mary Anne, perhaps with the same strength, loyalty, and admiration shared by both father and son. Moreover, though Mary Anne is focused on Chris, Pérez Firmat and Mary Anne are standing together. Their unity is remarkably different from Gustavo and Nena's sitting position in the Christmas Day photograph, which clearly suggests that father and mother are bonded by the children and not by each other. I wonder if exile had some personal benefits? It may have forced the protagonist to break from the traditional relationships known to his father and grandfather, rearrange his life, and establish connections that proved to be more meaningful. If we were to take a picture of the protagonist's current life, what would this picture reveal?

Pérez Firmat's *Next Year in Cuba* refers to the protagonist's exile experience but also to his transitions from exile to immigrant, from Cuban to Cuban American to American, with all of the complexities that the process entails.

While he attempts to keep alive his parent's culture and traditions, which are also a part of him, the protagonist does not live totally in the past, as a more traditional exile does, but is also influenced by U.S. culture, which has become an intrinsic part of his life. The movement is not necessarily in one direction, but oscillates back and forth. Whether it is "Next Year in Cuba," even though the author has stated he would not return to Cuba, or "Next Year in Miami," a place to which the author is more likely to embrace, Cuban and U.S. cultures are intertwined to produce a new synthesis of the Cuban and American experience.

For Pérez Firmat the past can only exist as a function of memory, and accessed metonymically, that is, through photographs and other artifacts Cuban exiles brought with them, the same ones they cherish so dearly. In *Next Year in Cuba*, the protagonist does not return to the island but to his and his father's recollections of a bygone era. They find comfort in the few signs that allow them to read and interpret the distant past. In either case, the physical past is inaccessible and lost forever. The past is in a constant state of decomposition or deterioration, regardless whether the process is natural or political. However, memory protects it as a museum preserves artifacts, as a collage of different thoughts and images, outside time and without any reference or context. Even so, memory is a function of the present; it is related to the time and society in which the protagonist lives, the same one that motivates the protagonist to look back and search for an earlier childhood identity. Memory erases the tension that would otherwise arise from different experiences such as the family Cuban past, the exile condition in Miami, a second exile from that city, and life in academia. It also encompasses more recent experiences, those of the society from which he lives and writes, which include his relationship with Mary Anne. U.S. culture and society become indispensable factors for understanding and writing about the memories of a Cuban past.

NOTES

1. See, for example, José Sánchez-Boudy's *Historia de la literatura cubana en el exilio*.

2. Alvarez Borland, *Cuban-American Literature of Exile*, 69, 72–73.

3. This idea is developed in Pérez Firmat's *Life on the Hyphen: The Cuban-American Way*.

4. For an analysis of this novel, see my *Dance Between Two Cultures*, 188–214.

5. Each English edition reproduces pictures, though they are not always the same ones. For example, the first edition has three pictures on the cover. One is a school picture of Pérez Firmat, another one is of the father and two sons on board the City of Havana, which has also been included in the second edition, and a third of the family on a terrace. In this one, the mother sits and holds baby daughter on her lap, and the father and sons stand. Unlike the second edition, none of the pictures appear in the book.

The second edition is the only one that contains the photograph of Pérez Firmat and Mary Anne, and their respective children. For the purpose of this analysis, I rely on this edition of *Next Year in Cuba: A Cubano's Coming-of-Age in America*, which offers the following information: "Cover design based upon family photographs provided by the author."

6. I am aware that the family picture of the first edition produces a different reading than the one I provide here. In that other picture, the family is divided into two groups: One is of the father, mother, Carlos and Mari; and the other, separated by space, of Pérez Firmat and Pepe, who stand to the right and wear identical clothing. However, there is another reading that divides the family by height, those who occupy the top part of the picture and those who are in a lower position. The mother is seated, with Mari on her lap, and her head is at the same level as Pérez Firmat and Pepe's. It is possible to even establish a third, lower, level, with Carlos and Mari. This interpretation separates the father from the other members of the family, and pairs the children, as Pérez Firmat does in "Billita, Who Am I?" (172). In any event, each picture tells a story about the Pérez Firmat family.

7. I read a version of this essay at the International Conference on Caribbean Studies. Gustavo Pérez Firmat, who had been invited as the keynote speaker, was present at my talk and later explained to me that his editor chose the pictures reproduced in the book. The conference was held in South Padre Island, Texas, from November 2–5, 2006.

WORKS CITED

Alvarez Borland, Isabel. *Cuban-American Literature of Exile.* Charlottesville: University of Virginia Press, 1998.

García, Cristina. *The Agüero Sisters.* New York : Knopf, 1997.

Luis, William. *Dance Between Two Cultures: Latino Caribbean Literature Written in the United States.* Nashville: Vanderbilt University Press, 1997.

Pérez Firmat, Gustavo. *Life on the Hyphen: The Cuban-American Way.* Austin: University of Texas Press, 1994.

———. *Next Year in Cuba: A Cubano's Coming-of-Age in America.* Houston: Scrivenery, 2000.

Sánchez-Boudy, José. *Historia de la literatura cubana en el exilio.* Miami: Ediciones Universal, 1975.

Sarmiento, Domingo. *Recuerdos de provincia.* Málaga: Anaya & M. Muchnik: Ayuntamiento de Málaga, 1992.

7

Writing in Cuban, Living as Other

Cuban American Women Writers Getting It Right

Eliana Rivero

I would imagine that the play on words in my title is apparent to most readers. But just in case: I take off on the fictional *Dreaming in Cuban* by Cristina García and change it around to propose a composite image. Let me articulate it from the start: Cuban Americans novelists, poets, essayists, and playwrights write/dream within a circumstantial, inherited (and as I will argue later, cultivated) context of exilic and migratory memories, nostalgic family remembrances, re-creation of transnational and deterritorialized imaginaries, and the everyday experience of "living as Other" in a society that—albeit national protestations to the contrary—highly values ethnic homogeneity even when it outwardly celebrates diversity. Let me also claim at the outset that, in spite of the gender qualifier in the second half of the title, I do apply the same observation to male writers, even though they are not the main subject of these pages.

I argue that Cuban American national identity can be viewed as a cultural artifact[1] open to a process of transformation, and more often than not it exhibits such a multiplicity of facets that it becomes almost essentialistic to speak about "*a* Cuban American literatura." How do we reconcile that oneness with a real diversity of individual visions and styles? There are certainly common denominators that can be recognized. We U.S. Cubans can not only imagine, but are able to see and configure ourselves as hybrid people, and indeed can frequently pass for border entities,[2] both in the social and in the metaphysical (or even spiritual) sense of the term: within the national political panorama, within the U.S. Latino cultural landscape, and some even within our own national subgroup—certainly those of us who are female, a condition that adds its own substance of marginality to our being. At the same time, all Cuban Americans are associated by birth or by kinship with a primal image: a peculiarly shaped extension of land surrounded by sea. Without a doubt, our borders with other societal groups are sites of translation.

When I read literary works by Cuban Americans (or when I myself write poetry or personal essays) I recognize a hybrid sensibility that we share with other ethnic minorities. Factually, the awareness of 'otherness' translates for some into a state of consciousness that can be quite oppressive at times, especially for the immigrants in our midst.[3] Fortunately, most of us seem to be able to imagine a collective ethnonational identity,[4] both at the existential and public levels, which can benefit from our very hybridity and not be narrowly framed by limitations of how we are perceived by society at large or by other groups.[5] Thus, in spite of the stereotypical classification of Cuban immigrants and Cuban Americans as "privileged" in American society, due in no small part to the widespread perception of our social and political conservatism as related to exceptional circumstances surrounding our migration, settlement, education, economic success, and/or insertion into the American middle class, our notions of individual social self-worth often vary from those common views.

But are we Cuban Americans really different? If so, from whom and how? And are our differences an integral part of our worldview, our arts, our literature? In their book *The Legacy of Exile: Cubans in the United States*, Guillermo Grenier and Lisandro Pérez reiterate the recurrent theme of Cuban exceptionalism found in many academic studies of Cuban exiles by insisting on the uniqueness of Cuban history (33). Although in a different vein, non-Cuban critics note a similar assumption when referring to "the myth of Cuban primacy" and its "discourse of uniqueness." For instance, in reviewing books on Cubanness, ironic comments are offered about Cuban cultural mythologies, in which the nation is seen by its citizens as "without comparison in her civilizational milieu" (Buscaglia-Salgado 290–91). Very often, these notions of exceptionality are also applied to Cuban Americans of all generations by other U.S. Latinos (and so further internalized by the group), especially when it concerns class, economic situation, and education. As David Rieff's informant Tony Quiroga says in Miami: "You should remember that Cubans are like all island peoples, and have an almost overdeveloped sense of their own specialness" (77). These factors, naturally, translate into singular expectations for the creative endeavors of writers and artists in our midst, whether women or men.

These notions of Cuban singularity—expressed in that peculiarly Cuban humorous vein of *choteo*—are often found in Cuban(a) American literary works: What reader of fiction can forget the satirical, hyperbolic definitions of Cuban male sexuality (indeed an area in which popular lore exalts our uniqueness) offered by Cristina García in her novel *The Agüero Sisters?* Expressing in an extreme way her view of Cuban exceptionality, the author describes Cuban males through the eyes of Reina, *la compañera amazona*, as she watches her fellow workers in the dining room of a hotel in El Cobre:

> They are all much too sure of their allure. This is a problem in Cuba. Even the most gnarled, toothless, scabrous, sclerotic, pigeon-toed, dyspeptic, pestilential men on the island believe themselves irresistible to women. (14–15)

By the same token, the success enjoyed by Cuban American Constancia and her line of cosmetic products in Miami (*Ojos de Cuba, Senos de Cuba, Cuello de Cuba, Codos de Cuba, Muslos de Cuba*, created "for every glorious inch of Cuban womanhood") is designed to embody "the exalted image Cuban women have of themselves as passionate, self-sacrificing, and deserving of every luxury" (131).[6]

Is Cuban Americanness then a sociocultural construct *and* performance of our own imagined unique identity, and does it extend to whoever is related to that *UrInsel*[7] by the circumstances of their birth, either by connections of place or kin? In addition, is the condition of "Cubanness" so strong, but so malleable, that it can be modified by the locational and personal circumstances of many "Cuban-plus" subjects,[8] and yet persist in morphed forms as it expands its cultural meaning and social significance? Here I posit that what I conceptualize as *Cuban Americanness* seeps into the imaginary constructs of fiction, poetry, essay, and theater as authors compose their works. And it most certainly permeates the texts of writers such as Cristina García, Dolores Prida, Achy Obejas, Ana Menéndez, and other women authors that are rapidly becoming part of our canon (although some of them are arguably canonical by now). In the pages that follow, I try to pinpoint and describe the Cuban American character—such as it is—of fictional works written by women authors of Cuban descent who were either born or reside permanently as immigrant citizens in the United States, and thus can be considered part of the burgeoning corpus of Cuban American literature/Latina literature/American ethnic literature recognized in humanistic, academic, and cultural circles today.

U.S.-Made Cuban(a)ness?

In terms of the Latina population in the United States, issues of gender, class, and sexuality are key categories that can aid our understandings of identity, and help us identify its markers. But how do we make all these fit our (at times vague) understanding of *diasporic Cubanness*, especially when the issue of national origin alone seems to have been the focus of most of the research in this field? My premise is, then, that the emotional content of exile memories (whether lived or inherited, cultivated or learned) compel many Cuban Americans toward a space of continuing, if not outright urgent questioning about their actual psychic relationship with a nation that lays divided, spread over a geography of space and time. This often happens for Cubana/Latinas in the context of gender and sexuality, colored by class customs and mores. Cuban American women (and men), both immigrants and their daughters (or sons), dispersed through many geographical and historical coordinates in the same manner as other cultural citizens with emotional ties to the island nation, often experience the effect of prolonged—although at many times low-level—emotional trauma, in the process of what I choose to call "unknowing the (Cuban) self." This can be portrayed as the mixture of confusion, ambiguity, uncertainty, denial, anguish, and/or paradoxical love-hate feelings toward things Cuban (and/or American) that may occur in the emotional evolution of a Cuban American, whether s/he belong to the first, second, or third generation of U.S. ethnics related to Cuba by birth or kin. In other venues I have dubbed this ontological cocktail as "Cubangst" (*Discursos* 56).

Unknowing, then, necessitates the epiphany of finding out, or getting to know: As such, the process of searching for a cultural identity that has remained elusive for so many Cuban Americans often takes place for women in a location defined by gender variables. This occurs, for instance, within the feminine dynasties created by Cristina García in her novels (Celia, Lourdes, Felicia, Pilar, Luz, Milagro in *Dreaming*; Blanca, Constancia, Reina, Dulce, Isabel in *Sisters*). In the case of Achy Obejas and the working-class protagonist of her novel *Memory Mambo*, identity search and construction fuses the cultural national with the sexual, as exemplified in Juani's descriptions of the provocative *machista* advances of her brother-in-law: "There is something disgustingly Cuban about him" (60). This also manifests through her queer self-identification in the figurative shape of an island, and in a jealous fit of rage at not knowing Cuba like her Puerto Rican lover, Gina (133): "I am as marked by genetics and exile as everyone else . . . but, though nobody much notices, I'm also a stranger in my own family" (79).

On the other hand, this "unknowing of the self" is the individual state of limbo that Cuban immigrants or ethnic Cubans[9] of diverse gender allegiances find themselves in as they struggle to (re)capture a familiar feeling of belonging that is no longer rooted in consciousness: "an awareness that there is another place where I feel at home in profound ways, even though that place has not been home for a long time [*or perhaps has never been except in my imagination—emphasis is mine*] and will never be again" (Espín 27).[10]

For first-, second-, and even third-generation Cuban Americans, I hope to show, this is the circumstantial background in literary works such as *Dreaming in Cuban, The Agüero Sisters, Memory Mambo, In Cuba I Was a German Shepherd, Loving Che, The Pearl of the Antilles*, and *Love and Ghost Letters* . . . the successfully published narratives by García, Obejas, Menéndez, Herrera, and Acevedo that I touch upon in these pages.

The Buenas Literary Club

Again, allow me to play with words and their multiple meanings. The title of Alisa Valdés-Rodríguez's first novel, *The Dirty Girls Social Club*, serves here to start naming what I would like to see as a recognized genealogy of Cuban American women writers. The *buenas autoras* who emigrated from Cuba as children in the sixties have been writing their hybrid cultural identities into being since the seventies, and the Cuban ethnic writers who were born in the United States follow suit. Of course, if we are truly Cuban-aware, we cannot fail to recognize in this linguistic exercise —as a not so subtle subtext—that glorious musical representation of Cubanhood popularized *ex-insula* as The Buena Vista Social Club.

But the pun gets better. In her fictional creation of a group of U.S. Latina friends who meet once a year to compare life notes and eat Caribbean food (yes, *tostones, pernil,* and *mojitos* are in/on order),[11] Valdés Rodríguez refers to her friends, Latinas who include two Cuban Americans, a Puerto Rican, a Colombian American, and two Chicanas, as "las sucias." This is an inversion of meaning: the author takes the term "buenas" (the logical result of associating those female members of a club with the musical group, and also with the made phrase "niñas buenas," good girls) and turns them into naughty/dirty girls, using also her writer's ear for a purposefully alliterative analogy between "*socia*" (in the Cuban sense of "buddy"), "social," and "sucia." The main character or narrator, Lauren, is supposedly modeled after the author's own family background: Cuban American father and "white trash" Irish American mother.

At some point in the novel, Lauren's therapist has told her she needs to get rid of ties to her father's people; she needs a surgical procedure to excise from her psyche all that weird Cuban stuff, epitomized by Papi's custom of eating boiled condensed milk for breakfast, "scooping up the sickly sweet paste out of the can" (11). She has already begun to pull away from being a Cuban American in order to become a full-fledged Latina, on her way to a crossover into the American mainstream (only relapsing when eating a plateful of *plátanos* and black beans once a year), and her transformation is punctuated by the food she chooses:

> Fine, okay. I'll stop talking about Papi now. My therapist would be proud of me. Cubadectomy . . . And me? I don't know where the hell I came from. I'll take a good Caesar salad any day. And I eat bagels for breakfast, with a schmear of salmon cream cheese. (11)

Lauren's deCubanization is necessary for her sanity, the psychologist says. The readers understand that she is suffering an identity crisis, and the cultural markers of food offer the clues for interpretation. She must say "no" to condensed milk, but "yes" to Caesar salads and bagels with lox, other ethnic foods gone mainstream now, but distinctly Italian or Jewish before. Obviously, the process of identity (re)construction integrates multicultural elements, even if it relapses into Cuban Americanness (integrally connected to "Latinness") once a year when she indulges in Cuban or Puerto Rican dishes. But the key sentence—buried in delectable morsels—is ". . . me? I don't know where the hell I came from."

This phrase on Lauren's lips can be directly compared to a similar one uttered by Pilar, the protagonist in *Dreaming in Cuban:* "Planet Cuba . . . where the hell is that?" (134). Supposedly, the word "hell" in English substitutes for the Cuban term "carajo," as in "No sé de dónde carajo soy," or "El planeta Cuba. ¿Dónde carajo está eso?"[12] Bilingually and biculturally, both phrases in the mouth of Cuban American young women, one of them an ethnic Cuban, signify the ethnonational limbo where they find themselves concerning any fixed notions of their origins. Although expressed in English, their dismissive black humor about their procedence fits in well with the Cuban penchant for self-deprecation or *autochoteo.*[13] For Pilar in García's *Dreaming*, as she sits in a night club in Brooklyn, her mother's obsession with the country of origin and her own fixation with the grandmother and the island family and surroundings she has not seen since 1961 (when she was literally pulled from Celia del Pino's arms at the age of two) place her in a state of disorientation mixed with exasperated, phony, and funny denial. Where is that other reality, that other planet where she was born? She finally decides to go back and buys a bus ticket for Florida. She will not make it to Cuba, however, until she forces her mother to travel with her.

As for Lauren, the journalist, in *Dirty Girls:* she does not even know the primal source of her being, where she hails from. She has to explain constantly to her editor that all Latinos are not the same, that they do not think like a block, although he still believes that "we all get on the phone with each other everyday to plot our next swarthy, mysterious, and magical move" (Valdéz-Rodríguez 304). This is the same *Gazette* editor who interviewed her for the job, and Lauren told him what he wanted to hear: "*Sí, sí*, I will be your spicy Carmen Miranda. I will dance the lambada in your dismal gray broadsheet" (7). For ads on billboards across Boston, her face is darkened on purpose by photographic means, and her other *sucia* friends ask her: "Hey, *Cubana*, when did you turn *Chicana* on us?" (9). As can be seen, identity issues weigh heavily on these characters, and while one is a full-blooded Cuban in the U.S. and the other is of mixed parentage, they both still deal with the Cuban heritage of unique, "weird stuff" as part and parcel of their cultural legacy.[14] Both young women are impulsive and question authority, one with her punk art and rebellion against her mother, the other with her refusal to be classified as a token Latina, although she acquiesces to her role because she needs a job. The generational gap between them and their parents is ironically accompanied by a fixation on things Cuban, which other mainstream Americans (or even other Latinos) consider a unique and extended form of madness.

"La locura nacional"

Engaging this issue, Ana Menéndez focuses on that very aspect of the Cuban American character (whether immigrant or ethnic) in the very first pages of her novel *Loving Che*. Narrated in the first person by a young woman who does not know her Cuban past (her grandfather who brought her to Miami refuses to tell her anything), the plot reveals later that she might have been born of a relationship between her mother and the Argentine revolutionary leader in Havana. Her thoughts turn philosophical when she considers what she thinks are "destructive traits in the Cuban character":

> Miami seemed to me in those years to be living in reverse. They named even their stores after the ones they had lost; and the rabid radio stations carried the same names as the ones they had listened to in Cuba, as if they were the slightly crazed sons of a once prominent family. This endless pining for the past seemed to me a kind of madness; everyone living in a asylum, exiled from the living, and no one daring to say it plainly. (2)

Menéndez's earlier collection of short stories, *In Cuba I Was a German Shepherd* exhibit traces of irrational behavior or happenings, seemingly echoes of that alleged dislocation of mind and spirit that accompanies the Cuban exile, the eviction from paradise, the loss of dreams. In "Miami Relatives," Aunt Julia bites like a dog: once her husband needed seventeen stitches, and another time she bit the mailman and her own sister, while their old mother goes up a mango tree to eat lunch everyday. One day, Julia climbs on the table and announces that she ate the sun, her grandfather has an antenna growing out of his ear, and at the end the narrator says: "We are crazy because of him[. . .]. And he is crazy because of us" (165–79). In "Her Mother's House," the last story in the collection, the protagonist's mother is half mad with longing for the home she left in Cuba, with all her photographs in it (206).

There are repeated and frequent instances of *la locura nacional* appearing in most of the works mentioned in these pages, and patent cases of split personalities that constitute, at least in one instance, the core format and structural underpinning for a text. For instance, in the bilingual play *Coser y cantar* by Dolores Prida, the characters She and Ella are two halves of one bicultural Cuban American self; in *Dreaming in Cuban,* Lourdes Puente seems "unhinged" with her obssessive behaviors: eating, having sex, and hating Fidel (ironically, she patrols her neighborhood at night like her *miliciana* mother used to do on the Cuban coast); in *The Agüero Sisters,* man-crazy Reina comes to Miami to find her supposedly cool and composed sister seeing her own face dissolving in the mirror, and their mother Blanca's face appearing instead.

Cuban American exilic or immigrant "craziness," identified and perhaps even justified by those who are in a position to know these hybrid subjects, is not the special province of women authors. In fact, one would find the same obssessions, wild idiosincracies, irrational behavior, and madness of characters in many of the works written by Cuban American male authors. I will mention just two texts in this regard: *Raining Backwards* by Roberto Fernández (one need only remember Mirta Vergara, who reconstructs Varadero Beach in her bathtub) and *Crazy Love* by Elías Miguel Muñoz (with the dreamy, "*mandona*" Abuela in action). There are many other examples, nevertheless, of ex-centric narrators and characters who exhibit this form of Cuban uniqueness. In my opinion such a trait might be adscribed, as well, to the performance of Cuban American hybridity one sees in Alina Troyano's *Carmelita Tropicana*, also characterized by the predominance of caricaturesque humor.

In the Beginning There Were Palabras

Cuban immigrant women in the United States began writing their texts in Spanish, but in the seventies a detail in English, a place name or a song title, would appear in a poem or a short story. The locale and narrative time would also place those texts squarely in the circumstances of exile; but some of the younger authors went even further and started engaging the experience of living in America. Among the first Cuban women authors who started showing traces of biculturalism and bilingualism, as well as a consciousness of duality or hybridity, were Lourdes Casal, Maya Islas, Mireya Robles, and Uva Clavijo (now Uva Aragón). Casal's poem "*Para Ana Veltfort*," although written in Spanish, spoke for a whole generation with the statement "Cargo esta marginalidad inmune a todos los retornos" (I carry this marginality immune to all returns), and bespoke the duality of exile and immigration as it declared the impossibility of choosing between New York and Havana.[15] Islas speaks in some of her lyric poems of those years about "el threshold de mis miedos"; Robles reflects on "Feelings" and the lyrics of a song "escrita para el subway"; Clavijo writes short stories about Miami with addresses in known Floridian locales, spelled out in English. Islas's *Sombras papel* (1978), Robles's *En esta aurora* (1978), and Clavijo's *Ni verdad ni mentira y otros cuentos* (1977) are "among the first works published by Cuban women in the U.S. that document American society through the authors' literary personae, bearing witness to the cultural impact of a very different lifestyle" (*ReWriting Sugarcane Memories*, 167).[16] In them, the reader can begin to detect, even if vaguely, a certain consciousness of belonging to an immigrant generation that is slowly starting to become something else; we (I count myself among them) turned extremely self-conscious about our differences from the dominant society in the seventies. We became "aware biculturals" and began a more or less effective utilization of a bilingual discourse that could capture our sense of hybridity. It was at that point, I have argued before, that Cuban immigrant writers began the process of becoming Cuban Americans . . . even if English appeared only at first as a point of contact and not as a form of sustained discourse.

Nevertheless, Dolores Prida staged her *Beautiful Señoritas* in 1977, and Achy Obejas published her first book of poems written in English in 1982 (*Come the Fox*). Obejas's stories can be read in collections appearing in 1983 (*Woman of Her Word: Hispanic Women Write*) and 1984 (*Third Woman*). Her composition "*Sugarcane*," characterized by a linguistic code-switching discourse and a mixing of AfroCaribbean cultural symbols and rhythms, was published in 1983. At that point, Obejas offered a poetic world vision that was bicultural, and engaged the Third World oppositional consciousness that characterized the Chicana and Nuyorrican women poets of the times. From that moment on, Obejas continued to create a discourse that, whether lyrical or narrative, shared many of the distinctive features of the English-dominant Hispanic/Latino literature of the eighties. This predates (at least in print) the English poetry written by Cuban Americans whose words were compiled by Carolina Hospital in *Cuban American Writers: "Los Atrevidos."* I suppose the label of "daring" could very well have been applied to these women.

The Cubana Boom

What launched Cuban American writing by women into stardom was, indisputably, García's *Dreaming in Cuban.* Nominated for a National Book Award, this book became paradigmatic of what it was to create fiction that, through evocative language, linked the two worlds of Cuban immigrant and island families and projected their exilic memories and their social and political hopes on both sides of the Florida Strait. Reviewers and critics waxed eloquent describing the new talent. García's writing became emblematic of what it meant to be Cuban American: Nostalgic family remembrances, re-creation of transnational and deterritorialized imaginaries, and the everyday experience of "living as Other"—all traits mentioned before—can be found in her novels, created and written in English.

It is also important to point out that, in the context of the Latin(a) American writer boom of the eighties and nineties,[17] *Dreaming in Cuban* had significant, if not numerous, predecessors. The success of Sandra Cisneros and Esmeralda Santiago can also be mentioned in this regard. The break in the publishing "glass ceiling" had come for Latinas in 1991, when Random House accepted Cisneros's short story collection *Woman Hollering Creek.* Thus, securing a contract from Alfred A. Knopf was a big event in the book world when it happened to Cristina García in 1992.[18] It was not until the year after, in 1993, when the same press published Santiago's *When I Was Puerto Rican.* By the time *The Agüero Sisters* was brought out by Knopf in 1997, only nine other Latina writers (Nicolasa Mohr, Julia Alvarez, Ana Castillo, Sandra Cisneros, Cecile Pineda, Denise Chávez, Esmeralda Santiago, Margarita Engle, and Helena María Viramontes) had been published by major New York-based commercial presses. Later in 1997, the novel *Yo!* by Dominican American Julia Alvarez was published by Penguin, so there were two Latina novels about Caribbean immigrant sisters' relationships circulating in the American literary world at the same time. Finally, in 1999, the floodgates opened for Latinas: Doubleday published Ana Castillo's

Peel My Love Like an Onion, Random House published Esmeralda Santiago's *Almost a Woman*, and Viking Press brought out the novel by young Dominican American author Loida Maritza Pérez, *Geographies of Home*.

The beginning of the new millennium has been good for Cuban American women authors: in 2000, Beacon Press in Boston published Alina Troyano, *I, Carmelita Tropicana*, and Ballantine Books brought out *Days of Awe* by Achy Obejas; Andrea O'Reilly Herrera's *The Pearl of the Antilles* was published by Bilingual Press in 2001; Grove Press published both of Ana Menéndez's books, her short stories in 2001 and her novel in 2003. Cristina García's third novel in her Cuban trilogy, *Monkey Hunting*, came out under the imprint of Ballantine Books in 2003; and the youngest Cuban American woman writer so far, Chantel Acevedo, published her first novel, *Love and Ghost Letters*, with St. Martin's Press in 2005. This last major firm, as mentioned before, has published three novels by Alisa Valdés-Rodríguez and published her first book for young adults, *Haters*, in October 2006.[19] Is this a "Cuban success story" or what?

Three Cuban Degrees of Separation

Born in Cuba of an American father and a Cuban mother and raised in Los Angeles, Margarita Engle has a background of experiences distilled from her summer visits to the island and engages history in her novels *Singing to Cuba* (1993) and *Skywriting* (1995). Even though these narrations contain autobiographical overtones, it is true—as Isabel Alvarez Borland has pointed out—that the perspective in *Skywriting* is more distanced from Cuba and things Cuban than other works (136). In *Singing to Cuba*, the lush world of the Cuban countryside, flora and fauna, is portrayed in a vein that some reviewers describe as evocative of magical realism (some of this can be attributed, no doubt, to Engle's professional work as a botanist and an agronomist). These novels by Engle contain echoes of the original narrative of exile that carried mournful and nostalgic tones, especially in their denunciation of political realities such as the plight of the *balseros* and political prisoners.

Unlike Margarita Engle, Andrea O'Reilly Herrera has never been to Cuba. The island nation and its culture are known to her through her mother in Philadelphia and her maternal great-aunts in Miami. She is exemplary of those ethnic Cubans that take their Cubanness/Cuban Americanness very seriously, and as such she has delved into family history to create a world that is imaginary and yet very real, both for the writer and for her readers. Herrera is known as a novelist and also as a chronicler of the Cuban American experience, as can be seen in the moving testimonials of *ReMembering Cuba*.

Herrera's *The Pearl of the Antilles* traces the lives of five generations of Cuban women. The story contains autobiographical elements of the author's own legacy, which yearns strongly for everything Cuban. Critics have pointed to the sensuousness of the world described in its pages, as well as to the fact that it is primarily a feminine universe, seen through female eyes. At the end, Lilly—Margarita/Daisy's daughter, who has learned about Cuba from her mother—finally becomes a writer and pens this novel, the story of all the strong and very Cuban women in her genealogy, beginning with her grandmother Rosa, "la perla de las Antillas."

It is this recapturing of some writers' versions of Cuban reality that a few Latino critics in the United States have not totally accepted, either from a political or from a feminist viewpoint. The depiction of the Cuban Revolution as a social turmoil of profound negative impact in the lives of exiled Cubans, who implicitly or explicitly bemoan the state of affairs in the now socialist nation while idealizing previous island history, does not seem to inspire much aesthetic enthusiasm in otherwise open-minded Latina literary critics. For example, a novel like *Loving Che* is praised above *Dreaming in Cuban* for the following reasons (I quote extensively to make the comparative point):

> *Dreaming* has been associated with the predominately male tradition of historical Caribbean writing despite the fact that it offers a feminized account of the events and outcomes of the Cuban Revolution . . . [On the other hand] Ana Menendez's Loving Che illuminates the historical tensions, traditions, cultural politics and diversity among Cubans living both inside and outside of the United States. In my view her writing is unique and important for a number of reasons. She is one of the few Cuban American writers who explores the tensions between global migration, identity politics and the transnational implications of U.S. Latina cultural formations. With language that is concise and poetic, Menéndez graphically represents the complex political predicament Cuban exiles confront. Loving Che probes deeply into what some have perceived as Cuba's continued infatuation with Che Guevara . . . Aesthetically speaking Menéndez's Loving Che builds upon Sandra Cisneros's approach to her short story *The Eyes of Zapata* in that it appropriates a revolutionary, male hero as a means for developing a creative exploration of love, culture, history and the female imaginary. (Quintana, online article)

It is easy to see that our literature in general is still stereotyped as representative of socially conservative (read anticommunist) immigrant values, rather than as an artistic embodiment of cultural ethnonationalism with a meritorious place in the American scene. This happens even with *Dreaming*, one among other Latino texts that denote a consciousness of oppression for women and people of color, and whose protagonist agonizes over her cultural, social, and familial commitments to both exile and island life. Dismissing such a foundational work as aligned with a masculine Caribbean tradition, and insinuating that its author is not prone to address the transnational implications for U.S. Latina cultural formations, is nothing short of baffling. So is the failure to recognize that Cristina Garcia's work illuminates cultural politics and diversity among Cubans living both inside and outside the island. Commentaries like the one above lead the reader to believe that political rather than aesthetic judgments are being offered, and sadly point to ideological/intellectual power struggles based on misconceptions and misperceptions about Cuban Americans in general. *Loving Che*, on the other hand, is considered a politically correct work, surprisingly so because it is written by a Cuban American author, or because—as the canonical work by Cisneros cited—it uses a revolutionary hero to search for a woman's truth in the context of myth. It would seem that too narrow a comparison is drawn between Cuban American and Chicano texts, when the historical records for such distinctly different ethnic literatures prove they are bound to represent quite different perspectives on American life and its connections to Latin/o cultures. Moreover, the positive statements expressed about Menéndez can be (have been) applied to García by innumerable literary critics in the last two decades, and it is apparent to anyone who reads the latter's novels, books, and interviews that García indeed lives and writes from the deep complexity of experiences of her Cuban exile and immigrant community.

Finally, *Love and Ghost Letters* (Acevedo) also inherits the penchant for recreating history and mystery that seem to frame many of the *Cubana* narratives published in the last fifteen years, but does so in the political mode expected of exilic literature. Set in Cuba and Miami, the story covers years in pre-Castro Cuba and in Florida between 1952 and 1965, and is centered on the life story of Josefina and her father (who writes mysterious letters to his daughter after he is presumed dead). One of the most interesting testimonials I have read about the persistently dual/hybrid existence of ethnic Cuban writers is the paragraph in the personal webpage of Hialeah-born and raised Acevedo, where she partly describes her life:

> As a Cuban-American, I am in a unique position to both understand what it is to be truly, legally, deep down American, and to be Cuban, exiled, and nostalgic for a past I never experienced except through storytelling—the stories of my family, friends, of the old women in Miami's hospital waiting rooms, and the old men who tell you their personal *cuentos* of exile as you wait in line together at the bank. I haven't met a Cuban yet who didn't have a story to tell. (http://chantelacevedo.com/author.html)

And so, for all these generations of Cuban American women writers (three and counting) who have a story to tell, the existential themes persist, the obsession with telling family stories and expressing their collective memories goes on, and the writing "in Cuban" while living as an ethnic "Other" continues. In the American cultural scene, these tales of life's transformation for Cuban immigrants and their descendants offer a rich motherlode of literary exploration in years to come.

NOTES

1. I use the term "cultural artifact" in the same sense as Louis A. Pérez in his book *On Becoming Cuban*, where he postulates the proposition of national identity "not as a fixed and immutable construct but rather as cultural artifact, as contested and contesting representations often filled with contradictions and incoherences, almost always influx" (8). I thank Raúl Rubio for pointing this out to me.

2. Ruth Behar and Juan León have spoken about "the borderland space that exists between the two Cubas" (one, the island itself; the other, all of us who are part of the Cuban diaspora).

3. Cuban American scholar Oliva Espín has researched the psychological effects of oppression for Latino and Latina immigrants in the United States. See her *Latina Realities*, 87–90, and her article "Psychological Impact of Migration on Latinas."

4. Throughout these pages, the term "ethnonationalism" is used as the social and political expression of transnational identities, those pertaining to transnational communities such as what I call "la Cuba global" (see Alonso Gallo and Domínguez Miguela 19–21).

5. Some U.S. Cubans, however, see their Cubanness and Americanness as two distinct identities. See David Rieff, *The Exile*. For years, I have consistently argued that one of the distinctive traits of Cuban Americans of the immigrant generations—as all hybrid cultural subjects—is their ability to be neither from here nor from there, and yet be part of both places while fitting wholly in none ("Cubanos y cubanoamericanos" 91). Nevertheless, where before I have used the term "dual" identity to refer to this "here-and-there" dichotomy, I now prefer the word "hybrid" with all its postmodern and postcolonial connotations. Also see Ofelia Schutte's "Negotiating Latina Identities," 66.

6. The Puerto Rican scholar Buscaglia-Salgado also points to this Cuban mythology of entitlement: "Cubans have a very healthy attitude—after all not uncommon in the rest of the world—of appropriating things foreign no matter where these may come from," which helps to explain their mastering of the U.S. consumer culture, a fact also due to Cuban "fascination with comfort" (292).

7. I am using this term here for the first time to signify "original, primal island," in the context of the lost paradise motif so common in the poetry of Cuban writers in the United States from the sixties through the eighties (see Burunat and García, *Veinte años* 70–73; 136); Rivero, "Hispanic Literature in the U.S." 184).

8. See "In Two or More (Dis)places: Articulating a Marginal Experience of the Cuban Diaspora" (194–215), where I discuss the notion of the multiple positioning of a diasporic "Cuban-and-other" subject who does not respond fully to the markings implied as paradigmatic in our hegemonic discourse of exile. I also argue that Cuban Americans reach phases in their self-awareness evolution and identity politics that denote a third option besides being Cuban or non-Cuban, that of being "Cuban-and-other," or "Cuband" (the latter is O'Reilly Herrera's term defined in her *(Re)Membering Cuba*, xxix). For the notion of "Cuban Americanness" as performance, see my discussion of Carmelita Tropicana in *Discursos desde la diáspora* 59–73.

9. I call "ethnic Cubans," those otherwise referred to as "members of Generation Ñ," Cuban Americans. Many of them have never seen Cuba and know about the national culture of the island by the transmission of family oral histories, memories, and ideologies, as well as by the Miami re-creations of "la Cuba de ayer" (see Rivero, *Discursos* 28–29; and Rieff 31–32). Views of Generation Ñ members can be appreciated in the film Café con Leche, an introspective, documentary-style look at the shared experiences of young Cuban Americans who grew up in Miami (http://www.channel2.org/cafe conleche/original.html).

10. Emphasis is mine. In like manner, Xavier Cortada, visual artist and social activist, is described in similar terms: "Coming up Cuban-American, caught somewhere on the gangplank between identities, Xavier Cortada always struggled to span the two worlds that defined him. He was the *Americanito* who knew Cuba only through his parents, and the *cubanito* who grew up praying to *La Caridad del Cobre*" (http://www.cortada.com/media/1998/generationN.htm).

11. The idea of a group of women friends and their assorted troubles has been the basis of many popular culture works, as far-flung as Terry McMillan's *Waiting to Exhale* and *How Stella Got Her Groove Back* (films based on novels), and the television series Sex and the City. In addition, Valdés-Rodríguez's book harks back to the classic 1963 novel by Mary McCarthy, *The Group*, a sexually outspoken depiction of eight Vassar graduates in the 1930s. Valdés's subsequent novels use a similar structure, with settings in the fashionable and glitzy locales of Los Angeles and Miami, respectively. Given the light, humorous, and entertaining character of her novels, centered on and addressed to young female audiences, Valdés-Rodríguez has been dubbed by some reviewers as "the queen of '*chica*' lit" (the Latina equivalent of "chick lit").

12. In the Spanish edition of *Soñar en cubano*, the sentence reads "El planeta Cuba. ¿Dónde diablos queda eso?" (182). García herself has said she is not happy with the translations of her novels (see Rivero, "Cristina García," 638). Apparently the book was translated primarily for a reading audience in Spain and contains such non-Cuban phrases as "patatas fritas" and "más loco que una cabra" (instead of "chiva").

13. I come up with this term by modifying the classic concept of this peculiarly Cuban type of humor as applied to oneself (see Mañach, *Indagación del choteo*).

14. This episode brings to mind an anecdote often told by a Cuban American professor of my acquaintance about her teaching times in California. At the end of an academic year, one student who had been in her classes approached her and said: "Now that I have finished my courses I can tell you. For a long time I thought you were crazy . . . and then I realized you were just . . . well, Cuban!" A Cuban Canadian academic affirms that most diasporic Cubans suffer from a special kind of obsessive craziness regarding things related to Cuba, and calls this malady "la locura nacional." Both these professors are also clinical psychologists.

15. Casal's poem was originally published in *Areíto*, 52. It was later included in Casal's posthumous volume *Palabras juntan revolución*. It later appeared in English translation in *Bridges to Cuba/Puentes a Cuba*, 23–24.

16. The poems by Islas and Robles, and the short story by Clavijo were reproduced by Margaret Randall in *Breaking the Silences*, 25; 31–32.

17. In a manner reminiscent of Latin American literature and the success of women novelists in the so-called post boom of the eighties, the "second wave" of the U.S. Latino literary movement in the nineties has been termed the "Latina Renaissance."

18. It had only happened before with another novel of Cuban theme: *The Mambo Kings Play Their Songs of Love* by Oscar Hijuelos. Born in New York of parents who had emigrated from Cuba before the revolution, Hijuelos would go on to win the Pulitzer Prize in literature for this work, later made into the film *The Mambo Kings*.

19. As of this writing, Bilingual Press and Arte Público Press have published ten books by Cuban American women: Dolores Prida, *Beautiful Señoritas and Other Plays*, 1991; Margarita Engle, *Singing to Cuba*, 1993; Beatriz Rivera, *African Passions* and *Other Stories*, 1995, *Midnight Sandwiches at the Mariposa Express*, 1997, and *Playing with Light*, 2000; Himilce Novas, *Mangos, Bananas, and Coconuts: A Cuban Love Story*, 1996; Raquel Puig-Zaldivar, *Women Don't Need To Write*, 1998; María del Carmen Boza, *Scattering the Ashes*, 1998; Teresa Bevin, *Havana Split*, 1998; and Andrea O'Reilly Herrera, *The Pearl of the Antilles*, 2001. Not included in the "success story" above is the novel by Carolina Hospital *A Little Love*, written under her pen name C. C. Medina, coauthored with her husband and published by Warner Books in 2000. Detective fiction has not been included in this survey either, but the Cuban American Carolina García-Aguilera and her Cubana/Latina sleuth Lupe Solano have quite a following: see her novels *Bloody Waters* (1996), *Bloody Shame* (1997), and *Bloody Secrets* (1998), published by GPPutnam; *A Miracle in Paradise* (1999) and *Havana Heat* (2000) published by Avon, and *Bitter Sugar* (2001), *One Hot Summer* (2002), and *Luck of the Draw* (2003), published by Harper/Rayo.

WORKS CITED

Acevedo, Chantel. *Love and Ghost Letters*. New York: St. Martin's, 2005.

Alonso Gallo, Laura, and Antonia Domínguez Miguela, eds. "Globalization and Ethnic Nationalism," in *Evolving Origins, Transplanting Cultures: Literary Legacies of the New Americas*. Huelva: Universidad de Huelva, 2002. 15–34.

Alvarez Borland, Isabel. *Cuban-American Literature of Exile: From Person to Persona*. Charlottesvile: University Press of Virginia, 1998. 135–47.

Behar, Ruth, ed. *Bridges to Cuba/Puentes a Cuba*. Ann Arbor: University of Michigan Press, 1995.

Burunat, Silvia, and Ofelia García, eds. *Veinte años de literatura cubanoamericana*. Tempe, AZ: Bilingual, 1988.

Buscaglia-Salgado, José F. "Leaving Us for Nowhere: The Cuban Pursuit of the American Dream." Review of Louis A. Pérez, Jr., *On Becoming Cuban: Identity, Nationality, and Culture*. In *The New Centennial Review* 2:2 (Summer 2002): 285–98.

Casal, Lourdes. *Los fundadores: Alfonso y otros cuentos*. Miami: Ediciones Universal, 1981.

———. *Palabras juntan revolución.* La Habana: Casa de las Américas, 1981.

Clavijo, Uva. *Ni Verdad Ni Mentira y Otros Cuentos.* Miami: Ediciones Universal, 1977.

Espín, Oliva M. "Psychological Impact of Migration on Latinas: Implications for Psychotherapeutic Practice." *Psychology of Women Quarterly* 11:4 (December 1987): 489–503.

———. "Roots Uprooted: Autobiographical Reflections on the Psychological Experience of Migration." In *Latina Realities: Essays on Healing, Migration, and Sexuality.* Boulder, CO: Westview, 1997. 19–29.

García, Cristina. *Dreaming in Cuban.* New York: Knopf, 1992.

———. *Soñar en cubano.* Trans. Marisol Palés Castro. Madrid: Espasa-Calpe, 1993.

———. *The Agüero Sisters.* New York: Knopf, 1997.

———. "Translation as Restoration." In *Voice-Overs: Translations and Latin American Literature.* Ed. Daniel Balderstone and Marcy Schwarz. New York: State University of New York Press, 2002. 45–48.

———. *Monkey Hunting.* New York: Knopf, 2003.

Hospital, Carolina. *Cuban American Writers: Los Atrevidos.* Princeton: Ediciones Ellas-Linden Lane, 1988.

Hijuelos, Oscar. *The Mambo Kings Play Their Songs of Love.* New York: Farrar, Straus and Giroux, 1989.

Islas, Maya. *Sombras-Papel.* Barcelona: Editorial Rondas, 1978.

Mañach, Jorge. *Indagación del choteo.* La Habana: Editorial del Libro Cubano, 1955.

Menéndez, Ana. *In Cuba I Was a German Shepherd.* New York: Grove, 2001.

———. *Loving Che.* New York: Grove, 2003.

Obejas, Achy. *Memory Mambo.* Pittsburgh: Cleis, 1996.

——. *Days of Awe.* New York: Ballantine, 2001.

O'Reilly, Herrera, Andrea, ed. *ReMembering Cuba: Legacy of a Diaspora.* Austin: University of Texas Press, 2001.

———. *The Pearl of the Antilles.* Tempe, AZ: Bilingual, 2001.

Pérez, Lisandro, and Guillermo J. Grenier. *The Legacy of Exile: Cubans in the United States.* Boston: Allyn & Bacon, 2003.

Pérez, Louis A., Jr. *On Becoming Cuban: Identity, Nationality, and Culture.* Chapel Hill: University of North Carolina Press, 1999.

Prida, Dolores. *Beautiful Señoritas and Other Plays.* Houston: Arte Público, 1991 [staging dates: *Beautiful Señoritas* 1977, *Coser y cantar* 1981, *Savings* 1985, *Pantallas* 1986, and *Botánica* 1990].

Quintana, Alvina. "The Future(s) of Latina Literature." http://www.word-power.co.uk/platform/The-Future-s-of-U.S.-Latina-Lit (April 7, 2006).

Randall, Margaret, ed. and trans. *Breaking the Silences: Twentieth-century Poetry by Cuban Women.* Vancouver: Pulp, 1982.

Rieff, David. *The Exile: Cuba in the Heart of Miami.* New York: Simon and Schuster, 1993.

Rivero, Eliana. "Hispanic Literature in the US: Self-Image and Conflict." In *International Studies in Honor of Tomás Rivera.* Ed. Julián Olivares. Special issue of *Revista Chicano-Riqueña* 13 (1985): 173–92.

———. "(Re)Writing Sugarcane Memories: Cuban Americans and Literature." In *Paradise Lost or Gained? The Literature of Hispanic Exile.* Ed. Fernando Alegría and Jorge Ruffinelli. Houston: Arte Público, 1986. 164–82.

———. "Cubanos y cubanoamericanos: perfil y presencia en los Estados Unidos." *Discurso Literario* 7:1 (1989): 81–101.

———. "From Immigrants to Ethnics: Cuban Women Writers in the U.S." In *Breaking Boundaries: Latina Writings and Critical Readings.* Ed. Asunción Horno-Delgado, Eliana Ortega, Nina Scott, and Nancy Saporta Sternbach. Amherst: University of Massachusetts Press, 1989. 189–200.

———. "Cristina García." In *Latino and Latina Writers.* Alan West-Durán, ed. Vol. 2. New York: Scribner's, 2004. 635–51.

———. *Discursos desde la diáspora.* Cádiz: Editorial Aduana Vieja, 2005.

———. "Cuerpo de Cuba: la construcción de un imaginario sexual cubano." In *Discursos* 91–101.

———. "In Two or More (Dis)places: Articulating a Marginal Experience of the Cuban Diaspora." In Andrea O'Reilly Herrera, ed., *Cuba: 'Idea of a Nation' Displaced.* New York: State University of New York Press, 2007. 194–215.

Robles, Mireya. *Tiempo Artesano.* Barcelona: Editorial Campo, 1973.

———. *Tiempo Artesano.* Bilingual edition. Trans. Angela de Hoyos. Austin TX: Dissemination Center for Bilingual Bicultural Education, 1975.

Schutte, Ofelia. "Negotiating Latina Identities." In *Hispanic/Latinos in the United States: Ethnicity, Race, and Rights.* Jorge J. E. Gracia and Pablo De Greiff, eds. London and New York: Routledge, 2000. 61–75.

Valdés-Rodríguez, Alisa. *The Dirty Girls Social Club.* New York: St. Martin's, 2003.

———. *El club de las chicas temerarias.* Barcelona: Seix Barral, 2004.

PART TWO

THE ART

Irremediable

No me pertenecen:
no les pertenezco—
ni Londres con su Westminster
y villancicos de Navidad,
ni Cleveland con su cielo rosa
ni Ginebra en su lago espejo
ni del todo San Juan.

Sé que en el Santiago natal
que no recuerdo,
lo mismo será.
—*Laura Imayo Tartakoff*

8

From the Vanguardia to the United States

Cuban and Cuban-American Identity in the Visual Arts

Lynette M. F. Bosch

The Avant-Garde of 1967 repeats the deeds and gestures of those of 1917. We are experiencing the end of the idea of Modern art.
—Octavio Paz, *Convergences: Essays on Art and Literature*

As a contribution to a volume that seeks to map the process of negotiating identity or identities, this essay focuses on the interaction between art and identity in Cuba and in the work of Cuban-American artists in the United States. As such, this essay addresses a variety of topics, including: the role that Modernism played in the formation of Cuban artistic movements; the definition of "lo cubano" in Cuba and in the United States; exile and immigration in relation to artists who have left Cuba at various stages following the 1959 revolution; and the manner in which Cuban-American artists negotiate their place in the continuum of Cuban and American art. The goal of this article is to present an outline for future work on the four groups of Cuban-born artists who have established careers in the United States and who have negotiated diverse definitions of Cuban-American identity.

Derived from the Latin *identitas* and *ficare*, identity is defined as an association or affiliation with a certain origin, nature, or definite characteristics. Identification implies that the process of ascertaining origin and characteristics is shared in agreement with others, thus identity is simultaneously an individual and a group process. The concept of negotiation is derived from the Latin *negotium* or business. To negotiate is to accomplish the business of reaching agreement in a successful transaction. However, the goal of negotiating identity is not easy or simple because, while it is possible to agree on the origin (Cuba), nature (Cuban and American), and characteristics (cultural markers and societal structures), it might not be possible to define a Cuban-American identity.

This essay is one approach to defining aspects of Cuban-American identity related to the formation of a Cuban and a Cuban-American artistic identity within the context of modernism and postmodernism. This process of negotiating identity began in Cuba with the Vanguardia Generation, in the 1920s and 1930s when Cuban artists began to travel out of Cuba in search for modernism and modernity. During those decades, Cuba emerged from the economic and social devastation of the 1898 War of Independence and its aftermath and began deliberately to develop a national identity.[1] The search for a national identity was enacted by writers, journalists, sociologists, anthropologists, and historians who sought to define "lo cubano." As a group, these intellectuals searched for a cohesive and unifying identity for Cuba's disparate population of diverse Europeans, Afro-Cubans, and Asians, mostly Chinese. In the visual arts, the business of negotiating a Cuban identity by introducing European modernism linked to a social agenda became the primary intentional goal of the Vanguardia. Thus, the negotiation of identity within an artistic context became an intrinsic part of Cuban culture at the beginning of the twentieth century.

In his book *Cuban Art and National Identity: The Vanguardia Painters, 1927–1950*, Juan A. Martínez traced how the painters of the Vanguardia linked Cuban art and the search for a Cuban identity to the type of European international Modernism predominant in Paris and Madrid (1–31). The Vanguardia's intentions were published as a manifesto in *Revista de Avance*, in 1927, "We want movement, change, advance, and we want absolute independence even from time" (10). The Vanguardia's spokesman, art critic Martí Casanovas, included an expanded form of their manifesto in his review of their art in the same magazine: "We fully condemn and negate the art of the Nineteenth Century, the servile instrument of the capitalist bourgeoisie. The highest aspiration of our young artists is to forget all that has existed, all the museums they have visited . . . We are trying to start anew, looking at art as a foundation of emotions . . . The central issue of modern art is to return to emotions: situate oneself with pure intentions before the spectacle of the world and of life and describe, with a simple and clear language, the emotions of everyday life" (Martínez 11). The Vanguardia artists also called for a vernacular art and free access to art for all of the people. As Martínez maintained (25), the Vanguardia brought modernism to Cuba and exported its art to an international audience, with the proof of their success being international exhibitions and their inclusion in the collection of the Museum of Modern Art in New York.[2]

The Vanguardia's manifesto with its rallying cry against the bourgeois and capitalism and its championing of a vernacular people's art contextualizes them among the socialist and Communist artistic movements of the early twentieth century (Mexican art immediately springs to mind as the model they followed). The veneration in which the Vanguardia artists are held and the place of honor they are given in Cuba's Museo Nacional, is, expectedly, the extension of their implicit socialist political allegiances as found in their manifesto. The Vanguardia's definition of modernism differed significantly from that of Parisian modernism, as such they became a countercenter focused on a localized search for identity instead of an international movement.

With their individualized interpretation of modernism, the Vanguardia succeeded in changing the stylistic tenor of Cuban art in the early decades of the twentieth century. By deliberately turning their backs on the academic traditions of their teachers at the Academia de San Alejandro, in Havana, the Vanguardia painters introduced styles of form and color that brought to Cuba the visual experiments of Picasso, Matisse, Braque, and Cezanne. Thus, Cuban modernism adjusted Matisse and Picasso to accommodate palm trees, campesinos, and cowboys as well as the mixed ethnic and racial groups that composed Cuba's upper and lower classes. In the paintings of the Vanguardia, Cuban anecdotal narrative replaced European-generated universalized imagery and form. Hence, as a Cuban national identity became realized in representational form, the individual members of the Vanguardia reinterpreted modernism on Cuban terms.

As Cuban modernists, the Vanguardia were successful in recycling into statements of identity stock Cuban themes, such as landscapes with palm trees, rural subjects (*campesinos* and *bohíos*), portraits, still-life paintings of tropical fruits, idyllic encounters between couples of recognizable Cuban ethnicity, Cuban country dances, Afro-Cuban carnivals, and representations of local flora. These visual tropes became the thematic material transformed by the Vanguardia into "lo cubano." It is within this revolutionary transformation of art that the images created by Carlos Enríquez, Fidelio Ponce, Eduardo Abela, Amelia Peláez, and Lorenzo Romero Arciaga can be viewed. Although each artist developed distinct visual styles, they are joined by a shared group move away from detailed realism toward a more abstract figural formation and dislocated color that indicated their familiarity with international art. As such, they brought Cuba's geography and its peoples into a modernity defined by the Vanguardia's contact with the world beyond the island and adjusted to accommodate the island's need for a visual definition of "lo cubano." In short, the Vanguardia enacted a successful negotiation between their interpretation of modernism and Cuban identity, which created a third identity—that of Cuban modernism.

Martínez argued that the Vanguardia's modernism drew attention to social inequality, racial prejudice, discrimination, and the class struggle in Cuban society by representing scenes featuring the poverty of the rural workers and the unemployment of Afro-Cubans. They were also responsible for problematizing the representation of the mulatto and the mulatta in Cuban society. It fell to the Vanguardia to indicate the exploitation of Afro-Cubans, mulattos, and Chinese by nineteenth-century artists and cartoonists by providing alternative characterization of these Cuban groups. This moralizing mode was contrapuntal to an exultant presentation of typical Cuban scenes, landscapes with palm trees, noble campesinos, horses and cowboys, and "la vida cubana" as a romanticized idealized world. In the former mode, there were Fidelio Ponce's representations of Cuba's poor rural and agricultural workers as Carlos Enríquez created images of starving campesinos. In the latter there were Enríquez's images of cowboys and landscapes with palm trees and picturesque vistas.

Additionally, there were departures from both programs that indicate that not all of the Vanguardia consistently adhered to their ideal intentions. Enríquez himself created a series of images of nude women, white and mulatta, depicted singly or in pairs, clearly linked to earlier erotic images and not so much to Cuba's socioeconomic class struggle. Furthermore, while paintings such as Alberto Peña's *Sin Trabajo* (*Unemployed*) give a poignant glimpse into the social plight of so many Afro-Cubans, it is difficult to see how the perky-breasted mulatta of Enriquez's *Tropics* enables social revolution. There is, nonetheless, no doubt that the Vanguardia did give visual form to their search for a national identity as they introduced an adjusted and negotiated modernism to Cuban painting.

In their search for a national identity, the Vanguardia also established a national art market as they expanded venues for exhibition and education. Cuba, at the beginning of the twentieth century, lacked art centers or galleries. Exhibitions were in private homes, private clubs, or in the few frame shops that existed in downtown Havana (Martínez 23–31). This situation would change as a result of the activities and efforts of the Vanguardia artists. By the time that this generation gave way to the next, Cuba had an established art market, recognized exhibition centers, and a growing awareness that visual art and national identity represented a significant contribution to the national enterprise of self-definition. Even if the Vanguardia artists did not always remain faithful to their higher aspirations, enough of their work recorded the plight of Cuba's underprivileged, thereby raising social awareness as they altered the intention, content, and style of Cuban art.

In the art of the Vanguardia, "lo cubano" emerges as a visual statement that relies on geography, flora (such as the ubiquitous Royal Palms of Cuba), social moments (the offering of a cup of *café cubano*), guitar strumming, dancing, carnivals, and the Cuban cowboy riding the essential symbol of Cuban masculinity—the galloping horse. The image of Cuba as a country where unemployment and hunger existed alongside joyful celebration and the intimate moments of daily engagement in the enjoyment of life is an accurate reflection of the economic, class, gender, and racial divides that formed part of Cuban society in the early twentieth century. It was precisely these social divides that would erupt to change Cuban society when Fidel Castro emerged as the catalyst for the dissatisfaction and alienation of the poor and the hard-pressed urban and rural workers. Thus, the roots of the Cuban Revolution of 1959 can be seen in the paradoxical imagery of the Vanguardia, split between the romanticized images of idyllic *cubanidad* and the more graphic expositions of life as it was for those who did not partake of Cuba's bounty.

Subsequent generations of Cuban artists have recognized and appreciated the groundbreaking efforts of the Vanguardia and they are venerated among exiled Cuban-American art collectors as the touchstone visual statements of Cuban identity. In the Miami art market, the work of the Vanguardia bring consistently high prices that have increased significantly from what they were in the 1960s. This veneration of the Vanguardia and the desire for their work on the part of exiled Cubans represents a fantastic paradox as they seek to buy (for increasing prices) the work of artists who consciously aligned themselves with the political and social forces that eventually led to the Cuban Revolution that rendered them exiles. Simultaneously, in Cuba, the Vanguardia artists are proudly exhibited while the Museo Nacional de Cuba retains the right to legitimize the attribution and provenance of Vanguardia works that appear on the international art market.

Thus, both groups of postrevolutionary Cubans, those inside and those outside Cuba, enshrine the same group of artists, claiming them as being representative of visions of "lo cubano" as it was understood in the 1920s and 1930s, that cannot help but clash ideologically. To the Cuban exiles, the Vanguardia's pictures represent "old Cuba" as it was in its heyday. To the Cubans who place the Vanguardia at the center of their display of Cuban artistic talent in the Museo Nacional, they represent the ideological vanguard of the revolution. Clearly, the Vanguardia's imagery and their representational mode is so central to the recognition of "lo cubano" that not even the politics of being Cuban on the right or the left can shake them from their primacy across the political and geographic divide. As such, the Vanguardia have established a base for Cuban art and identity that continues to signify "Cuba" to the generations that followed their pioneering efforts.

The modernist style developed by the Vanguardia was not, however, uniform in its formalist goals as each member of the group exhibited individual preferences and diverse artistic creativity. Amelia Peláez, for instance, painted in a manner that evoked stained glass windows (such as those seen in the doors of Cuban homes) and an adaptation of Cubism, with hints of Cezanne. Carlos Enríquez combined aspects of Expressionism with hints of Impressionism and the daubing technique of the Italian Macchiaoli. Antonio Gattorno adopted a naïf style somewhat evocative of Mexican painting with a touch of Gaugin. Wilfredo Lam opted for a type of Cubism similar to Picasso's *Demoiselles d'Avignon* laced with tropical flora and allusions to the synchretic practices of Santería. In so doing, his style mirrored the blend of African and European found in Santería, wherein the identity of African deities (Orishas) were masked by the use of images of European saints. Although today, with hindsight, the Vanguardia artists can be seen to share a "period style" associated with the early part of the twentieth century, this period style does not extend to an easy identification of a group style. Thus, individualized diversity and not uniformity or conformity is an early marker of style in the history of Cuban art. It is a marker that would be passed on to subsequent generations of Cuban artists, who have not yet produced a cohesive group style. In the same way that there is no one way of being Cuban or of looking Cuban, there is no group style that can define Cuban identity or Cuban art.

The ideological mission of the Vanguardia was not wholly transmitted to the next generation of Cuban artists. The artists who came of age in the 1940s and 1950s, such as Rafael Soriano, Baruj Salinas, Eladio González, Antonia Eiriz, Agustín Fernández, Gladys Triana, Lourdez Gómez Franca, and Enrique Gay García, among many others, were not interested in searching for "lo cubano."[3] This generation, essentially an interim generation between the Vanguardia and the revolution, was the generation that left Cuba in large numbers in the 1960s and 1970s, settling in the United States, Europe, and Latin America. The group that settled in Miami eventually became known as La Vieja Guardia. In Cuba, the interim generation's artistic interests were focused more on establishing themselves within contemporary modernist currents than in defining Cuban identity. Cuba, in the 1940s and 1950s, was no longer in the grip of an identity crisis. After forty to fifty years of grappling with the need to meld its diverse population into Fernando Ortíz's *ajiaco*, these early efforts had yielded a modus vivendi for the Cubans of the next generation (Martínez 37).

In the 1940s and 1950s, the increased American presence on the island at a time when New York City was becoming an artistic mecca meant that it was easier for the artists of the interim generation to focus their attention on the world outside the island. New York was an accessible artistic center as travel between Havana and New York was easier than travel had been in the 1920s and 1930s between Havana and Paris and Madrid. Cuban artists of the interim generation could easily familiarize themselves with what was happening in New York through magazines and books that featured contemporary art and artists. Increasingly, Cuban artists adopted the movement toward abstraction favored by the New York establishment, championed by critics such as Clement Greenberg, into the modernist standard.[4] By the late 1950s abstraction and color field painting defined the avant-guard in art, and artists in Cuba developed styles that reflected these trends. An overview of the artistic production of the interim generation demonstrates that their work was keeping pace with international currents in terms of artistic quality and formalistic concerns. Line, space, and color were the real subjects that preoccupied these artists and this can be seen in the work of individual artists and in the work of the generational group. Cuban identity was not a concern for this group, although as with the Vanguardia, a group style was never developed.

Post-1959 this would change for many of these artists, as they became refugees and exiles. Suddenly, the interim generation found itself being defined not through participatory similarity with their peer artists in other countries, but by their cultural difference as Cubans. The shock of difference, accompanied by the trauma of exile, caused them to revaluate their identity as Cubans and, for those who settled in the United States, as new Americans. Some of these artists explored these new issues in their work (Baruj Salinas and Eladio González), while others continued the same trajectory of thought and intent they had in Cuba (Rafael Soriano).

Life in Cuba during the 1940s and 1950s was good for the upper classes and somewhat better for the working classes.[5] During those decades, Cuba enjoyed a level of overall prosperity that was enviable to the rest of the Latin American world. Its proximity to the United States and a steady flow of American money and influence into its capital city and its resort areas meant that Cuba could then define itself in contrapuntal juxtaposition to "los Americanos." Thus, it can be said that there were Cubans who through marriage, education, and affinity became Cuban-American in Cuba. Many of these Cuban-American Cubans were among the first waves of exiles to arrive in the United States from the island. One example among artists is Baruj Salinas, who had studied at Kent State University where he earned a degree in architecture before returning to Cuba to pursue a career as a painter.

In the United States, the group task of the newly exiled artists, who became La Vieja Guardia, was parallel to that of the Vanguardia generation in Cuba. It was up to this group of artists to employ modernism as a tool for negotiating and defining identity within a community that did not have clearly delineated art market practices. This had not been the situation in Cuba for the interim generation, as Cuba's art market was established by the 1940s and 1950s and the rudimentary art exhibits and the dearth of galleries encountered by the Vanguardia belonged to another age. Although Cuba's art scene was not comparable to that of New York or Paris, it was, by the late 1950s, an established part of Cuban culture. The interim generation was accustomed to easy travel in and out of Cuba, an audience interested in art in Cuba and venues throughout the island for exhibition and employment. But when these artists arrived in the United States it was up to them to create a market for their work as they sought to define themselves in their new identity as Cuban exiles in the United States. Once again, in the history of Cuban art, it was necessary for a generation of Cuban-born painters to negotiate art and identity in a developing art market.[6]

In *Cuban-American Art in Miami*, a description is given of how the Cuban art market was founded in Miami by the first group of exiled artists, assisted by collectors and the owners and directors of galleries that began to sell the work of these artists.[7] The beginnings were not promising and did not hint at the Latin American art market that exists in Miami today. Sales took place in private homes and in garages. There were galleries that opened and closed in the blink of an eye. Slowly, in the 1970s and later, spaces such as the Bacardí Gallery, the Meeting Point Gallery, and area colleges and libraries became venues for regular exhibitions of art by Cuban-born artists. By the late 1970s, it can be said that La Vieja Guardia had established Cuban art as a force in the art market they formed as they formulated the original parameters for a definition of Cuban-American art. Thus, La Vieja Guardia initiated the process of negotiating artistic identity with a Cuban and an American identity seen from the perspective of exiles.

The stylistic diversity found in the work of the Vanguardia can also be seen in the work of the artists of La Vieja Guardia. The abstract sculptures of Agustín Cárdenas, while evocative of those of Henry Moore, and similar in the use of negative and positive space to the paintings of Rafael Soriano and the sculpture of Enrique Gay García and Eladio González, nonetheless occupy their own niche because of marked differences in color and form. Soriano's ineffable spaces and his mesmerizing colors distinguish his painterly style marked by his immediately recognizable personalized formalist idiom. González's edgy sculptures with their eroticized planar complexity are significantly different from Cárdenas's sweeping forms. Gay García's forms could be associated with those of Constantin Brancusi, yet they differ in the rhythm of the lines and spaces so much that they too are an individualized product exemplary of the spatial experimentation characteristic of these decades.

By the late 1970s, the generation of Cuban children and adolescents who came to the United States between 1959 and 1979 began to make inroads into the Cuban-American art market established by La Vieja Guardia. These artists became the first hyphenated generation of exiled Cuban-American artists. It fell to them to create an art of exile, unique in its conceptual base and in its varied yet distinct stylistic manifestations. Included in this group of artists are Humberto Calzada, Emilio Falero, Arturo Rodríguez, Mario Bencomo, Maria Brito, Demi, Juan Carlos Llera, Alberto Rey, Luis Cruz Azaceta, Paul Sierra, María Lino, and Ramón Guerrero.[8] It was this group that began to define "lo cubano-americano" as they negotiated their identities as artists, as Cubans, as Americans, and as Cuban-Americans. Much as the Vanguardia had done, they also negotiated their place within contemporary modernism and postmodernism as it developed in the 1980s and 1990s in the United States.

Thoroughly American in their approach to the art world found in the United States, by the late 1970s, Cuban-American artists of the hyphenated generation were ready to compete for attention with their American peers. Their work was featured in a series of exhibitions from the 1970s to the 1990s and from exhibitions such as "Outside Cuba" and "Cuba/USA: The First Generation," it is clear that their styles were diverse and defied easy classification.[9] Realism and abstraction were evident throughout these exhibitions. Subjects and messages were equally diverse as some artists concentrated on issues of identity, feminism, gender orientation, exile, or fantasy. Some artists were contemporary in their stylistic references, while others recontextualized traditional imagery into new configurations of meaning. Some favored traditional easel paintings while other created elaborate Santería altars. White, black, and mixed race and ethnicity was evident everywhere in the group as a whole. A group style was impossible to discern. Yet, all shared the division of their creative roots into their Cuban and American sides, their memories of Cuba, their experience of exile, their process of assimilation to the United States, and their acceptance or rejection of American culture. As such, their group dynamics functioned to unite them in intention yet separated them in the manner of expression. Additionally, they were distinguished by their diverse experiences and perceptions of their cultural situation and by their acceptance or rejection of mainstream modernism. Much like the Vanguardia artists and La Vieja Guardia, younger Cuban-American artists retained a strong individuality as they forged their personal visual vocabulary, although some comparisons can be made to link this group of artists to the artists of previous generations.

For example, it is clear that the abstract flora and organic forms of Mario Bencomo's paintings are kin to the floral abstractions of Amelia Peláez. Arturo Rodríguez's forms and colors are somewhat evocative of those of Carlos Enríquez. Humberto Calzada's paintings of stained-glass windows can also be seen to be similar in spirit to those of Amelia Peláez. Demi's representations of children can be viewed within a context provided by Fidelio Ponce and by Lourdes Gómez Franca's early paintings of children. Yet, even though such similarities can be indicated, the differences that separate the younger Cuban-American artists from the Vanguardia are so much greater that one can't even properly speak of influence. As with the Vanguardia, while it is possible to discern some similarities of approach in the Cuban-Americans, their diversity resists classification through the identification of a group style. If anything, it can be said that stylistic disunity is an important element in the characterization of Cuban art from the twentieth into the twenty-first centuries, with stylistic diversity being a parallel to the racial and ethnic diversity of Cubans.

Nonetheless, despite their stylistic diversity, the shared purpose of the younger Cuban-American artists was to transmit the experience of exile and their personal interpretation of this experience. As a group, this generation has evolved visual languages and personalized symbolic systems intended to convey the emotions of exile to those who have experienced it and to those who have not. For their peer group of exiles, their images have created a world of memory and events with which they identify because their experience of exile with its alienation, uncertainty, dislocation, trauma, renewal, and assimilation is a given in their work. Much as the Vanguardia generation had done in Cuba for defining "lo cubano," the younger Cuban-American artists provided a visual vocabulary for how it was that "lo cubano" became "lo cubano-americano."

For the younger Cuban-Americans, negotiating their search for identity and their experience of exile with contemporary modernism and postmodernism was not an easy fit. The predominant artistic styles in the United States during the 1960s and 1970s still reverberated with the abstraction introduced in the 1950s and 1960s by artists such as Jackson Pollock, Louis Morris, and Louise Nevelson. Abstraction is inadequate for recording human experience in a manner that makes it recognizable to the spectator. Thus, representationalism is a better choice for artists wishing to explore identity and seeking to express emotion directly in a manner that is more easily recognized by the spectator. In the 1970s and the 1980s, figurative American art meant Pop Art, and Andy Warhol was the master to follow. If Pop Art was not the lodestar, figurative expression could be found in currents of ongoing installation (Ed Kienholz), Surrealism (Salvador Dalí was still in the news) or Dada (Marcel Duchamp was still king). Alternative options included Joseph Cornell or Joseph Beuys. Nowhere in these mainstream movements was there a place for the exploration of a group experience of exile and assimilation for artists who had been half-formed in their native country and brought to maturity in a foreign country that had become theirs.

Immigrant artists, such as Wassily Kandinsky or Wilhelm De Kooning or expatriate artists such as Picasso had made the transition to other countries individually, not as members of a group.[10] But the hyphenated Cuban-Americans were taken from their original homes and moved by their parents as a group. They, thus, became a generation marked by their divided identities and by circumstances beyond their control, and as a group they grew up in Miami's Cuban enclave or, if taken elsewhere, they were brought to Miami periodically to reconnect with their Cuban origin. Theirs was an unusual position in the chronicle of exile and theirs was a singular opportunity for making their mark in the history of art with a unique contribution to the visual culture of modernism and postmodernism.[11]

Thus, much as the Vanguardia generation had done, the younger Cuban-Americans on the mainland of the United States sought to negotiate the search for identity with their search for an individual artistic voice within the context of contemporary modernism and postmodernism. Yet, during those decades, the established American mainstream that controlled the art world was approving thematic agendas that were counter to the personalized intentions based on emotions and on the experience of exile that was the thematic base of the work of the younger Cuban-Americans. It is not, therefore, surprising to find that the mainstream art world of New York City in the 1960s and into the 1980s was unable to recognize or address the implications or the significance of the work being created by the Cuban-American artists of both generations.

An additional barrier to recognition or acceptance by American critics and art historians was the employment of Spanish by Cuban-Americans as a language of communication. Furthermore, Miami, the center of their activities, although a short airplane ride from New York, was not at all recognized in the 1960s to the 1980s as being an artistic center comparable to the established art world of the northeast. Older Cuban-American artists had studied at San Alejandro, which was not a recognized institution in the United States. Younger

Cuban-American artists were either self-taught or had been educated in local Miami area schools. They, therefore, lacked the contacts and context guaranteed to American artists coming from colleges and universities favored by the American art world. To the New York art establishment, Cuban-American artists were provincial foreigners intent on creating works of art that reflected an experience and emotions that were unfamiliar to the settled institutions and individuals who defined modernism and postmodernism during the middle to the end of the twentieth century. There were also ideological conflicts that barred the Cuban-American artists from access to the mainstream.

Part of modernism's artistic agenda was a destruction of what can be termed "the real," the actuality of existence, experience, and of the technical accomplishments inherent to artistic traditions. Modernism favored the avant-garde accompanied by the dissolution of "academic" elements, such as technical and visual quality in art, and fostered a break with the history of art that sought to obfuscate the past in favor of a present dislocated from its sources and origins. Hence, references to past art, whether in materials, representational style, quotations, incorporation, appropriation, and the employment of content and subject that emerged from the emotional, psychological, and social world of the artist was censored as being "retardataire" and "ahistorical." For Cuban-American artists coming of age in the 1970s and 1980s, mainstream modernism was incompatible with their artistic intentions as their work was about the very things that modernism denied—experience, emotion, historical references, and technical accomplishment. Their insistence on the portrayal of personal experience based on emotion and memory rendered them as being behind the times to New York critics, who, if they came across their work, immediately moved on looking for work that suited their framework for modernism. In effect, the provincials adhering to a narrow exclusionary view of the art world were the New Yorkers, but, as they had control of the journals, venues, and critics, they had control of making or breaking artists and movements. Additionally, Cuban-American artists exiled to the United States, between 1959 and 1979, implicitly and explicitly (by their presence in the United States) rejected the modernist metanarrative of a leftist utopia.

On the other hand, postmodernism promised a more open agenda within which the work of Cuban-American artists could be placed. In *After the End of Art*, Arthur Danto placed the end of early twentieth-century modernism, as a cultural and artistic movement, in the late 1960s (14). Danto attributed its demise to a tendency to be "too local and too materialist, concerned as it was with shape, surface, pigment, and the like as defining painting in its purity" (16). Identifying Clement Greenberg as the catalyst for the establishment of the modernist movement in art, Danto pointed out that the art that Greenberg had seen as embodying modernity and the "truth of art" was simply, "a certain local style of abstraction" (18). For Danto, truth in art, "would have to be consistent with art appearing every possible way," and he added that in his view, "the major artistic contribution of the decade was the emergence of the appropriated image—the taking over of images with established meaning and identity and giving them a fresh meaning and identity" (22). Danto thus implicitly argued for the type of pluralism evident in Cuban-American art in the work of the hyphenated Cuban-Americans.

As Latin Americans, who grew up immersed within a culture that has always been intimately bound with the Surreal and the Magical Real, the unexpected and the chaotic irrational, Cuban-Americans are quintessential postmodernists. As the descendants of cultures that were never designed to meet, much less coexist and blend into a larger whole, Cuban-Americans instinctively understand and embody a postmodernist aesthetic. Because Cuban-American artists matured within the technological explosion that characterizes the latter half of the twentieth century, they naturally took advantage of the wealth of global information made available in the postmodernist era. The resulting pluralism is evident in their work. However, postmodernism did not embrace the work of Cuban-American artists during the decades of the 1970s to the 1990s.

Thus, Cuban-American artists continue to lack merited recognition as a group and as individuals. Possibly this lack of recognition is the result of ignorance on the part of American critics who are not sufficiently flexible in their critical assessment of movements within contemporary art to cope with the problematization of a group of artists whose work does not fit their parameters of significance. Thus, it has fallen to Cuban-American critics and art historians to attempt to integrate this group within modernist and postmodernist current, a process that is only now beginning. Despite their lack of recognition by the New York mainstream, in the 1970s and 1980s, the combined efforts of the artists of La Vieja Guardia and the younger Cuban-Americans established an art market in Miami during the 1970s and 1980s that by the turn of the century had become an artistic center in its own right.

The themes that gave both generations of Cuban-American artists their place in Miami and barred them from acceptance to the American mainstream were the themes they shared with their peer group of Cubans. Exile, displacement, alienation, assimilation, multiple identities, and the assumption that a return to Cuba was barred for the foreseeable future and could exist only in memory. As a result old photographs and films became their inspiration and motivation. Thus, the artists representing the community's psychological and geographic situation had a very specific mission, the transference into visual form of the process of negotiating the emotional experience of being divided and of being denied the possibility of a return to unity. The younger Cuban-Americans had an even more specific thematic goal, that of conveying their divided identities as well as their exile experience, an experience that was often accompanied by financial struggle and by the dissolution of their families.

For children and adolescents, the trauma of exile is augmented by divided loyalties and confused allegiances, which add to their trauma. It is precisely this territory that is explored by the work of Demi and María Brito. In María Brito's paintings, installations, and sculptures, the artist presents her personal understanding of what it means to negotiate social and cultural identity with her identity as an artist. The often conflicting dilemmas that are presented by the individual's attempt to simultaneously fulfill every role and to play at being all of the parts means that conflict, tension, and anxiety attend the attempt to become too many things to too many people. Demi's work, primarily centered around the depiction of children, presents the spectator with the effects that exile and trauma have had on the members of her generation. Her work addresses a population that is frequently forgotten in the process of displacement because children lack the forceful voice of adults and the power to decide. By focusing attention on children, Demi reminds the spectator of their own experiences, which parallel hers and her generations', and of the experiences of other children caught in similar traumatic moments.

Conversely, for other younger exiles, family can provide a supportive structure that assists their assimilation. And, it is this perspective that is found in the portraits Juan Carlos Llera has made of his father. Memory and the attempt to reconstruct the past is also the purview of the exile, and it is this aspect of exile that is explored in the architectural paintings of Humberto Calzada whose work brings the spectator to an idealized Cuba delineated by its architecture brought to life in Calzada's assembled interiors. Composed of archaeological knowledge of Cuban architecture and evocative memories of his childhood and adolescence spent looking at Cuba's buildings, Calzada takes the spectator into an imagined world that is of a time and place and yet beyond any time or place. His is the reality of fantasy employed to record a fragmented past negotiated through memory and by identity.

Once easier access to Cuba began in the late 1980s and 1990s, Cuban-Americans have begun a slow process of temporary return to the homeland from which they had been banned for so many years. For some Cuban-American exiled artists, the call of home has been too strong to not answer and for artists such as Mario Bencomo and Alberto Rey, the return to Cuba has represented a cathartic moment in their artistic process where memory and reality have intersected to form a new nexus for their work. Mario Bencomo's repeated returns to Cuba have been the catalyst for a series of works about Cuban flora. Other series have considered the process of negotiating place between Cuba and the United States or Cuba and Canada, an example of which is his series *If Quebec Were in the Tropics*. Alberto Rey initiated a series of portraits of Cubans inside the island and on the mainland prior to his travels to Cuba as well as a series of videos that record his emotional journey to a home he did not remember because he left Cuba at the age of three.

Until Cuban-American exiled artists began to address the experience of exile and divided cultural identity as an area of artistic inquiry, the visual arts did not have a cohesive artistic voice for articulating these concerns. Hence, the younger Cuban-American artists are the first group of artists to have consciously and deliberately sought to unite their efforts to transform an existential experience into an arena for artistic expression. Certainly other immigrant or exiled artists had expressed similar experiences and memories in their work—one thinks of Marc Chagall and other transplanted Jewish artists, or the Yuan painters of China, who were exiled from their capital to the provinces. But, unlike the Yuan painters, Cuban-American exiles had lost their country and unlike individual immigrant or exiled artists they worked together as a group localized in a community that supported their search for a group voice with which to address the reality of their lives and the negotiation of their divided identities.

Thus the hybrid generation addressed a situation as old as Hebrew Scripture or the chronicle of the Egyptian Sinuhe from a completely contemporary perspective that has become a daily part of our perception of our world. And their diasporic experience with its echoes of Jewish displacement was especially resonant to a group of artists, among whom some had Jewish roots (Baruj Salinas and Mario Bencomo). Because their work was centrally concerned with negotiating issues of identity and social culture as well as gender, race, and class, their work in the 1970s and early 1980s anticipated the exploration of these issues by American artists in the later 1980s and 1990s. Thus, the younger Cuban-American artists constitute a postmodernist avant-garde enacted on the mainland of the United States by Cuban-born artists who had left Cuba from 1959 to 1979.

In 1980, the base group was joined by artists who escaped Cuba with the Mariel boatlift, which brought artists such as Carlos Alfonzo, Luis Vega, and Juan Boza to the United States.[12] As with the other groups of Cuban-born artists, the art of the Mariel artists exhibited stylistic diversity and a search for their Cuban identity once they reached the United States. The Mariel artists were approximately the same age as the older and younger groups established in Miami. Their experience was in many ways similar to that of earlier arrivals, yet different in significant ways.[13] The sudden release by the Castro government of the Mariel exiles meant that Miami was suddenly inundated with refugees that could not be easily absorbed. The INS center (the Freedom Tower on Biscayne Boulevard), which processed the original exiles, had already closed by 1980 and the new arrivals were processed in public parks. The difficulties of housing the Mariel arrivals meant that they became problematic within the Cuban community and for American authorities. As many of the Mariel exiles had been released from jails and mental institutions or came without adequate literacy or job skills, their arrival changed the perception of Cuban-Americans as a relatively easy group to integrate. The artists arriving with the Mariel group had initial difficulties. Nonetheless, once the Mariel artists had negotiated the initial stages of assimilation into their new surroundings, they found that the first waves of artists had created an art market where they were recognized and accepted. Their adjustment to the United States, however, was negotiated more along the lines of that of the Vieja Guardia than that of the hyphenated Cuban-Americans because they arrived as adult Cubans and mature artists.

By the end of the 1980s and the beginning of the 1990s, there were three distinguishable groups of Cuban-American artists living and working in Miami and the city's art market was receiving national and international recognition among curators and critics in the United States and in Latin America. It was becoming clear to the art world outside Miami that a countercenter had been established and that countercenter identified itself as being a market where the negotiation of identity in art was a legitimate thematic concern that reflected the experience of a significant population of naturalized Americans.

In the 1990s, following the collapse of the Soviet Union and the economic stresses that were created in Cuba as a result of the withdrawal of Soviet support, another group of Cuban-born artists arrived in the United States. As with previous waves of Cubans, this group also settled predominantly in Miami. But the Miami they came to was a dramatically different place from that which the first arrivals had found. Instead of the sleepy Southern town that reluctantly absorbed the first exiles and the Mariel group, Miami, in the 1990s, was a highly developed cosmopolitan city with a diverse Latin American culture. Additionally, the artists coming in the 1990s also found that, unlike the first arrivals, it wasn't necessary to sell their work in garage sales because Miami's Coral Gables and the surrounding areas had dozens of galleries ready to exhibit and sell their work. The international art fairs—Art Miami and Art Basel—increased visibility for the artists who came in the 1990s and their adjustment to the United States was not attended by the language or employment difficulties or the trauma of being political exiles who had been persecuted by the Castro regime that defined the experience of earlier exiles. There was another significant difference between the artists who came in the 1990s and those who were already in the United States, and that is their accessibility of return to Cuba.

As travel from the mainland to the island and back was available to the artists arriving in the 1990s, a return to Cuba was a matter of choice. Hence, although many of the artists arriving in the 1990s chose to remain on the mainland, some do travel back and forth. The availability of travel in and out of Cuba meant that the generation of the 1990s can be classified as being transnational by choice as opposed to being exiled by political necessity. Despite the possibility of immediate and consistent return to Cuba and the economic, cultural, and political difference of their situation compared to that of earlier exiles, the artists of the 1990s also began to address issues of identity. Yet, their work differs significantly from that of the earlier arrivals because their experiences of being Cuban and being American and of leaving Cuba and settling in the United States were not the same as those of the earlier groups.

The artists who arrived in the 1990s represented a generation that, in Cuba, had been identified as the generation of 1980, as is described by Luís Camnitzer in *New Art of Cuba*.[14] This group had been trained in Cuba and assisted in the promotion of their work by the Cuban government's system of exporting the work of Cuban artists to the international market. Unlike their contemporaries, the younger Cuban-Americans and the Mariel group who struggled to find time and money for the production of their work as they competed with their American counterparts for attention, the Cuban generation of 1980 enjoyed the privilege of being able to spend all of their time and energy being artists. The generation of 1980 also benefited from government-sponsored cultural exchange programs and from the invitations to Cuba extended to art critics and collectors by the Cuban government for the purpose of showcasing Cuban art. Their career privileges meant that, when they arrived in Miami, the generation of 1980 was greeted by collectors, critics, curators, and gallery dealers who were already familiar with their work. As a result of the Cuban government's efforts on their behalf, with relative ease, they became Miami's generation of the 1990s.

Earlier Cuban artists had arrived impoverished, traumatized, suffering from language and culture shock, and wondering how they were going to survive economically in a foreign country. The generation of 1980 (now known as the generation of the 1990s) need never learn English, as Spanish is the lingua franca of Miami. When they arrived, the generation of the 1990s found venues and galleries ready to exhibit and sell their work. Thanks to Cuba's policy on arts management, many members of the generation of the 1990s enjoyed the privileges of capitalist profit from the day they arrived in Miami. While some members of the generation of the 1990s have become financially successful (José Bedia, Rubén Torres Llorca, and María Magdalena Campos-Pons), others have found that they could not adapt to a freemarket economy where their sales and exposure were not guaranteed by government programs. Many of these artists have faded from the art scene.

As with all other groups of Cuban-born artists, the generation of the 1990s differs in the visual styles and media they employ. However, those who have been successful in this country do not have the conflicted relationship with modernism or postmodernism that characterized the negotiation of art and identity for other groups of Cuban-born artists since the Vanguardia because their work's design fit within the parameters set by the American mainstream critics. Those who have been the most successful in the United States have crossed the identity gap with artistic styles that closely echo in form, style, and content the acceptable artistic categories defined by the New York establishment. Hence, as Mark Denaci has argued, María Magdalena Campos Pons has been well received by a critical establishment that places her work alongside that of Carrie Mae Weems and Lorna Simpson.[15] José Bedia has received acceptance among critics accustomed to the installations of Joseph Beuys, while Rubén Torres Llorca, whose work can also be aligned with that of Beuys, combines elements akin to those of the constructions of Jasper Johns and Joseph Cornell, thus his visual vocabulary is familiar to American critics.

Because these artists work fits the norms and forms of American modernism and postmodernism, their work fulfills the expectations of a critical establishment that has defined the parameters of critical acceptance. Additionally, their work comes with bonafide credits as Cuban international production, as these artists are wholly Cuban in their training and artistic origins and were already integrated into the international art market by Cuba's artistic policies. The artists of the generation of the 1990s therefore do not represent a disturbing presence on the American landscape as hyphenated Cuban-Americans because they are considered by American critics to be completely and truly Cuban. As such, they can be seen to fit a category—that of foreign émigré artists working in the United States. Thus, American critics are comfortable with their status as "others" and their use of Spanish is acceptable instead of being cause for unease as it is with the Cuban-Americans.

The coterminous existence of these four groups of Cuban-born artists in Miami since the mid-1990s has meant that the process of exile definition and identity formation for Cuban-born artists has undergone several stages of adjustment and negotiation. Because these groups do not proceed in uniform parallels neatly categorized into specific canonized formulas, it is difficult to talk about these issues without devolving into superficial generalization. Yet, the substantive differences in their knowledge of and in their experience of being Cuban as represented by the different and diverse groups of artists means that for each group the reception of their identity as artists and as Cubans in America has varied considerably. Thus, each artist's negotiation of their experience of being Cuban, of adapting to America, and of representing these adaptations in their work is markedly different. However different these groups are, one shared element unifies them all and that is their stylistic diversity and a universal concern within their work and their lives to try to create a record of their experience as Cubans who have come to the United States. Nonetheless, it should be noted that among these groups of Cuban-born artists, only the younger Cuban-Americans legitimately possess the territory of articulating the specific dual identity that is the result of their exile as children and adolescents and their maturation in the United States.

"Lo cubano-americano" in the hands of the younger Cuban-Americans is indicated by images that are fragmented, split into separate parts, sectioned off to indicate the divided identity and the divided self negotiating with two or more cultures in order to arrive at a definition of the self that combines aspects of each. For this group, their half-Cuban and half-American lives are an intrinsic part of their identity and of their artistic process. When they address the experience of exile, they address it simultaneously from both sides of their personal cultural divide. When the artists of La Vieja Guardia address identity, they address it from the perspective of Cubans who now live in a foreign country into which they have assimilated more or less willingly. The same is true of the Mariel artists and of the artists of the generation of the 1990s. For them, their Cuban identity was always whole. They came into exile as fully formed Cuban adults and as mature artists, secure in their artistic vocabulary and in their Cuban identity. They confronted American culture *as Cubans*, and the unity of the imagery in their work indicates that their perspective on their experience is seen from their Cuban identity, which perceives American culture as foreign. On the other side of the divide, when they transmit information about their Cuban identity, it is transmitted whole as they are confident of their identity as Cubans.

When issues of identity surface in the art of Cuban-born artists living and working in the United States, the art of the Vanguardia resurfaces in kind if not in like. As the generation of artists known to all Cuban artists, the imagery initiated by the Vanguardia to define Cuba continues to recur in the work of subsequent generations who employ figural motifs to address issues of negotiating identity. The geography of Cuba, its palm trees, its subtropical flora, its diverse population of Europeans (Christian and Jewish), Afro-Cubans and Santería, as well as traces of Asian Cubans emerge along with topical references to the food, local customs, gender and class relations that form part of Cuban society continue to provide the source material for an ongoing presentation of "lo cubano."

Fifty-eight years of a Cuban diaspora have generated a significant art of exile and immigration that needs to be studied further as a uniquely unified phenomenon that can be separated into different stages and generations of artists. All are Cuban in the depths of their souls. All have become American to a lesser or greater degree. All draw upon their familiarity with the Cuba that was first depicted by the Vanguardia as being the quintessential island the source of "lo cubano." All negotiate their place in the streams of artistic culture identified as modernism and postmodernism as they seek to record an experience that is unique to them, yet basic to the human condition of movement, displacement, and cultural accomodation.[16] Future studies of these artists will enable a better understanding of their contribution to art, to history, and to the history of their two countries, which, in the near future, must learn to negotiate a new path with the survivors of this lengthy and unusual exile.

NOTES

1. See Juan A. Martínez, *Cuban Art and National Identity: The Vanguardia Painters, 1927–1950* for a discussion of Cuba's economic and social situation in relation to the Vanguardia's political agenda (32–49).

2. The collection assembled at MOMA was put together by Alfred Barr working with the advice of Cuban critic, José Gómez Sicre.

3. For a discussion of the work of these artists see Lynette M. F. Bosch, *Cuban-American Art in Miami;* and Carol Damian, *Breaking Barriers.*

4. See Mark Denaci's chapter in this volume for a discussion of Cuban-American art and modernism and postmodernism.

5. For a discussion of Cuba before Castro, see Jaime Suchlicki, *Cuba: From Columbus to Castro;* and Luís Pérez, *Cuba and the United States.*

6. For an early grouping of the first arrivals, see José Gómez Sicre, *Cuban Art of Exile.*

7. Bosch, "The Founders of Cuban-American Art in Miami," 35–41.

8. For this group, see Bosch and Damian.

9. For a discussion of the phenomenon this group represented in literature and art, see also Isabel Alvarez Borland, *Cuban-American Literature of Exile;* Giulio Blanc, *The Miami Generation* and *Cuba/U.S.A.: The First Generation;* and Ileana Fuentes-Pérez et al., *Outside Cuba/Fuera de Cuba.*

10. On this phenomenon, see *The American Experience;* and Cynthia McCabe Jaffee and Daniel J. Boorstin, *The Golden Door.*

11. See Denaci's chapter in this volume for a discussion of modernism's and postmodernism's precepts. Also see Danto's *After the End of Art.*

12. For the Mariel artists, see Damian.

13. On the Mariel boatlift, see Hamm, *The Abandoned Ones: The Imprisonment and Uprising of the Mariel Boat People;* Holly Ackerman and Juan Clark, *The Cuban Balseros;* Alex Larzelere, *The 1980 Cuban Boatlift.*

14. See Luis Camnitzer, *New Art of Cuba,* for a description of the Cuban government's establishment of art as a national enterprise.

15. As quoted by Denaci in chapter 9 of this volume.

16. It is beyond the parameters of this publication to fully illustrate the works of artists discussed in this essay. Reproductions of the work of the included artists, can, however, be found in the publications cited herein.

WORKS CITED

Ackerman, Holly, and Juan Clark. *The Cuban Balseros: Voyage of Uncertainty.* Miami: Policy Center of the Cuban-American National Council, 1995.

Alvarez Borland, Isabel. *Cuban-American Literature of Exile: From Person to Persona.* Charlottesville: University of Virginia Press, 1998.

The American Experience: Contemporary Immigrant Artists. Philadelphia and New York: Balch Institute of Ethnic Studies, 1985.

Blanc, Giulio. *The Miami Generation.* Miami: Cuban Museum of Arts and Culture, 1984.

———. *Cuba/U.S.A.: The First Generation.* Washington DC: El Fondo del Sol, 1991.

Bosch, Lynette M. F. *Cuban-American Art in Miami: Exile, Identity and the Neo-Baroque.* UK: Lund Humphreys, 2004.

Camnitzer, Luis. *New Art of Cuba.* Austin, TX: University of New Mexico Press, 1994.

Damian, Carol. *Breaking Barriers: Selections from the Museum of Art's Permanent Contemporary Cuban Collection.* Florida: Fort Lauderdale Museum of Art, 1997.

Danto, Arthur. *After the End of Art.* Princeton: Princeton University Press, 1997.

Denaci, Mark E. "Challenging Orthodoxies: Cuban-American Art and Postmodernist Criticism." Chapter 9 in this volume.

Fuentes-Pérez, Ileana, et al. *Outside Cuba/Fuera de Cuba.* New Brunswick: Rutgers University Press, 1987.

Hamm, Mark S. *The Abandoned Ones: The Imprisonment and Uprising of the Mariel Boat People.* Boston: Northeastern University Press, 1995.

Larzelere, Alex. *The 1980 Cuban Boatlift.* Washington, DC: National Defense University Press, 1988.

Martínez, Juan A. *Cuban Art and National Identity: The Vanguardia Painters, 1927–1950.* Florida: University Press of Florida, 1994.

McCabe Jaffee, Cynthia, and Daniel J. Boorstin. *The Golden Door: Artist-Immigrants of America, 1876–1976.* Washington, DC: Smithsonian Institution Press, 1976.

Pérez, Luis. *Cuba and the United States.* Athens: University of Georgia Press, 1997.

Gomez-Sicre, José. *Art of Cuba in Exile.* Miami, FL: Editorial Munder, 1987.

Suchlicki, Jaime. *Cuba: From Columbus to Castro.* Washington, DC: Pergamon Brasseys, 1987.

9

Challenging Orthodoxies

Cuban-American Art and Postmodernist Criticism

Mark E. Denaci

What sorts of challenges does Cuban-American art pose to mainstream art criticism in the United States? That is at least one of the questions implicitly raised by the appearance of Lynette Bosch's 2004 book *Cuban-American Art in Miami: Exile, Identity, and the Neo-Baroque*, as well as the more recent exhibition and catalogue *Layers: Collecting Cuban-American Art*, by Bosch, Jorge Gracia, and Ricardo Viera (in conjunction with the NEH seminar on Cuban-American Philosophy, Art, and Literature that resulted in the present edited volume). The challenging aspect of this art from the perspective of contemporary academic criticism might not be immediately apparent; after all, one of the most striking features of recent criticism has been the attempt to deal with art and artists falling outside the mainstream of white North American and European traditions, with a particular focus on hyphenated identities. Yet, for several important reasons, much Cuban-American art does not fit comfortably within this critical paradigm.

Some of the reasons for this lack of fit involve the medium and style preferred by many of the artists: The work in these publications is dominated by representational painting, with very little in the way of the sort of multimedia experimentation favored by the critical establishment. Other reasons, ironically, may relate to biases inherent in many varieties of the multiculturalism referred to above: Art critics interested in a global perspective might tend to pay closer attention to art from Cuba itself, which, for some, might fit more comfortably the criterion of an exotic "otherness" to be uncovered and explored. This phenomenon might be seen as a more specific variation on the neglect long faced by U.S.-based Latino artists even as those from Latin America have received increasing attention and resources.[1] But while the second, more culturally based issue may be the greater problem for Cuban-American artists in terms of visibility and success in art world institutions, the first, more formally based issue is probably more responsible for the neglect of this art by the academic critical establishment in particular.

Due to the current nature of art criticism, the particular stylistic and formal characteristics of so much of the art featured in these recent publications raises a number of questions for art critics and historians interested in promoting a more multicultural understanding of contemporary art: Should these artists continue to be ignored? Should they be condemned for what might be considered formal conservatism, or defended for their resistance to current fashions and trends? Should they be juxtaposed to those currently working from the island, or would that amount to an overly simplistic and perhaps biased reductionism? I would suggest responding to these questions by embracing the very aspects of this art that seem most troublesome, and using them as opportunities for self-critical reflection; rather than asking how my own critical assumptions can be used to critique or evaluate Cuban-American art, I propose a kind of phenomenological reversal, whereby I might ask instead how Cuban-American art might be used to critique or evaluate those critical assumptions.

Before considering how this might be done, I need to outline in somewhat greater detail the history of what I am calling the mainstream art critical paradigm, which emerged most directly from the debates over the definition of the term "postmodermism" in the late 1970s and early1980s, and more indirectly from the mid-twentieth-century writings of Clement Greenberg.[2] Most academic art criticism over the past two decades identifies itself either explicitly, or more often implicitly, with a particular strain of anti-Greenbergian thought, among the earliest and best articulations of which was Douglas Crimp's canonical exhibition and essay titled "Pictures" (175–87). Crimp's direct target in that essay was not Greenberg himself, but one of his most influential followers at the time, Michael Fried. Essentially, Crimp both accepted and rejected the argument made by Fried in "Art and Objecthood." In that now classic 1967 essay, Fried argued from a Greenbergian position against the then-flourishing Minimalist movement, claiming that in reducing the work of art to a single basic object or series of objects with no complex interrelationship of parts to be contemplated, minimalism encouraged viewers to experience—rather than contemplate —the work in their own time and space, a type of experience he labeled "theatrical" (116–47).

Fried's position was based upon Greenberg's notion of "self-criticism," itself derived from the eighteenth-century German philosopher Immanuel Kant, whose philosophical critiques of pure reason, practical reason, and judgment used the methods of philosophy to determine philosophy's own proper areas of competency. In Greenberg's conception, the history of modern art consists of artists' progressive divestment of all nonessential formal conventions in an attempt to discover what is essential to each medium; most famously, in the case of painting, its fundmental characteristics included flatness and "opticality." According to Fried, for sculpture this essential condition involved the articulation of forms in space, an articulation noticeably absent from most minimal sculptural works. This absence, he argued, left room for a theatricality that he saw as potentially subsuming all other forms of cultural expression and leading to an anti-intellectual "experientialism," wherein we lose the ability to appreciate works for their inherent quality, but instead demand that they provide us with experiences.[3]

In "Pictures," Crimp actually accepted almost all of Fried's points, with the important exception of the latter's conclusions. Agreeing with Fried that the theatricality was both the defining feature of minimalism and a threat to Greenbergian self-criticism, and finding Fried's predictions to be prescient in terms of subsequent movements such as performance art, earth art, and conceptualism, Crimp mainly differed with Fried on the ultimate implications of this theatricality. Rather than leading to a dumbed-down experientialism, Crimp saw the postminimalist movements as representing a more thoroughgoing criticality, one that refused to take even its own specific medium for granted as in Fried's preferred conception. Instead of a threat to sustained, aesthetic critical attention, Crimp saw in these movements an attempt to rescue critical art from an ivory tower of aesthetic autonomy and bring it into dialogue with lived material reality. The main subjects of his exhibition and essay, of course, were not those aforementioned movements of performance art, earth art, and the like, but rather the then-emerging practices to which Crimp wanted to apply the term "postmodern": These generally involved a return to two-dimensional images (the "pictures" of the title), but in a way that rendered problematic their representational coherence. Instead of making claims for originality and authenticity, as was arguably the case for modernist artists, the artists in question undercut such claims through such strategies as appropriation, quotation, and framing (Crimp, "Pictures" 186).

One of the difficulties for theorists of the postmodern—a difficulty that Cuban-American art throws into sharp relief, as I hope to demonstrate—has always been the question of how similar or different postmodernism really is from modernism, and to what extent modernism would or would not be understood from a Greenbergian perspective. In "Re: Post," Hal Foster argued that most of the strategies claimed by Crimp and other theorists such as Craig Owens on behalf of the postmodern had already enjoyed an important role in the modernist tradition, and that the ability to bracket them off under a new category of "postmodernism" depended on conceding to Greenberg and Fried their limited definition of modernism (Foster 189–201). This point is debatable, and depends on the extent to which movements such as Dada are considered central or exceptional in relation to modernism. But what may be more ironic than the necessity of using Greenberg as a foil in the definition of postmodernism is the extent to which even the most explicitly anti-Greenbergian formulations rely on fundamental principles similar to those of Greenberg. In particular, the notion of self-criticism remains paramount: While postmodernist critics avoid using that term, and would never accept Greenberg's medium-specific definition of it, most of the anti-Greenbergian critics do share with Greenberg the fundamental assumption that the point of art is to be critical, and that this criticality is dependent at least in part on artists' self-awareness of the critical tradition preceding them. Much postmodernist criticism of the late seventies and early eighties, for example, was devoted to resisting the phenomenon of Neoexpressionism, which was accused of emptying the modernist tradition of its criticality by reproducing its techniques outside of their historical contexts. The idea of "turning back the clock" was often evoked, and with it the presumption that art had to progress by building critically on the achievements of the art of the immediate past.[4]

To a large extent, their position was simply a broader application of Greenberg's general principle, a kind of self-criticism of self-criticism. Certainly if, in its rejection of internally articulated parts, minimal sculpture was abandoning the Greenbergian self-critical position of Abstract Expressionist sculpture, it was operating no less critically in relation to that position. To some extent, the shift from modernism to postmodernism could be argued to have been from an apolitical self-criticism to an activist social criticism, and this was the position argued by Crimp in later essays dealing with activist art.[5] Yet, for the most part, these critics did not champion the work of such socially engaged artists as Leon Golub, for example, presumably because it lacked criticality at the formal level. Although postmodernist formal experimentation could blur Greenberg's rigid medium-based boundaries, a formalist self-critical tendency remained a requirement for art to be taken seriously by postmodernist academic criticism.

Among the many changes in the art critical climate nearly thirty years after the first debates about postmodernism in the visual arts are a seriously diminished level of interest in the term "postmodernism" and a far more pronounced interest in global and multicultural issues in art. While the former might appear to be a major shift, a look at the essays in the recent anthology *Theory in Contemporary Art 1985* suggests that while the term "postmodern" has receded into the background, the critical principles (such as site specificity, appropriation, and fragmentation) articulated by academic critics in the postmodernist debate are alive and well, as well as the latent Greenbergian basis for those principles. While Greenberg's thought is engaged directly in such essays as David Joselit's "Notes on Surface: Toward a Genealogy of Flatness," other essays, such as Liz Kotz's "Video Projection: The Space between Screens" engage in a medium-based formal critique whose debt to Greenberg is as notable as it is unacknowledged. The following passage from Kotz's conclusion illustrates the continued art-critical tendency to look for art that explores what is "essential" to its medium:

> Thus the pixel and scan lines are the visible mark of the intervention of technology and its abstracting effects (hence the very goal of "high definition" television

> is to repress this structure, to make video look more like film by reducing pixilation below the threshold of visibility). Video, as a temporally generated grid, produces a continual transformation of the image. Signal interference and disruption are integral to its workings, as are the decays and distortions introduced by recording and storage processes. It is in the interplay between this screen of scanning—that translates electrical signals into moving images—and the screen of projection—that transmits these optical images into architectural space—that video occurs. As we continue to wait for more artists to explore the many unpredictable things that happen there, perhaps we are beginning to see that the video projection work that was so celebrated during the last decade was less of a disruption of mass-media signal than a sign of the times. (101–12)

For Kotz, then, pixel and scan lines, signal interference and disruption, decays and distortion, are what constitute the reality of the medium of video, and she calls on artists to use these characteristics rather than suppress them. What I am trying to highlight about this strain of criticism is the emphasis it places on the work of art as a means of critiquing its own medium, a distinctly Greenbergian emphasis in spite of the post-Greenbergian insistence that this medium-based self-criticism also function as social criticism (to which Kotz alludes in her final sentence, implicitly criticizing video projection art for reflecting, rather than disrupting, contemporary mass media culture).

In such a critical climate, as I suggested earlier, traditional representational painting—regardless of its style or subject matter—is not likely to be taken particularly seriously. This is not necessarily a problem in itself, as an insistence on formal experimentation certainly can be (and has been) defended on multiple grounds. But I wonder whether some of the more "conservative" Cuban-American artworks don't offer an implicit critique of the very critical assumptions that could potentially be used to dismiss them. Before getting to that point, however, I want to acknowledge that the work of several Cuban-American artists fit very easily into what I am calling mainstream critical paradigms. The most well known of these is probably José Bedia, who was already a successful artist before emigrating to the United States. Gerardo Mosquera's 1992 description of his work underlines Bedia's direct engagement with the postmodernist critical project:

> His work intelligently takes advantage of openings, resources and sensitivities from current art of the centres, to confront us with a different vision. This syncretism also occurs in his technique, effortlessly integrating technological, natural and cultural elements, drawing and photography, ritual and mass-cultural objects, all within the sobriety of an analytic discourse. He also appropriates "primitive" techniques, but not in order to reproduce their programmes: he creates elements with them that articulate his personal discourse and iconography.

> Bedia is making Western culture from non-Western sources, and therefore transforming it towards a de-Europeanisation of contemporary culture. But simultaneously we could say that he is making postmodern Kongo culture. (218–25; 221)

Through the mixing, appropriation, and transformation of different media, techniques, and discourses, Bedia's work is an example of precisely the types of strategies called for by Crimp, Owens, and other postmodernist critics so many decades ago; whether or not it is promoted by contemporary critics on its individual merits, Bedia's work speaks the language of that criticism and fits comfortably within its parameters.

Like Bedia, Rubén Torres Llorca developed an international reputation while still in Cuba, and since settling in Miami has continued to produce conceptually based, multimedia installations that engage with most of the concerns of postmodernist art criticism. His 2005 collage titled *The Annunciation* offers a particularly appropriate example: Not only does it combine different media, but its art historically loaded title also creates friction in juxtaposition to the 1940s popular illustration style of the "Mary" figure. Moreover, the figure appears threatened by a series of circles containing texts specifically referring to art world institutions: art options, art fairs, art collections, art market, art magazines, art dealers, and art critics. This type of art world self-reflexivity engages directly academic postmodernism's paradigmatic form of "self-critical" activity, the practice of institutional critique long associated with artists such as Daniel Buren and Fred Wilson.

Likewise, the photographic work of María Magdalena Campos-Pons engages directly with mainstream academic art-critical discourse. Remarkably, her work has little in common, at least formally, with that of other Cuban and Cuban-American artists, but is very closely related to the work of several important African American photographers, including Lorna Simpson and Carrie-Mae Weems. Like Simpson, she presents portraits—often self-self-portraits—in a way that emphasizes their constructed quality through fragmentation, repetition, the inclusion or intrusion of texts, and other postmodernist strategies. Like Weems, she presents identity as enmeshed within a complex network of discourses, including folkloristic or religious traditions as well as oral histories, in addition to those of hegemonic racial oppression. While Cuban cultural motifs are integral to her work, she uses them to engage in a much broader international artistic dialogue concerning race and identity. As such, her work is immediately comprehensible within the critical paradigms already in place for the reception of the work of Simpson, Weems, and similar artists.

As I pointed out earlier, however, such work is somewhat exceptional in the context of the Cuban-American art presented in these recent publications. An obvious temptation for critics schooled in the postmodernist tradition might be to focus exclusively on artists such as Bedia, Llorca, and Campos-Pons, possibly dismissing the other artists as conservative or even retrograde. But something about these other artworks—perhaps the insistent quality of their resistance to these familiar critical modes—seems to demand my attention, and I don't think that treating that demand as something purely personal and subjective would constitute a satisfactory response. Instead, like Michael Ann Holly, who suggests that works of art might have something to say about the art historial practices that purport to interpret them, rather than strictly vice-versa as is usually assumed, I propose a phenomenological reversal in looking critically at Cuban-American art: Instead of using an art-critical apparatus to gain insight into Cuban-American art, I want to see to what extent Cuban-American art might offer some insight into that critical apparatus.[6]

In so doing, I want to begin by looking at some artworks that do not fit into that framework as seamlessly as that of Bedia, Llorca, or Campos-Pons, but nonetheless do not appear to reject it entirely. These include works by the late Juan González, María Brito, and Alberto Rey. Among the many qualities that these artists share is a tendency to combine a focus on strong, representational painting technique with sustained attention to issues of framing and quotation. While the first characteristic allies their work to the modernist notions of unmediated artistic genius that postmodernist criticism has attempted to challenge, the second characteristic concurrently implies their own destabilization of those notions.

González, who died of AIDS in 1993, differed from both Brito and Rey in that he was already in his twenties when he arrived in Miami in 1966 (Bosch 69). His mature works feature a Dalí-esque hyper-realism, but consistently call attention to their own status as representations through the inclusion of various framing devices. One of the most jarring examples of this juxtaposition of different levels of representation occurs in his 1976 portrait of his daughter Teresa, who is depicted in several trompe l'oeil frames, including one that recreates the portrait as a devotional reliquary and another that suggests that it will soon be closed off behind the kind of roll-down metal door used on the back of trucks or to safeguard large store windows at night. While this attention to framing might be dismissed as merely an exercise in Baroque illusionism, an untitled painting from two years earlier shows clear affinities to the proto-postmodernist work of Sigmar Polke among others in its juxtaposition of different registers of appropriated imagery: According to Bosch, the work "manages to combine a peacock from Domenico Ghirlandaio's *The Last Supper* (1480), a reference to Francis Bacon's *Two Figures* (1953), and references to Eadweard Muybridge's photographs" (Bosch 69). Additionally, the background consists of several overlapping surfaces that, in the tradition of modernist collage, both suggest and subvert the possibility of reading the images as figures on a stable, illusionistic ground.

Five years younger than González, María Brito came to the United States as part of the "Peter Pan" program whereby children were sent to the United States ahead of their parents in the years immediately preceding the Cuban Missile Crisis. Brito's highly personal artworks often deal with fragmented and partial identities, and her earliest works, multimedia installations such as *El Patio de Mi Casa*, arguably make an even stronger claim to membership within the more postmodernist category occupied by artists like Bedia and Campos-Pons than do her more recent paintings. Nevertheless, even the paintings, like those of González produced with a nearly photorealistic technique reminiscent of Northern Renaissance masters, maintain elements of sculptural installation, such as the bucket at the foot of her monumental *The Traveler: Homage to B.G.* (1993) or the arm extending beyond the boundaries of the already dimensionally ambiguous frame of *Self-Portrait as a Swan* (2001). The latter work is a particularly good example of the play of presence and absence of self that occurs throughout her works: If the swan is her self-portrait, does that mean that the hand holding its leg is not? Could it be a split portrait? Brito's own location within the work is as ambiguous as the richly patterned geometric space behind the swan. Like that of González, her recent work emphasizes a strong representational painting technique but undercuts its own formal unity through framing, fragmentation, and quotation.

Although very different in style from either González or Brito, Alberto Rey shares with them a similarly ambivalent relationship to contemporary critical models. Currently living near Buffalo, New York, Rey left Cuba in 1963 when he was only three years old, and unlike many of the artists featured in the recent publications spent most of his life in the United States outside of Miami, though he maintained close connections to family there. While not quite as meticulously photorealistic as that of either González or Brito, Rey's technique is nonetheless highly naturalistic, with hints of expressionist exaggeration and simplification. Though less inclined to the direct appropriation of specific Renaissance and Baroque styles than either of the aforementioned artists, he has used appropriation from those same sources at the level of content, most obviously in his 1993–1995 *Madonnas in Time* series. Again, in a very different way from that of either of the other two artists, he subverts his technique's suggestion of unmediated naturalism through a direct acknowledgment of framing. Unlike González's trompe l'oeil frames or Brito's sculptural additions, Rey often calls attention to the various ways in which his paintings act as their own frames. Instead of painting on canvas, Rey works primarily on boxlike plaster panels, and in his recent series of decomposing steelhead trout (provocatively titled *The Aesthetics of Death*), he leaves a kind of border around the edges of his panels, putting the naturalistic fish and their elaborate backgrounds into a kind of floating cloud reminiscent of Mark Rothko. Similarly, the boxlike supports of the *Madonnas in Time* series lend them an aura of being devotional shrines, objects in this world as opposed to merely illusionistic images of another world. This framing takes on particular significance for his *Las Balsas* series commemorating the dangerous journey faced by the wave of Cuban refugees who made the treacherous journey to the United States in the wake of the economic depression following the collapse of the Soviet Union in 1990. In this series, the paintings themselves often "float" within a black shadowbox-like structure, transforming the painting within into a sculptural object while also calling attention to the nature of the rafts themselves, floating on dark waters. Even the painted images suggest this floating within a sea of blackness, as Bosch describes in the following passage: "Painted in *grisaille*, Rey's *balsas* float in pools of silent light on glassy seas that isolate each boat" (Bosch 142). By framing these works as he does, Rey asks us to view his paintings as objects, perhaps for devotion, perhaps for inspiration, but decidedly not as illustrations, imitations, or even pure expressions; like the rafts themselves, these works seem designed to have an important function in the material world.

Despite their many differences, then, the three artists I have discussed all use different framing strategies to confront and challenge, but not necessarily destroy, the illusion of unmediated access to an alternate reality that their highly developed painting techniques might otherwise convey. At the same time, they all are unambiguously painters, producing easily commodifiable objects to be hung on walls. Of course, the same can be said of much of Bedia's work, for example, but the mere fact that he does not emphasize mastery of traditional, representational painting technique as do each of the previously discussed artists makes the conceptual qualities of his work stand out in greater relief, thereby making the work more accessible to academic criticism. The subversive qualities of González, Brito, and Rey are more subtle and depend to a greater extent on the very traditions that they subvert.

Finally, I want to consider briefly some artists whose works are more unambiguously marginal to the discourse of mainstream academic art criticism, artists whose works display a similar emphasis on representational technique to those of González, Brito, and Rey, but who do not employ any of the postmodernist strategies that complicate the apparent traditionalism of those latter three. I should be careful here to point out that I am not referring to such artists of the Vieja Guardia as Baruj Salinas and Raphael Soriano, whose resolutely modernist Abstract Expressionist styles, while outside the parameters of postmodernist criticism, lie so comfortably and securely outside that they do not challenge those boundaries in any meaningful way. Rather, I am talking about such figurative painters as Arturo Rodríguez and Demi, whose works at least display some characteristics associated with postmodernism, such as the use of appropriation and allegory. Still, I would not attempt to claim that these characteristics should be sufficient for a work to be considered postmodern in the sense outlined previously; to use just one very direct example, in *Appropriating Appropriation*, Crimp argued convincingly against precisely such an identification of a handful of general aesthetic strategies with postmodernism, claiming, for example, that the sort of appropriation he was writing about in "Pictures" was the appropriation of actual material rather than style.[7] In fact, the appropriation of historical styles, which on some level is the shared concern of virtually all artists included in Bosch's book, was the object of sustained attack by the postmodernist critics at the same time that they were attempting to define the term "postmodernism." The attack was directed against the then-current revival of figurative painting, primarily in Germany, Italy, and the United States, which was given the title of neoexpressionism. As I pointed out in discussing the vestiges of Greenbergianism in this body of criticism, the appropriation of historical styles was seen as a denial of history, and with it a denial of the ability of art to foster meaningful social change.

Much like neoexpressionist paintings, the works of Rodríguez and Demi do not seem to acknowledge even the advent of abstract expressionism, let alone conceptualism and the kind of postmodernism practiced by artists such as Barbara Kruger, Mary Kelly, and Sherrie Levine. Still, the visceral power of both artists' works would be difficult to deny. Rodríguez, who after leaving Cuba lived for a year in Madrid before arriving in Miami in 1973, paints harrowing expressionist allegories involving alienation and exile. While he appropriates stylistic elements from artists ranging from El Greco and Goya to Gino Severini and Max Beckmann, he has also made more explicit iconographical references to Giorgione in his *Tempestad* series. Demi's influences are also numerous, but she does not engage in that same literal level of quotation. After growing up in hiding following the execution of her father in 1960, Demi came to the United States in 1971, settling in Miami in 1978. Her shimmering, almost pointillist canvases generally feature children who tend to look both delicately beautiful and tragically vulnerable; the latter characteristic comes forth most dramatically in works like *The Park*, the lush setting of which only amplifies the horror of seeing a group of naked, armless children who have ironically been given a ball with which to play. While the works of both artists may be critical, then, of the kinds of conditions that lead to the kind of suffering that they depict, they do not appear to be particularly *self*-critical in that Greenbergian sense that seems to remain fundamental even to the contemporary criticism that sets itself against Greenberg in other ways.

At this point I want to emphasize that I am not condemning contemporary art critics for their adherence to the principle of self-criticism. In fact, I consider the self-critical attitude, at least in the conventional rather than strictly Greenbergian sense of the term, to be a worthy aspiration. To view contemporary art as commenting upon the art that preceded it, and upon its own conditions of possibility, is to approach art seriously and analytically, an approach that I personally would be skeptical of abandoning. But the critical attitude must itself be subject to self-criticism as well: How might it respond to the critical tradition of which it is a part, and what are its conditions of possibility? What inessential conventions can it abandon while retaining its power as criticism? Thinking about the Cuban-American art featured in these recent publications has forced me to confront many of these questions. If the work of artists like

Rodríguez and Demi does not seem up-to-date in terms of formal experimentation, is it therefore unworthy of serious attention, regardless of its content? And if stylistic and iconographical appropriation appears to be a striking characteristic of literally dozens of Cuban-American artists, can such strategies be casually dismissed without thereby dismissing the legitimacy of a specific culture's distinct form of expression?

One way of approaching that latter question is to consider the differences between those artists whose work fits into the postmodernist critical paradigms and those whose work does not. Bedia, Llorca, and Campos-Pons are all relatively recent immigrants, who moreover immigrated to the United States as adults, whereas most of the other artists whom I have discussed left Cuba in the 1960s or 1970s. While this might not immediately seem like a particularly relevant distinction, a closer look at the history of Cuban immigration to the United States suggests that the distinction is crucial. In arguing against the continued special status enjoyed by Cuban immigrants to the United States, Ted Henken convincingly claims that while some Cuban immigrants really are victims of political persecution, most of the post-1990 immigration from Cuba is motivated primarily by economic opportunity. Recent Cuban immigrants, from this perspective, should be considered just that: immigrants, as opposed to exiles or refugees (Henken 1–18). On the other hand, those Cubans who left the island during the early years of the revolution were often escaping threats of impending executions, imprisonment, and forced separation from family members. Ironically, some sociologists call this generation the "golden exiles" in reference to the lack of restrictions on their immigration and the institution of programs such as the Cuban Refugee Assistance Program (3). However, from all accounts the real situation of those exiles was anything but "golden." Instead of looking forward to a new life of greater opportunity, that generation of Cubans came to the United States in the wake of the destruction of the very worlds through which they gained their senses of identity. This is the experience of trauma; as Bosch writes, "This destruction of cultural unity and self-definition disrupts an individual's ability to project a future self confidently located within a cultural continuum" (64). For this generation, then, "Cuban-American" means something very different than it does for earlier or later generations. It does not involve only or even primarily a dual, multiple, or even fragmented sense of identity experienced by so many people with various "hyphenated" identities, but rather a loss of self. Everlyn Nicodemus vividly describes the loss of self as a result of trauma:

> Traumatic disorders can be about distorted memory. And because all trust is taken away from the traumatized individual, it can mean disconnection from almost all human relationships—a loss of trust in oneself, in other people, in justice. It can even mean a shattering of the whole construction of the Self. Traumatized people often fixate on the trauma, thinking of nothing else. This emotional imprisonment

> means an erasure of their individual history outside the trauma. And when history is abolished, identity also ceases to exist. (258–73; 261–62)

According to Nicodemus, artists responding to such trauma fall into two categories: "those that narrate or symbolically represent experienced historical events and catastrophes of a traumatizing nature, and those that testify to the impossibility of narration and representation of such experiences" (263). I would suggest that the Cuban-American artists of the "golden" generation straddle the line between Nicodemus's two categories in that they attempt to represent traumatic events, but seem unable or unwilling to represent them as coherent narratives, confirming Nicodemus's speculation that "works of art containing a dimension of testimony to trauma can be expected in most cases to show signs of a breakdown of narrative language" (263).

Now, such narrative breakdown is not what makes Cuban-American artists of the "golden generation" so problematic to contemporary critical paradigms, which often celebrate the terminologies of rupture, trauma, and narrative breakdown. Rather, it is their paradoxical attempts to convey the more-or-less stable subject positions of modernist or even Renaissance and Baroque-style painters, with the claims to mastery that such positions entail. This subject position, according to the late Craig Owens, was the main target of postmodernist theory and criticism. In his now canonical essay "The Discourse of Others: Feminists and Postmodernism," Owens responded to feminist criticism that postmodernist theorists were "killing the author" just as women's voices were starting to be heard by asserting that the "subject" under postmodernist attack was a very specific one: white, male, and heterosexual (Discourse 166–90). The question that comes to mind in the context of Cuban-American art, then, is to what extent victims of trauma—even those who may be white, heterosexual males—have untroubled access to that privileged subject position. This question is, of course, even further complicated by the unstable status of race in Cuban-American culture: Whereas some may consider those of predominantly Spanish ancestry to be "white," Spanish culture already constitutes a complex racial mixture, which may make attempts to distinguish neatly between "black" and "white" somewhat arbitrary. This situation is hardly confined to Cubans or Cuban-Americans, as Adrian Piper's well-known *Cornered* installation has explored in the context of U.S. racial categorizations (182–86).

Can or should artists be expected to be overtly critical of the type of subjectivity of which they were traumatically stripped? This question gets to the core of what I find challenging to my own long-held critical assumptions in this art. As a gay man, my experience of identity and subjectivity has always been extremely complex, fragmented, and contradictory; the kind of work produced by artists such as Campos-Pons, with its implicit and explicit criticisms of essentialized subjectivity, therefore, always made sense to me. However, a complex, fragmented, and contradictory sense of self is very different from a lost one, and I cannot assume that an analogous form of criticality is or should be available or desirable to artists who have experienced a traumatic loss of self.

If, as I argued, the demand for certain types of formal criticality in contemporary art retains at least vestiges of Greenberg's version of Kantian self-criticism, Pierre Bourdieu's criticism of Kantian "critical disinterest" may be relevant here. Bourdieu claimed that to take a position of disinterest was to assert a particular kind of class distinction, because only people with relative immunity from physical necessity could view the material world with such disinterest.[8] Again, in relation to Cuban-American art, I would ask whether a disinterested critique of subjectivity is a desirable or even a possible response for those artists who experienced such a traumatic loss of so many markers of their subjectivity.

I experience these works, therefore, as testimonies to that trauma and insistent calls for that testimony to be heard. Interestingly, those artists who do add elements of critical distanciation to their work also tend to be somewhat more removed from traumatic loss; Juan González, for example, was already an adult when he left Cuba, so his sense of self may have been much more resilient than that of the many artists who came as children and young teenagers. Alberto Rey, on the other hand, was probably too young to have experienced the full effects of the trauma and, furthermore, grew up far from the Miami enclave where that trauma would have been an unavoidable part of the social fabric. María Brito is an interesting exception here, a product of the Peter Pan generation who manages to combine some very postmodern distanciating elements within her powerfully autobiographical work. While her example demonstrates that Cuban-American artists' work cannot be reductively pigeonholed on the basis of when and how they arrived from Cuba, the connection between explicitly personal, narrative figural work with the "golden" exiles is difficult to ignore, and that connection, I contend, is the basis for this work's challenge to the contemporary critical paradigms in which I have been trained. What might well be considered conservative or lacking in criticality in certain cultural contexts may in fact be courageous and critical in others, and art criticism risks falling into its own kind of parochialism if it refuses to acknowledge this reality. This may be one of the most important lessons to be learned from the current resurgence of attention to Cuban-American art.

NOTES

1. Mari Carmen Ramírez has summarized this argument particularly succinctly: "The mainstreaming of Latin American art as 'marginal' has further complicated the tensions between these groups of artists. For, while Latino art has served to broker the ac-

ceptance of Latin American identity in U.S. institutions, it has not gained equal access to them. Mainstream public museums, under pressure to represent Latino artists, invariably manage to displace their responsibility by buying Latin American art, whose value is well established in the market." See Mari Carmen Ramírez, "Brokering Identities: Art Curators and the Politics of Cultural Representation," 21–38; 33.

2. Greenberg's notion of self-criticality is articulated in "Modernist Painting," *Arts Yearbook*, later reprinted in *The New Art* and discussed by Crimp, "Pictures."

3. See for example, this passage from page 139: "At this point I want to make a claim that I cannot hope to prove or substantiate but that I believe nevertheless to be true: *viz.*, that theatre and theatricality are at war today, not simply with modernist painting (or modernist painting and sculpture), but with art as such—and to the extent that the different arts can be described as modernist, with modernist sensibility as such." See also 141–43.

4. For well-known examples of this body of criticism, see Benjamin H. D. Buchloh, "Figures of Authority, Ciphers of Regression," 107–34; and Craig Owens, "Honor, Power, and the Love of Women," 143–55.

5. In the introduction to his collection of early essays dealing with postmodernism in contemporary art, Crimp suggested that the essays seemed to him in retrospect to be more about "the end of modernism," whereas the truly postmodern work might better be exemplified by the art of AIDS activism, which he characterized as "often anonymously and collectively made; appropriating techniques of 'high art,' popular culture, and mass advertising; aimed at and constitutive of specific constituencies; relevant only to local and transitory circumstances; [and] useless for preservation and posterity." Douglas Crimp, "Photographs at the End of Modernism," 2–31; 22. See also Crimp, Ed., *AIDS: Cultural Analysis;* and Crimp and Rolston's, *AIDS Demo Graphics.*

6. See Michael Ann Holly, *Past Looking: Historical Imagination.*

7. "The strategy of appropriation no longer attests to a particular stance toward the conditions of contemporary culture. To say this is both to suggest that appropriation *did* at first seem to entail a critical position, and to admit that such a reading was altogether too simple." Referring to such "appropriationist" painters as David Salle in contrast to what he viewed as the more radical practices of photographer Sherrie Levine, he argues that "the rejection of photography as a possible tool guarantees the atavism of the painters' recent pastiches, since they remain dependent on modes of imitation/transformation that are no different from those practiced by nineteenth-century academicians. Like Graves and Mapplethorpe, such painters appropriate style, not material, except when they use the traditional form of collage." Crimp, *On the Museum's Ruins*, 127–37; 127, 129.

8. "Thus, the aesthetic disposition is one dimension of a distant, self-assured relation to the world and to others that presupposes objective assurance and distance. It is one manifestation of the system of dispositions produced by the social conditionings associated with a particular class of conditions of existence when they take the paradoxical form of the greatest freedom conceivable, at a given moment, with respect to the constraints of economic necessity." See Bourdieu, *Distinction*, 56.

WORKS CITED

Bosch, Lynette. *Cuban-American Art in Miami: Exile, Identity, and the Neo-Baroque*. London, UK: Lund Humphreys, 2004.

Bourdieu, Pierre. *Distinction: A Social Critique of the Judgment of Taste* (1979). Trans. Richard Nice. Cambridge: Harvard University Press, 1984.

Buchloh, Benjamin H. D. "Figures of Authority, Ciphers of Regression." Brian Wallis, ed. *Art after Modernism: Rethinking Representation*. New York: New Museum of American Art, 1984. 107–34.

Crimp, Douglas. "Pictures." Brian Wallis, ed. *Art after Modernism: Rethinking Representation*. New York: New Museum of American Art, 1984. 175–87.

———, ed. *AIDS: Cultural Analysis/Cultural Activism*. Cambridge: MIT Press, 1988.

———, with Adam Rolston. *AIDS Demo Graphics*. Seattle: Bay Press, 1990.

———. "Photographs at the End of Modernism." *On the Museum's Ruins*. Cambridge and London: MIT Press, 1993.

Foster, Hal. "Re: Post." *Art after Modernism: Rethinking Representation*. Ed. Brian Wallis. New York: New Museum of American Art, 1984. 189–201.

Fried, Michael. "Art and Objecthood." *Minimal Art: A Critical Anthology*. Ed. Gregory Battcock. New York: Dutton, 1968. 116–47.

Greenberg, Clement. "Modernist Painting." *Arts Yearbook* no. 4 (1961). Reprinted in *The New Art*, ed. Gregory Battcock. New York: Dutton, 1973.

Henken, Ted. "*Balseros, Boteros*, and *El Bombo:* Post-1994 Cuban Immigration to the United States and the Persistence of Special Treatment." *Latino Studies* (2005): 1–24.

Holly, Michael Ann. *Past Looking: Historical Imagination and the Rhetoric of the Image*. Ithaca and London: Cornell University Press, 1996.

Kotz, Liz. "Video Projection: The Space between Screens." Zoya Kocur and Simon Leung, eds. *Theory in Contemporary Art Since 1985*. Oxford: Blackwell, 2005. 101–12.

Mosquera, Gerardo. "The Marco Polo Syndrome." Zoya Kocur and Simon Leung, eds. *Theory in Contemporary Art Since 1985*. Oxford: Blackwell, 2005. 218–25.

Nicodemus, Evelyn. "Modernity as a Mad Dog: On Art and Trauma." *Over Here: International Perspectives on Art and Culture*. Gerardo Mosquera and Jean Fisher, eds. New York: New Museum of Contemporary Art, 2004. 258–73.

Owens, Craig. "Honor, Power, and the Love of Women." *Beyond Recognition: Representation, Power, and Culture*. Berkeley and Los Angeles: University of California Press, 1992. 143–55.

———. "The Discourse of Others: Feminists and Postmodernism." *Beyond Recognition: Representation, Power, and Culture*. Berkeley and Los Angeles: University of California Press, 1992. 166–90.

Piper, Adrian. "Cornered: A Video Installation Project." Zoya Kocur and Simon Leung, eds. *Theory in Contemporary Art Since 1985*. Oxford: Blackwell, 2005. 182–86.

Ramírez, Mari Carmen. "Brokering Identities: Art Curators and the Politics of Cultural Representation." *Thinking About Exhibitions*. Ed. Reesa Greenberg, Bruce W. Ferguson, and Sandy Nairne. London and New York: Routledge, 1996. 21–38.

10

Cuban Artists and the Irony of Exile

Carol Damian

It is difficult to find a common thread among the artists in exile in Miami and beyond who share their Cuban heritage and what has so often been discussed—their sense of loss. The situation of exile, for anyone anywhere, is traumatic. Today, as we consider their art from the perspective of outsiders (Cuban or not, we are outside the island), we are forced to view its development from afar and from the voices and visions of a fifty-year Diaspora. I set about writing a chapter about the early years of the Cuban exile artists, but I was not satisfied with the necessity of limiting the discussion to a few artists. I needed to find a common thread in order to organize them. Who are the artists of the early years? There are artists, among them Agustín Fernández and Rafael Soriano, who are considered to be the older generation, and now called "masters" of Cuban art. Then I decided to focus on the so-called Miami generation and first generation that left the island in the 1960s as children and adolescents. This included Emilio Sánchez, Agustín Fernández, Paul Sierra, Arturo Rodríquez, Humberto Calzada, Juan González, Emilio Falero, Miguel Padura, María Brito, Demi, Connie Lloveras, Lydia Rubio and others.[1] All of them have enjoyed (some are now deceased) great respect as artists, the majority of them in Miami. How could I overlook the most recent arrivals, the artists who have arrived during the last ten to fifteen years and who were born and raised in revolutionary Cuba? These artists, the generation of the 1980s, put Cuba's avant-garde on the world stage. In 1984, the first Latin American Biennial was held in Havana to showcase their work. Since then, the art world has flocked to Havana for the biennial and to witness the survival and tenacity of the small country still in the grips of the Castro dictatorship, where art endures in astonishing ways, despite the fact that at the same time as the world was paying attention, conditions had actually been deteriorating for years for those very same artists, and many of them had realized the futility of any possibility of change and were forced to reconsider their future. Already, in 1980, the Mariel exodus to Miami was the solution for some, long-term stays in Mexico and other countries for others. The generation of the 1980s would become the generation of the 1990s and their presence in Miami and beyond changed the international character of Cuban art. For this reason their inclusion among the established exile community of artists adds a valuable layer to any discussion of Cuban art, and a challenge to put it all together.

What could I do to bring them together artistically in a way that was valuable and more than a brief review of artistic accomplishments? The more I looked, the more I began to move away from the subject of a chronological survey of Cuban art in Miami. I did not want to repeat the well-written books on Cuban art history that told their story within the context of Cuba, before and after the revolution.[2] An alternative approach to Cuban art was inspired by my conversation with José Bedia during one of his exhibitions. When asked by someone about how "dark" his work was, Bedia responded that his work was not dark, but ironic and witty and that he wanted people to look beyond the obvious and realize how ludicrous life can be—especially for exiles (*The State of Things*).

In today's world we are confronted by concerns of war, terrorism, and our need for safety and health. An exile not only shares these same concerns, but his/her existence is further complicated by looking at the world from the point of view of a stranger, an outsider so to speak. For Cuban exiles in the United States, Miami in particular, it is difficult to let go of the past. This situation promotes and often favors nostalgia (Hutcheon 1). In this ironic set of circumstances people often see things with a strange clarity—as Bedia does. So I began to look around at the artists with whom I was most familiar and realized that many of them—early generations to the most recent—used irony in their work. Irony is the deliberate contrast between apparent and intended meaning. In art, we see the visual incongruity between what is real and what is imagined. It can be humorous, even absurd to create something that is so deliberately the opposite of its literal meaning. Actually, so much is ironic these days that the word is often used as a synonym for cool cynicism, or detachment. In art, irony is associated with postmodern constructs, even manipulated to echo the self-referential that is basic to its description. In this postmodern category, art is constantly recycled, as are the subjects and ideas that inspire its creation. For artists in exile, irony is a means to create the necessary distance from, and a new perspective on, the past. Irony exists on many levels in visual imagery and I found with these artists that their work could be read many different ways.

I decided on a group of fourteen artists that includes the Miami generation and the generation of the 1980s (in the United States, called the generation of the 1990s), Cuban-born artists who were raised and educated during the Castro regime, and some who are not easily categorized. The story of the art of Cuba and the impact of the revolution has been told by many, in many ways. There is no denying that the sociopolitical situation, on and off the island (perhaps most apparent in Miami), has again proven that artists are resourceful and dedicated individuals. With irony as the focal point of this discussion, the work of this diverse group of artists may be seen as an emotional and expressive response to these dire circumstances or as something altogether different—a sardonic commentary on life's twists and turns that is common to everyone. They use their art to both adapt and subvert conventional painting and sculpture by underpinning the images with evident conceptual strategies that frequently employ ironic counterplots.

José Bedia (1956 Havana—1991 Mexico—1993 Miami) inventively joins religious symbols and mythologies drawn from disparate cultures—Native American, African, Mayan, Mexican, Spanish colonial—which have shaped and complicated Cuban identity over the years. He prefers to work directly on the wall, on unframed papers and cloths, and with objects. As he crosses boundaries between the cultural mainstream and ritual, he maintains connections to sacred origins with a contemporary mindset. He is also very witty and, despite the apparent seriousness of the concept of ritual that is so pervasive in his work, has a wry sense of humor. This is evident in his elongated figures, his sensitivity to the representation of animals, and in the use of a comic-book style with its voice boxes. One of his most important installations is titled *Viva el quinto centenario (Long Live the Fifth Century), 1992*, which criticizes the whitewashed history of Spanish imperialism and the methods of education determined by European rationalism. He uses a classroom setting with a tree falling on the desks, beneath which ritual herbs are placed. Nature has been destroyed, replaced by industry and inaccurate books. A student has been forced to repeat "viva el quinto centenario" on the blackboard, but ends it with his own ironic comment, in Nahuatl (the Mexican indigenous language): *Nehua omatocac*, a Mexican obscenity.

The use of irony continues throughout Bedia's career, and with the latest works he addresses subjects ranging from the military, evident in the tanks and ships, and monuments to heroes now exaggerated in the forms of giant lions who dwarf them. He says they do not refer to Iraq or any one war, but to the irony of making heroes of killers with the invention of war machines, and to the clash between First and Third World countries symbolized by the cold industrial machines versus active spirituality.

The same interest in rituals and traditions appears in the work of María Magdalena Campos-Pons (1959 Matanzas—1991 Boston). The constant search for her African-Cuban roots is a paramount influence on her concept of using art as a transformation of ordinary things into new forms. The imagery that results is not part of its original purpose, and this irony drives her creativity. She uses the substitution of one meaning for another to give her subjects new life. She keeps her family history alive in her mind and gives it validity through her work. It is especially a history of a people who are not heroes and the domestic work of black Cubans becomes a symbol of their lives. Childhood memories, her grandmother's stories (her grandmother was involved with the Afro-Cuban cult called *Santería*), the watchtower of the sugar mills resonate with meaning for her today. Campos-Pons explores the irony of the past through her modern eyes and the realization that what she remembered as a child, its pleasant associations, were really based on slavery and oppression. She works with photography and video to create, rather recreate, installations about time and place, and uses her body as the canvas for rituals renewed. She empowers herself, like an African fetish figure, to contain the past and maintain its presence. There is a pantheistic quality as her body blends with objects and symbols to become new signifiers of myth.

How language can also become a signifier is crucial to the ironies presented in the work of Rubén Torres Llorca (1957 Havana—1993 Miami). Torres Llorca employs the language of art to construct a practical object with connotations based on religion, culture, and tradition, and overt references to sociopolitical subjects, often with the attitude informed by mass-media aesthetics and objects. However, he strips them of their ideological character to present a new icon with the same sense of being an artistically authentic image, but without any magical associations. "Sensitive to the influence of U.S. movies, television, and comics in his upbringing and the influence of his mother's seamstress trade, he tried to synthesize all these experiences in a quasi-therapeutic fashion" (Camnitzer 24). The viewer confronts a new object, or series of objects. There is an ironic subtext that exists—sometimes obvious and other times puzzling. How to explain a wall full of identical little *Santería* figures that upon close examination bear the names of local collectors, dealers, and other acquaintances? Torres Llorca is a jokester.

Luís Cruz Azaceta (1942 Havana—1960 New York—1992 New Orleans) has been creating works dealing with the journey since the late '60s, not just the Cuban journey but also the universal, philosophical journey of life that affects us all. His figures are distortions of his own self; self-portraits gone awry in the turbulence of survival. They often appear tormented, as they confront urban life and its accompanying anxieties. Harsh colors, dizzying patterns, and a disturbing symbolic language are used to express the irony of new-found freedom. While his early, most recognizable works are the self-referential technicolor nightmares inspired by his arrival in the overwhelming city of New York, Azaceta continues to voice his concerns about AIDS, immigration, exile and identity. The artist uses a mixed-media approach to the production of his art to capture the world around him—his keen wit and dark irony looming in the distance.

The carefully drawn landscapes of Glexis Novoa (1964 Holguin—1993 Miami) are far from bucolic and his ironic recreations of Cuba's skyline onto that of Miami, or any other futuristic cityscape, become reminders of progress and its social implications, not to mention revolution. There are also recognizable architectural elements from history and the imagination floating in his seas. Noticeably devoid of the human presence, these cityscapes portend a dark future, from the perspective of bleak memories of Havana. How ironic that, as others envision the Havana of the past as a pristine colonial city, his outlook is quite the opposite. Novoa uses the notion that the exiles have maintained their

"Cubanness" in an infinite nostalgia that becomes an obsession. It is a Cuba no longer there for them, but that lives on in their imagination. His imagery exists at an intersection between reality and artifice, remembrance and experience and his precise drawings—part old, part new, part apocalyptic—rise from the horizon and float like traces. Novoa's images evoke disquieting ironies and incongruities as they relate to exile, loss, political power, cultural ascendancy as monuments, towers, high-rises, ships—appear and reappear.

Arturo Rodríguez (Las Villas, 1956—Spain 1970 Miami 1974) has long explored the dysfunctional and the disturbed in his figurative paintings. In works from the 1990s, he includes water and boats not only as the symbols of the voyage of exiles (especially the Cubans who journeyed over the dangerous Florida straits to freedom), but as metaphors for the human condition that results with displacement and loss. He uses figures to express his ideas and is particularly interested in painting as an aesthetic means of expression based on its most formal elements. "His figures often appear to cavort aimlessly, but they have actually been carefully calculated and composed. A consummate draftsman, he draws upon numerous sources: art history, literature, music, poetry and philosophy" (Damian, "Arturo Rodríguez" 152). His latest series is called *The Human Comedy* and features large canvases with enormous distorted heads. They are not portraits in the usual sense but social archetypes and caricatures of people from popular culture who are frustrated with an oppressive society. In *The Tempest (La Tempestad III)*, 1998, the waters swirl and the world is topsy-turvy, but in the midst, there is birth and hope. The irony of loss survives with the paradox of rebirth.

María Brito (1947 Havana—1961 Miami) deals with essential existence as defined by emotions, sensations, personal memory, and psychological situations. Her imagery, whether painting, sculpture, or installations, is symbolic of the process of self-discovery developed from her identity as a woman, a mother, a wife, an exiled Cuban, a naturalized American and a Catholic. Her experiences as a woman growing up in a close (claustrophobic?) Cuban family in Miami—and the expectations for her to be a wife/mother/traditional woman (not an artist)—affected her work from the beginning of her career. Brito began mixed-media installations in the 1980s which allowed her to compare/contrast her bicultural experiences. *El Patio de mi Casa*, 1991, is a two-part installation that has Miami on one side and Cuba on the other and is based on a Cuban nursery rhyme. Throughout her life, she found it ironic that as much as she tried to be an American, the more demands she faced from her Cuban family. There was no escaping. Often the context is seemingly innocent, even childlike, but the concerns are serious—physical repression, vigilance, and the search for a means of escape.

María Lino (1951 Havana—1964 Miami) has also worked with feminine issues and the difficulties of rising to the expectations of her family. At one point, she went back to school for a teaching certificate (MA) to disguise her artistic passions. Finally, last year she returned to Florida International University, this time to pursue an MFA. She began as a sculptor and painter, and now uses mixed media and video. Her most recent work involves drawing, animation, video, and digital media juxtaposed in complex overlays of meaning. She explores the concept of "home," using video to sift through layers of sound and images to find its elusive and complex definition. The irony of home for many women is a universal one—as are expectations. Lino's latest project is inspired by a woman who lost her vision and searches for her new image. She has forgotten how she looked when she had sight and the irony of her predicament results in a series of questions involving the kind of image of self we all create in our minds, dreams, and visions.

There is no doubt that artists often use their work as a vehicle for autobiographical exploration. Demi (1955 Camagüey—1971 Miami) uses children in magical fantasies that reflect an escape from the travails of her own childhood. Despite the apparent elegance of their appearance, her children are painted with both a technical and conceptual veil of pain. The surfaces are layered with exquisite drawing and thick impasto that belie a sharp precision within their decorative beauty. Children are the victims of loss, change, and violence; their only means of survival are rooted in fairy tales and theater and the dreams of innocence she so wishes were real. Demi confronts the heartbreaks of life through the irony of dolls and children and a fictional recreation she hopes will substitute for the tragedies of the past. The dolls become personalized characters in a surreal drama that she continues to reveal before our eyes.

The cast of characters that populates the paintings of the elder statesman of the group, Cundo Bermúdez (1914 Havana—1968 Puerto Rico—1996 Miami), has its origin on the streets of Havana, in the "clubs de señoritas" full of lavishly dressed women in elegant settings, popular folklore, and dancers, musicians, and other performers, but they have been transformed into personalities now definitively "cundo-esque." Their clothes are created out of yards of ribbons and their headdresses are absurd ribbon-wrapped turbans. Cundo sees these figures as caricatures of what once was, now redetermined by his unique aesthetic. They are often inspired by images of regional Spanish women he found in a book and thought interesting for their unusual headdresses, veils, and ethnic garments. Cundo makes them his own, now set in the tropics and in his Cuban neighborhood. Another ironic image of a woman is that of *La Macorina*, 1978, which celebrates the first woman to drive a car in Havana. She was a special attraction in her red convertible and Cundo has redressed her in his own image with ribbons and in colonial surroundings. Other women in his oeuvre are the *gusanas*, a term meaning worms, used by Castro in a speech in 1959 to refer to the exiles that had deserted the island because they were against the government. These women were actually lonely servitors who lived in the past and hoped for the return of their family and friends as they maintained their belongings in a cluttered household. Cundo depicts them lounging wistfully in the confusion of their abandoned homes (Damian 152). Such characters and all their finery are excuses for his painting now. Ironically, they have now lost their identification to most of the people who are familiar with his work and collect his "women." At the venerable age of ninety-two, Cundo has just completed a major commission for Miami's new CPAC (Carnival Performing Arts Center)! The work reflects his interest in music, dance, art, and theater.

There is no doubt that each of Ramón Carulla's (1938 Havana—1965 Miami) characters appears to be involved in a journey to nowhere, at least nowhere recognizable to the ordinary viewer. They parade in their strange finery, alone or isolated within a group, and even converse while dressed in ridiculous hats and costumes. Somehow they are all related as human beings who are in a state of concern over their plight. They may also be seen as personalities in the process of metamorphosis into or with some animal or bird. They emote, gesture, and socialize as if nothing was wrong with their very bizarre appearances. There are groups in boatlike constructions that cannot possibly float, and certainly make references to the exile communities of South Florida and their voyages, with which the Cuban-born artist is all too familiar. His hats are a ubiquitous element in his works and he uses them as part of a masquerade, an ironic identifier that refers to something only he, the artist, knows about the person, past and present. Always questioning the human condition, Carulla accumulates expressions and experiences that turn the existential nature of his subject matter into something remote and humorous.

The magnificent architectural facades with their classical elements, iron balconies, and stained-glass vitrals that Humberto Calzada (1944 Havana—1960 Miami) recreates with the precision of an architect (he began his career as an engineer) are completely invented. Based on memory, their beauty is ironic within the context of the Cuba of the past. Cuba is no longer a city of classical palaces. It is a city in ruins. In fact, his city has really never existed in the way he describes—at least not since the nineteenth century. Symbolism abounds—universal, not just Cuban. Roman ruins are an ironic element in his works—fragments that are as incomplete as the memory of the city of Havana. The viewer is enticed to live in the dwelling of the artist's imagination, which is now merely a stage set. There is a tension that develops between the serenity of the scene and the impossibility of its reality. In Miami, the focus is no longer what was remembered, but the faculty of remembering itself, and Cubans are especially willing to consciously accept its fictiveness as a necessary reality in everyday life. It is an ironic fiction, which negotiates between internal and external scenes.

The youngest of the group, Hugo Mora (1954 Havana—1966 New York—1999 Miami) is a latecomer to making art. He began as a ceramicist and sculptor and has always created objects as a mockery of the traditional. His obsessive work with details and planning has translated into projects that are far more imaginative than one would expect from one who approaches his art so meticulously and describes it as a reflection of an unusual attitude toward Cuban upbringing. Mora came from a family of homemakers, blacksmiths, and carpenters always involved in making things. He claims that his obsessive method for creating art should leave no room for discovery, but found just the opposite to be true. As soon as a piece was symbolically complete, a new element randomly emerged that changed it into an ironic joke. He has made perfect *quince* cakes, table settings, and other objects to flaunt Cuban family traditions in a new artistic context. For the Havana Biennale in March 2006, he created an installation of hundreds of objects based on the shapes of the stone street markers in Havana. He made a cast of one and then recreated them in cardboard. They are useless—as are so many things in Havana.

Gory (Rogelio López Marín) (1953 Havana—1991 Miami) was trained as a painter and his crossover to photography has always revealed his dual interest, as he often uses both in the same work. His work is about handling and reinterpreting images directly derived from reality, through the eye of the camera. He manipulates with chemicals, sometimes uses pigments on canvas, and often combines both. Always, he refers to photographic reality as the basis of his work. There follows a juxtaposition and fragmentation that is the key to his vision. Reality becomes something else, still recognizable, but not possible. A close examination of his works reveals an astute eye for detail and spatial constructs. Disparate images seen and captured from strange perspectives and viewpoints reflect life's often bizarre twists and turns. There is a sense of wit and irony as he looks at something quite familiar and ordinary and transforms it into something else—forcing the viewer to remark: "I never noticed that."

These thirteen artists represent only a small selection of the many who have left Cuba in the past fifty years to pursue their education and careers in the freedom of the United States. It is a diverse group in age and experience and each has met the challenge of exile with artwork that ranges from cathartic and nostalgic recreations to acerbic comments forged from ironic visions of old and new worlds. "Given irony's conjunction of the said and the unsaid—in other words, its inability to free itself from the discourse it contests—there is no way for . . . [these artists] to separate themselves from the culture of which they are a part" (Hutcheon 8). In fact, there is no way for these artists to separate themselves from the *two* cultures of which they are a part: Cuban and American. That is the irony of exile.

NOTES

1. For a discussion of the Miami generation, see Gomez Sicre; Blanc; Fuentes-Pérez et al.; Bosch.

2. For the history of Cuban art of the twentieth century, see Zeitlin; Camnitzer; Fuentes-Pérez et al.; Martinez; Veigas et al.; Damian; Bosch.

WORKS CITED

Bedia, José. *Exhibition: José Bedia: The State of Things*. Miami: Frederic Snitzer Gallery, 2006.

Blanc, Giulio. *The Miami Generation: Nine Cuban-American Artists*. Miami: Cuban Museum of Arts and Culture, 1984.

Bosch, Lynette M. F. *Cuban-American Art in Miami: Exile, Identity and the Neo-Baroque*. UK: Lund Humphreys, 2004.

Camnitzer, Luis. *New Art of Cuba*. Austin: University of Texas Press, 1994.

Damian, Carol. *Breaking Barriers: Forty Years of Cuban Art*. Fort Lauderdale: Fort Lauderdale Museum of Art, 1997.

———. "Arturo Rodríguez: The Tempest." *Arturo Rodríguez: Recent Works*. Panama: Legacy Fine Art, 1998. 149–71.

———. "Voyage into Exile." *Cundo Bermúdez*. Miami: Cuban-American Endowment for the Arts, 2000.

Fuentes-Pérez, Ileana; Graciela; Cruz-Taura, and Ricardo Paul-Llosa, eds. *Outside Cuba/ Fuera de Cuba: Contemporary Cuban Visual Artists/Artistas Cubano Contemporaneos*. New Jersey: Rutgers University and University of Miami, 1989.

Gomez Sicre, José. *Art of Cuba in Exile*. Miami: Editora Munder, 1987.

Hutcheon, Linda. "Irony, Nostalgia, and the Postmodern." http://library.utoronto.ca/utel/criticism/hutchinp.html. 1.

Martínez, Juan A. *Cuban Art and National Identity: The Vanguardia Painters, 1927–1950*. Florida: University Press of Florida, 1994.

Veigas, José, Cristina Vives, et al. *Memoria: Cuban Art of the Twentieth Century*. California: CIAF, 2001.

Zeitlin, Marilyn A. *Contemporary Art from Cuba: Irony and Survival on the Utopian Island/ Arte Contemporáneo de Cuba: Ironía y sobrevivencia en la isla utópica*. Tempe: Arizona State University Art Museum, 1999.

11

Cuban-American Identity and Art

Jorge J. E. Gracia

In a recent article published in *The New Yorker*, entitled "*Die Weltliteratur*: How We Read One Another," Milan Kundera makes an astute observation:

> [The] nations [of Central Europe] have never been masters of either their own destinies or their borders. They have rarely been subjects of history but almost always its objects. Their unity is *unintentional*. They were kin to one another not through will, not through fellow-feeling or linguistic proximity, but by reason of similar experience, of common historical situations that brought them together, at different times, in different configurations, and within shifting, never definitive borders.

What many Europeans mean when they speak about nations is seldom simple, and always difficult to pinpoint, including such different strands as ethne, races, and states. Kundera, however, has focused on an important claim that seems to apply to ethnic groups in particular: They are more often the targets of action than the initiators of it, they are not the products of design, and they lack features that characterize their members throughout their histories, whether fellow-feelings or linguistic ties. The unity of these groups needs to be understood rather in terms of experiences based on the history that brought them together in diverse and changing contexts. The pressures of nationalism, racism, and ethnicism, on the one hand, and of postmodern subjectivism and relativism, on the other, however, often combine in our age to create a climate in which this commonsense view is rarely espoused.

The opposition to it comes from two camps. One sees ethne as groups of people who necessarily share particular properties, an essence that accounts for their unity. For some, the properties are cultural—language, religion, values—for others they are physical—looks, skin color, bodily shape—and still others combine them into cultural-racial profiles. This view of ethnicity goes by the name of *essentialism:* Members of an ethnic group share an essence.

The problem with this view is that, when one leaves behind ideological commitments and unquestioned assumptions and turns to the facts, there are no such properties common to all members of an ethnic group throughout the history of the group. What is it that members of an ethnic group have in common? Not their taste, not their language, not their religion, not their values, not their political views, not their physical appearance, not their ancestry, and not the place where they live or even were born. So where does the notion that they have, and must have, such common characteristics to account for their unity come from? From hasty generalizations based on limited samples found in particular contexts.

If essentialism is wrong and there are no such properties common to all members of ethnic groups, the opponents of this position argue that we must abandon the view that ethnic groups are anything more than imaginary myths, vacuous notions lacking substance. Indeed, the whole idea of ethnicity must be eliminated from our discourse insofar as it is groundless and raises unwarranted expectations. This position is known as *eliminativism* because it advocates the elimination of the notion of ethnos from our conceptual framework.

But is this view right? Don't many members of ethnic groups think about themselves as a group, don't many of them act as a group, and don't many have common interests and properties they share in particular contexts? Is it false that a great many members of ethnic groups like the same foods, share a longing for a mother country, and experience a sense of kinship and comfort among other members of the groups? Our experience vouches for this, which leads to the conclusion that eliminativism must also be wrong.

But we cannot go back to essentialism, can we? So how can we account for the unity of ethne? How can we preserve the notion of ethnicity without falling into false generalizations and unwarranted presuppositions? Before I propose a solution to this dilemma, let me turn to the particular case of Cuban-Americans, for they serve as a good example of an ethnic group.

Cubans

Cuban-Americans face the kind of group-identity challenges that many other ethnic groups encounter. Cubans have come to the United States for different reasons and under different circumstances. Prior to the most recent waves of exiles resulting from the establishment of the revolutionary government in 1959, groups of Cubans had lived and sometimes settled permanently in the United States. Those who immigrated permanently were primarily in search of economic opportunities, and those who came for limited periods of time were usually fleeing political oppression. These groups were relatively small. Mass exodus from Cuba into the United States occurred only in the aftermath of Fidel Castro's revolution. This recent diaspora may be divided into several periods and groups.

The first to leave the island were associates of the dictator Fulgencio Batista, government people who lost their jobs and were afraid of reprisals for their actions under the dictatorship. They fled almost immediately, and many of them were able to take substantial resources with them. Closely after and continuing until 1962, an exodus of professionals from the middle to the upper class began in earnest. The expropriation of property by the revolutionary government and the increasing assaults on the private sector prompted members of these groups to leave the island. The exodus accelerated after the Bay of Pigs invasion in 1961 and the declaration of Cuba as a Marxist-Leninist state, when it became clear that the political situation in Cuba was not going to change in the foreseeable future.

Among this wave of exiles were the children who participated in the Peter Pan program. These youngsters were sent to the United States through the auspices of the Catholic Church for various reasons: fear of their removal to the Soviet Union, fear of having them grow up in an antireligious environment, fear that their exit would be denied if the parents waited to emigrate, and fear that they would have to suffer deprivation under the increasing shortages of goods. By this time the revolutionary government had abolished private religious education and had expelled all priests, nuns, and members of religious orders who were not Cuban citizens. When the children arrived in the United States, some were placed with families, but most of them were sent to camps, sometimes with insufficient supervision.

These initial groups of exiles increased in number after the Bay of Pigs fiasco. They were given refugee status and provided with special assistance by the United States government in the form of a small monthly allowance and army food rations. A system of educational loans was also put in place to help those accepted in colleges and universities. Many of the Cubans who arrived between 1959 and 1962 stayed in Miami, but some settled in other parts of the United States. These exiles assimilated quickly into the American workforce and eventually regained their status in the professional classes.

After 1962, it became more difficult to leave the island, until 1965, when the Cuban government allowed some exits in what came to be called "Freedom Flights." These lasted until 1973. Those who left at this time were primarily family members of exiles already settled in the United States, and belonged mostly to the middle class. Many of them were owners of small businesses and workers in various trades.

The next large exodus occurred in 1980, when Castro opened the port of Mariel, presumably to anyone who wished to leave Cuba. Among those who left were persons the government considered undesirable, such as homosexuals, drug addicts, mental patients, criminals, and political dissidents. This group is known as *Marielitos*, a name derived from the place from which they left. Most of these Cubans have stayed in Miami, many still being detained in jails or in mental institutions.

The nineties saw a different kind of exodus. After the collapse of the Soviet Union and its support for the Castro government, economic conditions in the island became desperate. People began risking their lives at sea, in makeshift rafts (the notorious *balsas*) to reach United States shores. At the same time, criticism of the Castro regime within Cuba became more pronounced and certain groups of intellectuals and artists were allowed to leave the island in order to prevent unrest. These Cubans had been born under the Castro regime and knew nothing other than revolutionary Cuba.

The waves in which Cubans have come to the United States has reproduced a microcosm of prerevolutionary Cuban society in this country. Whereas other immigrant groups have a certain degree of homogeneity insofar as most of them have come under similar conditions and at roughly the same time, Cubans have come here for different reasons, under different circumstances, and at different times. Also important is that a large proportion of Cubans have stayed in Miami, creating a city with a strong Cuban flavor. Miami includes every class, ethnicity, and race within the Cuban population.

Although Cubans have come to the United States for a variety of reasons, and they differ in education, economic and social status, and personal goals, they constitute a cohesive ethnic group, easily identifiable. They effectively function as *cubanos*. They regard themselves as Cuban or Cuban-American and they are so regarded by American society, the U.S. government, and the press.

Identity

To speak about Cuban-Americans is to speak about their identity. So let me turn to four questions about identity in order to explore further the notion of ethnicity in general, how best to conceive it, and how this affects Cuban-Americans: How do identities function? How are identities formed? How do identities endure? And, what does having an identity entail? The answers to these questions require considerable development, but here I will give them skeleton answers, concentrating on what appears more obvious and important before I turn to art in order to show how this cultural phenomenon illustrates the way I will propose to understand Cuban-American identity.[1]

The answer to the first question is that identities are sources of action and feelings. Why do I collect Cuban-American art and not, say, Russian icons? One answer is that it is because I am Cuban-American. Why did I think of organizing a National Endowment for the Humanities Seminar around the topic reflected partly by the title of this book, and not about the identities of Chinese Americans? Again, because I am Cuban-American. My Cuban-American identity functions as a source of many of the actions in which I engage. Of course, not all my actions are related to my Cubanness. Neither my interest in metaphysics nor my love of Verdi have anything to do with my Cuban-American identity. But at least some of my actions can be easily seen as a result of this identity. The same can be said about some of my feelings. I like being with Cubans, at least some of the time. I relate to them, I feel at home with them. I sympathize with their plight, and I feel sad when I hear some of the horrors they have had to suffer in a way that is different from my feelings when I hear of the horrors that Iraqis have had to endure.

But how did I become Cuban-American? The answer to this question cannot be brief, because identities are formed through a long drawn-out historical process, but here we will have to do with a general suggestion instead of a worked-out answer. I am not Cuban-American just in virtue of having been born in Cuba. The child of a Protestant missionary born in Cuba can be as gringo as any other gringo, and be nothing like a Cuban-American. There is much more to becoming ethnically Cuban than being born in the island, or even living in the island for a long time. There has to be a meshing with other Cubans, a belonging that develops only with time and connections. Identities are products of long historical processes, all contingent, but nonetheless present and effective. They are not one thing, but many.

And how have I endured as Cuban-American? Why am I still Cuban-American, after having lived in Canada and the United States for most of my life and in places that have no Cubans to speak of? Most people think of an account of identity in terms of staying the same, but identities require change. Think about how species endure in the natural realm. They do so through adaptation to the challenges of a changing environment. Whoever cannot adapt must perish, and this goes for identities also. We are nuclei of change. To be who I am I had to learn to adapt. To survive in the United States I had to master English, to adopt gringo ways, to eat what was put before me, and even like it. If I had wanted to live on *dulce de guayaba* and *queso crema* alone, which would probably have been my choice, had I had one, I would be dead now. To keep being Cuban-American I had to become something different from what I was as a Cuban, and this process has not ended, but goes on.

But what is entailed by Cuban-American identity? If change seems to be of the essence of identities, and they are formed through processes that are historical, long, and composed of contingent elements, it is clear that there cannot be a set of necessary properties that makes Cuban-Americans, so for all times and places. It is, as Kundera understood so well, in the history, in the kinship, in the contextual relations and experiences that tie Cuban-Americans and separate us from Mexican Americans and gringos. Of course, these relations generate properties in context. My accent is probably similar in some ways to the accent of some other Cuban-Americans. Like some other Cuban-Americans I like *arroz con frijoles negros*. And I like "our" music. My feet leave me when I hear a good *guaracha*; the music sticks to them until I cannot but follow. But is this true of every Cuban-American? Obviously not. I have Cuban-American friends who speak English with a British accent, hate *arroz con frijoles negros*, and have square feet, just like most gringos. Are they less Cuban because of that? Surely not, because they are tied to me and other Cuban-Americans in other ways that also separate them from gringos and Mexican Americans.

So, how is it that we should conceive the Cuban-American identity? In the way that we should conceive all ethnic identities, that is, in familial-historical ways. It is the historical context that renders us Cuban-Americans. The solution to the dilemma between essentialism and eliminativism posed at the beginning is to abandon the assumption that the only way in which an ethnic group can be justified is by reference to common properties among its members, that the unity of Cuban Americans is based on common characteristics we all share.

Cuban and Cuban-American Art

This point is most evident in art. Many Cuban artists have found inspiration in Cuban themes, but not all of them have explored the same motifs or have done so in the same ways. There is no uniformity of topics or styles. Yes, many Cuban-American artists seem to be explicitly concerned with Cuba or the events precipitated in 1959 by the triumph of Fidel Castro's revolution. Some use iconic images related to the island, such as forts, palm trees, or Cuban landscapes, and include portraits of Cubans, whether ordinary citizens or political leaders, in their work. And the work of some deals with the particular social and political issues that have concerned many Cubans for the past fifty years. The images used in the art are particular and so are the themes of the work, even if the overall message, when there is a message, is universal.

This is in line with the efforts of many Cuban artists in the twentieth century who tried to integrate recent artistic developments in Europe.[2] In doing so, they attempted to explore Cuban culture, lo cubano, and embed the developments of European art in a local context. The use of African motifs by some of the masters of twentieth-century art in Europe, such as Picasso and Modigliani, becomes for Cuban artists the use of Afro-Cuban themes, or of motifs that have to do with the Cuban landscape and the Cuban reality. The great master of the Vanguardia of Cuban art, Wilfredo Lam, produced Cubist paintings inspired by Afro-Cuban topics. His most famous painting, *La jungla* (*The Jungle*, 1943), is an example of this approach.

The trend to explore the Cuban situation in art has continued in the work of more recent artists. For example, until recently most of José Bedia's work explored the Cuban religious traditions that can be traced to an African heritage, and even his recent work goes back to events in the history of Cuba.[3] Gustavo Acosta has painted many Cuban buildings. Much of the work of Leandro Soto refers to the island. And Arturo Rodríguez frequently incorporates motifs related to the Cuban situation in his paintings. Even Alberto Rey, who left Cuba when he was three years old, has a series of paintings of Cuban icons, ordinary

Cuban cultural objects, and even portraits of Cubans. Much conceptual art from Cuban artists involves political and social criticism, as is the case with some of the pieces by Ana Mendieta and Glexis Novoa. Indeed, the work of some artists seems to be completely absorbed by the exploration of Cuban themes.[4] Even an artist like Baruj Salinas, whose work has a very strong abstract component, has occasionally introduced Cuban elements in his painting. Of course, many artists have stayed away from Cuban topics, such as Rafael Soriano, Paul Sierra, Mario Bencomo, and Carlos Estévez. These artists tend to avoid anything typically Cuban, or even distantly related to Cuba, although in some cases one can still provide interpretations that relate the art to Cuban history and the Cuban or Cuban-American experience.

These points can be illustrated with reference to eight Cuban-American artists whose work was included in the exhibition, *Layers: Collecting Cuban-American Art*, held in conjunction with the National Endowment for the Humanities Seminar mentioned earlier: Gustavo Acosta (b. 1958; Miami 1991), José Bedia (b. 1959; Miami 1991), María Brito (b. 1947; Miami 1961), Humberto Calzada (b. 1944; Miami 1960), Emilio Falero (b. 1947; Miami 1961), Alberto Rey (b. 1960; USA 1963), Baruj Salinas (b. 1935; Miami 1961), and Pedro Vizcaíno (b. 1966; Miami 1999). Only one of these belongs to a generation of Cuban artists who was already established in Cuba before the revolution, Salinas. Three were teenagers when they arrived in the United States in the early sixties and were trained in the United States: Brito, Calzada, and Falero. Acosta and Bedia were trained in Cuba and were established artists there during the revolution; they arrived in this country in the early nineties. Vizcaíno is younger, and although trained in Cuba, formed part of a group that offered resistance to the artistic guidelines imposed by the revolutionary government. And Rey was brought to the United States when he was a three-year-old baby.

All these artists, except for Rey, have settled in Miami, but their experience of the Cuban diaspora is very different. Those who arrived early were exiles and refugees, but those who arrived in the nineties were immigrants. Some have become fully integrated into American society, know English well and, although living in Miami, have adopted many of the ways associated with the American mainstream. Others, however, are still struggling with the language in spite of their success as artists, and continue to live in a primarily Cuban environment. These factors affect the conception these artists have of who they are, the way they are perceived by others, and their work. Are they Cuban, Cuban-American, or American? Or are they all three? And does their art display elements that tie them to Cuba, to Cuban America, or to America? How do their struggles concerning their social identity reveal themselves in their work?

These questions require the kind of investigation that is not possible in a short article like the present one. Nonetheless I shall illustrate some of their dimensions, and how they fit within the ideas about ethnicity presented earlier, by referring to a work from each of these artists.

Eight Cuban-American Works of Art

Acosta's *Missing Link* (2005, acrylic on canvas, 36″ × 14″) has at its center an impressive neoclassical building at the end of what looks like a broad park with red and light colored tiles. Rows of trees stand on either side. The tiles provide a perspective that, together with the trees, leads our gaze toward the building, which is not only the center of the picture, but also of our attention. Above, stormy skies signal trouble, although we also have glimpses of a lighter and safer blue. Acosta is known for his interest in architecture, and he is a master of perspective, so one would have expected a perfectly symmetrical and anchored building. But surprisingly, the building is leaning slightly to the right, similar in a way to the notorious leaning tower of Pisa. There is clearly a point to the inclination as there is about the title: *Missing Link*.

Acosta does not tell us anything explicit, and if we did not know that the building in the work is the Cuban Presidential Palace, it would be difficult for us to make a connection between this painting and the Cuban situation. But once the building is identified, we are led to certain questions. What is the missing link to which Acosta is referring? Is he telling us something about the abandonment of democracy in Cuba and about the revolutionary dreams that have been ignored and crushed under a repressive political regime? Is he lamenting the absence in Cuba of all those generations of people, including leaders, that have had to leave the island and settled in foreign lands? Does the inclination of the building signal the precarious political and social Cuban situation? Clearly, the painting has to do with Cuba and with the Cuban circumstances. Its message, however, is universal, because its moral could be generalized to other societies that also have suffered conditions similar to those of Cuba and Cubans.

Bedia's *Acerca del viaje* (2001, mixed media on amate paper, 15.5″ × 23.5″) is typical of his early work. Bedia is one of the best-known Cuban artists today. On the right side of the painting we see one of the usual figures that populate Bedia's art, a man drawn in very simple lines. From his mouth come two lines. One turns back toward the man, and the other branches out into three lines in the way a stylized version of tree branches would do. The lines have various things attached to them. The top line has half a human head peeking back at the man. The first branch of the other is further subdivided into two, one turning into a knife and the other into the head and torso of a woman whose legs appear to be two further branches, each ending in leaves in place of feet. The original branch from which this second line issues continues, supporting some kind of African-looking animal, probably an eland. Then it opens up into two other branches, one displaying another half human head and a hut, and the other supplying support for a bird and ending with a jet plane. Every line consists in fact of two parallel lines, one black and one red. And so does the title of the work, which is drawn in uneven letters, some capitals and some lower case.

The title means "concerning the journey," and suggests what this work is about. But there are other indications of this theme. One is the jet, and another is the human head that lies on a branch and is moving away from a hut, which presumably represents home. Two birds and the migratory African animal further signal a journey. But a journey where? The jet would seem to suggest the one undertaken by Cubans who have left the island, who have settled away from their ancestral homes. But there is a strong African flavor to the painting, as in most of Bedia's work. And there is the woman and the knife. The color red that accompanies the black lines could mean blood. Is Bedia suggesting some other journey, the one of Africans to the island, with all the pain and suffering it caused? Or is there another journey involved, the spiritual trip believers in Afro-Cuban religions engage when they fall into a trance and are possessed by spirits? The leaves suggest the herbal elements used in these ceremonies, and so does the knife, which points to sacrifice, perhaps not so much of the woman, but of the birds and the African animal depicted in the work.

In any way we interpret the work we end up with signs and elements suggesting a Cuban experience of passage. But this does not entail any kind of particularity in the work, for its message can be given a broader significance. It can be applied to all peoples who have been forced to leave their native lands and to all those who are seeking spiritual comfort in religious searches.

Brito's *Self-portrait as a Swan* (2001, oil on wood, 29″ × 18″ × 4″) is a three-dimensional piece consisting of an arm holding a swan by a leg located in front of a box. The swan is desperately trying to get away, some of its feathers flying around, and its head turned to the hand in angry protest and perhaps even attack. On the box there is a small rectangular opening, a sort of window or door, which gives a glimpse of a hidden garden, full of vegetation, a secure hiding place the swan is trying to reach.

This work, both simple and complex, is full of meaning and can be the locus of many interpretations. Brito is known for her interest in identity, self-identity in particular. At one level one could see in this work her search for a freedom she longs for. The hand holding her is actually that of her son. She might be telling us that her family and social commitments are keeping her from escaping to a place in which she might find solace and freedom. If interpreted in this way, the work has little to do with Cuba or Cuban identity. The reference of the work goes back to classical Greece and Leda. But there are at least two other possible interpretations of the work that suggest something about Cuba. In one, the arm holding Brito is the Cuban culture and society and the hiding place is the refuge she seeks outside it. Cuban society can be overwhelming and stifling in many ways, full of norms and taboos, and the artist wants out of this trap. The other interpretation is that the arm stands for the Cuban Revolution, the government that almost kept Brito in Cuba against her will and that of her family. And the place of refuge is her adopted country, where she has found the freedom to be what she wants to be as a person and as an artist. The messages of these three interpretations are all universal, but they are rooted in the personal experience of a Cuban exile. That Brito herself may have other views about the significance of the work, would be a further testimony to the versatility and universality of her statement.

Calzada's *Island in Crisis* (2005, acrylic on canvas, 32″ × 22″) refers unabashedly to Cuba and the experience of Cubans. Its title could hardly be more explicit. The island in question is Cuba, and the architecture displayed in the painting is typically Cuban. We see the corner of a room with one full door, two partial doors, and the ceiling. The room has a high wooden ceiling and the top parts of the doors have colored glass. One door is partially open; we do not see enough of another to be able to tell; and of the third we see only what corresponds to a panel, which is also open. Light filters through the colored glass and projects itself on one of the walls. The most obvious feature of the room is that it is flooded. Through the doors we see an endless ocean and sky. But the flood is not only of water; light pours into the room profusely.

Clearly, something terrible is happening. The building is flooded and it needs to be evacuated, or perhaps it has already been evacuated, for there is no sign of a human presence. The water needs draining, but there is no evidence that drainage will come. This is a crisis, obviously, and a serious one. Still, there is reference to a happy and beautiful dimension represented by the light and the colored glass, which contrasts with the dangerous predicament indicated by the water.

The reference to the Cuban situation is unquestionable. Calzada is known for work inspired by Cuban architecture, but in this painting he goes beyond the mere representation of that architecture. He is connecting us to the soil and political situation of Cuba, although the lesson he seems to be voicing could apply to other places as well: to all places where a catastrophe has undertaken a country, where its people have had to flee, and where in spite of everything, there is still hope.

Falero's *Across* (2006, oil on canvas, 48″ × 48″) is an example of art about art. He has taken a Christ painted by José de Ribera, and incorporated it into the work. The reproduction is faithful, as only Falero's extraordinary technique could produce, but the Christ anachronistically rests on a balsa, a typical raft of the ones that Cubans have used to brave the waves and reach the United States. The Christ is somewhat emaciated, but peaceful; he looks alive, though sleeping. His wounds are visible and he seems to have abandoned himself to Providence. There is no struggle, but peace. The balsa is made of a tractor inner tube covered with jute to guard against the implacable sun and heat. Under the Christ is a box, probably a cooler or supply cabinet that serves also as a prop. An oar lays to the right. It is night time, and the moon illumines the scene, with a hint of a cross on its reflection on the dark ocean waters. The view we have is from above, and the title suggests a crossing, a crossroads, and a cross.

Falero is a spiritual painter who regularly explores religious motifs. His interest in baroque and Spanish art is well known. In this painting he puts all these elements to work to give us a piece that speaks of sacrifice, passage, hope, redemption, and peace. The painting clearly has to do with Cuba and the experience of Cubans who have come across in rafts. It also harks back to the Spanish past, the great Spanish painters of the baroque, and migration. And it speaks of universal themes of persecution, intolerance, pain, abandonment, and the finding of peace and tranquility in the midst of a catastrophe.

Rey's *Balsas Artifacts: Cross and String* (1998–1999, oil on plaster, 15.5″ × 12″ × 4″) is, like Falero's painting, about the Cuban raft experience. Rey lost his grandmother in one of these *balsas* and feels a special connection to this phenomenon. He produced a series of works that are either paintings of *balsas* or of artifacts found in *balsas*. The paintings are framed in wood boxes that make them appear almost like sacred objects, icons of devotion. The pieces in the series on the *balsa* artifacts are painted as frescoes, on a surface whose edges are black, with wide margins of gesso. Each work displays different artifacts. In the one I have chosen here, among other things we see a part of a coat with a button, an instrument of observation, a crucifix, and the string used to hang the crucifix on the neck. The cross and string are the most prominent objects in the painting, suggesting the role that these adventures gave it and giving the work its title.

Without knowledge of the Cuban *balsa* phenomenon, we would be hard pressed to understand this painting. Yet, once this fact is revealed through the title, the painting opens for us the whole question of diaspora and people fleeing, taking with them what is dearest and they consider most important in their lives: a coat for the cold in the voyage, an instrument of travel, and an object of faith to sustain them through anticipated adversity. The objects refer to a particular situation, a Cuban experience, but the lesson is universal. How many people have had to abandon their lands and venture into the sea, under precarious situations, because of political persecution or economic necessity? This is a universal plight with which many can identify.

Salinas's *Flow-Up* (1998, acrylic on canvas, 26″ × 36″) is in many ways an abstract painting. On the center and right we see green and white brush strokes that could be an eruption, a plant, or a branch. Behind it on the right is a reddish half moon, and on the left side at the top a broken circle. This painting belongs to a series Salinas made about palm trees. Once we know this, we see that the green and white flow do in fact resemble the top of a palm tree under heavy wind. The red half moon could be an image of the island of Cuba. And the circle is a broken mandala.

Salinas comes from a family that has experienced the vicissitudes of persecution and diaspora. He is a Sephardic Jew, whose parents came to Cuba from Turkey. In Cuba, a new diaspora was imposed on him, and his art gives us a vivid picture of the significance of this event. The royal palm tree is the symbol of

Cuba, but in this painting it could also refer to Salinas himself. Here he is, having been born in Cuba, swept away by the winds of the social and political storm unleashed by the Cuban Revolution. The mandala represents a broken peace, security, happiness, and the wholeness that comes with belonging, as well as the loss of part of himself in this maelstrom. This is an experience common to most Cuban-Americans of his generation, but it is also universal, because it extends to other people. Where is Salinas's identity now? Who is he, after he has been blown away from his roots by the winds of social change?

Vizcaíno's *Taxi* (2005, color pencil, styrofoam on cardboard, 31″ × 42″ × 6″) is perhaps the work, among the ones that I have chosen, that least of all connects to the Cuban situation. Here we have a kind of sculpture and painting of a New York City taxi made up with discarded materials from the supermarket where the artist used to work. The work does not try to imitate what a taxi looks like in reality, but presents us with a disjointed, comical, and engaging artifact. Vizcaíno's work has a childlike quality, an emphasis on pop art and the contraptions of everyday experience.

Still, *Taxi* represents an instrument of travel. Is this work telling us something about the artist's condition as an immigrant? Does the broken-up and disjointed appearance suggest the experience of diaspora? And does the use of discarded materials tell us something about how immigrants put together a new identity based on pieces that come from a variety of sources, the discards of the societies from which they come and from the societies that they join? Perhaps this is the subtle message of Vizcaíno's work. Perhaps it is a reflection on the very nature of diasporic identity in general and Cuban-American identity in particular. There seems to be nothing ostensibly Cuban about the work—no Cuban symbols and no reference to any particular event—but there is something in it that can be related to the Cuban situation.

Cuban-American Identity

Let us go back now to the questions we posed earlier: Do these paintings show any element that ties them to a Cuban-American identity? If you consider the paintings themselves, apart from their titles and anything surrounding their historical circumstances, there seems to be nothing that is common to all of them, or even that, except for one, suggests anything that is peculiarly Cuban and reflects the Cuban-American ethnos.

The only work that appears to have something Cuban about it is Calzada's *Island in Crisis* in that it portraits a common feature of Cuban colonial architecture, the use of large doors with colored glass. The rest of the paintings suggest nothing like this. But even the Calzada piece could have been painted by someone else, and in fact tourists and artists visiting Cuba have often painted such buildings. So, is there something Cuban-American about the picture? Only if we consider its title, history, and author do we find anything. An island in crisis makes sense in the Cuban-American context; this is a view of Cuba from exile, partly nostalgic, partly political.

Now that we have come back to history, we can see also that the other works mentioned can be tied to the Cuban-American ethnos, but not because the members of the ethnos to which their authors belong have necessarily anything in common. Rather, it is because their history has brought them together. Acosta's Presidential Palace becomes a symbol of the Cuban situation, again seen from outside Cuba, by members of the Cuban diaspora. Bedia's journey brings up connotations of Africa, emigration, and spiritual renewal. Brito's swan may depict an attempt to escape from an unwelcome exile, a repressive regime, or the pressures of a culture that can be sometimes stifling. Rey's artifacts are telling because they come from one of the rafts in which Cubans escaped to Florida. When one realizes that his grandmother perished in one of these attempts, and that he was trying to capture what is considered important in a moment of escape, the piece becomes extraordinarily Cuban-American. Salinas's palm is a metaphor for the Cuban self, uprooted by the circumstances. Falero's Christ on a balsa evokes suffering and redemption. And Vizcaíno's taxi brings us back to a journey and adaptation.

In short, it is the history, experiences, and kinship that make the art we have examined relevant to Cuban-American identity. Art, like ethnicity, means nothing outside its history, a point effectively made by a work of another Cuban-American artist, Carlos Estévez. On a black background, he draws a ballet dancer whose head lies at her feet, and entitles the piece *Art without History* (2001).[5] The art works we have examined effectively illustrate the understanding of Cuban-American identity in particular, and ethnic identity in general, in familial-historical terms. They also reveal the complex ways in which identities intermingle and flourish, something which is possible precisely because identity is never rigid and well defined, but is a living thing subject to the contingencies of events. That these experiences are shared by other groups in other places and in other times links the Cuban-American experience to the human reality and condition everywhere. Yet, a special context identifies this particular diaspora, its history, and the individuals that are part of it as Cuban and Cuban-American.

NOTES

1. For the details of the theory that supports this view, see Jorge J. E. Gracia *Latinos in America*, ch. 1; *Hispanic/Latino Identity*, chs. 2 and 3; and *Surviving Race, Ethnicity, and Nationality*, ch. 3.

2. See, for example, Juan A. Martínez, *Cuban Art and National Identity;* Lynette M. F. Bosch, *Cuban-American Art in Miami;* and José Veigas et al., *Memoria: Cuban Art of the Twentieth Century.*

3. See my interview with Bedia in Jorge J. E. Gracia's webpage, *Cuban Art Outside Cuba: Identity, Philosophy, and Art.*

4. For revealing interviews about the work of Cuban artists, see Gracia, Bosch, and Alvarez Borland, eds., *Identity, Memory, and Diaspora: Voices of Cuban-American Artists, Writers, and Philosophers;* also see two web sites established by Jorge J. E. Gracia: *Cuban Art Outside Cuba,* and the website for the 2006 NEH Summer Seminar: *Negotiating Identities in Art, Literature, and Philosophy.*

5. This image is reproduced on the cover of this volume. For more information on Carlos Estévez's work, see J. Gracia, *Images of Thought.*

WORKS CITED

Bosch, Lynette M. F. *Cuban-American Art in Miami: Exile, Identity and the Neo-Baroque.* London, UK: Lund Humphreys Press, 2004.

Gracia, Jorge J. E. *Images of Thought: Philosophical Interpretations and Carlos Estévez's Art.* Albany: State University of New York Press, 2009.

———. *Latinos in America: Philosophy and Social Identity.* Oxford: Blackwell, 2008.

———. *Negotiating Identities in Art, Literature, and Philosophy: Cuban-Americans and American Culture* (http://philosophy.buffalo.edu/contrib/events/neh06.html).

———. *Cuban Art Outside Cuba: Identity, Philosophy, and Art* (http://www.philosophy.buffalo.edu/capenchair/CAOC/index.html).

———. *Surviving Race, Ethnicity, and Nationality: A Challenge for the Twenty-first Century.* Lanham, MD: Rowman and Littlefield, 2005.

———. *Hispanic/Latino Identity: A Philosophical Perspective.* Oxford: Blackwell, 2000.

——— Lynette M. F. Bosch, and Isabel Alvarez Borland, eds. *Identity, Memory, and Diaspora: Voices of Cuban-American Artists, Writers, and Philosophers.* Albany: State University of New York Press, 2007.

Kundera, Milan. "*Die Weltliteratur:* How We Read One Another," *The New Yorker* (January 8, 2007): 32c.

Martínez, Juan A. *Cuban Art and National Identity: The Vanguardia Painters 1927–1950.* Gainesville: University Press of Florida, 1994.

Veigas, José, et al. *Memoria: Cuban Art of the Twentieth Century.* Los Angeles: California/International Arts Foundation, 2002.

12

Cuban Art in the Diaspora

Andrea O'Reilly Herrera

As an island—a geographical space with mutable and porous borders—Cuba has never been a fixed cultural, political, or geographical entity. Over the centuries, as a result of its strategic location, Cuba has borne witness to a series of voluntary and forcible migrations to and from the island. In consequence, the island has been a receptacle to all manner of interventions and exchanges. The sea that circumscribes it suggests this perennial ebb and flow, this constant movement and cultural cross-pollination that have become the defining features of Cuban culture and Cuban identity formation.[1]

As a result of these continuous and multiple out-migrations and scatterings, Cuba has also become a moveable nation, a traveling, prismatic site of rupture and continuity. Though the lush landscape and the incandescent tropical light continue to figure largely in the Cuban cultural imagination and have assumed almost iconic significance, the idea that this nation can be self-contained, defined according to geopolitical boundaries, or reduced to a single factor denies its historical and cultural complexity. Rather, Cuban culture is a composite of widely diverse elements and influences beginning with the Taíno, the indigenous population that inhabited the island prior to the arrival of the Spaniards in 1492. It has been stratified and striated by the multiple ethnic *presences* that have inhabited the island and transformed by the *poly-rhythmic repetitions*[2] that have occurred outside the island and are characterized by continuity and permutation as opposed to mimesis. One such example of this particular form of *repetition* is the itinerant exhibition *Café: The Journeys of Cuban Artists*, the central focus of this chapter.

First conceived by artists Leandro Soto, Yovani Bauta, and Israel León, and consequently curated by Soto, *Café* has had five showings since its original presentation in 2001.[3] The exhibition, which is indefinitely ongoing, features alternating, multigenerational groups of artists (including those who have remained on the island and those born outside Cuba) working with a range of mediums including oil, acrylic, watercolor, installation and/or performance art, photography, video/film and sculpture.[4] Nearly all of the participating Cuban-born artists left the island either voluntarily or forcibly in the wake of the 1959 revolution, seeking asylum in various parts of the world as a result of government censorship and the consequent constraints placed upon them in regard to their personal and creative freedom.

The actual inspiration for *Café* first came to Leandro Soto during a trip to the Yucatán. One evening while sitting in the central plaza in Mérida sharing conversation and coffee prepared *the Cuban way* with Yovani Bauta and Israel León, the three men began to reminisce about their lives in Cuba and the family members and friends they had left behind. As the evening wore on, Soto, Bauta and León—all of whom received their art training on the island—began talking about how they had managed to preserve their Cuban artistic identities in exile, as well as incorporate new cultural elements into their work. At the time all three artists were working on a series of paintings in which coffee pots were depicted expressionistically in order to invoke what Soto describes as *the essence* of the island. As they sipped their *café*, Soto, Bauta, and León collectively mused over the significance of the fact that they were all undertaking similar projects and were reunited in Mérida, a place that physically and architecturally resembled the island yet was also distinctly foreign. Suddenly it occurred to Soto that the *café* they were drinking had been the emotional stimulus for their conversation. "I realized at that moment that *café cubano* could serve as a poetic metaphor for an essential component of Cuban identity, regardless of where it is prepared and served."[5] And so on that night beneath a canopy of trees, they came up with the idea for *Café*.

Each showing of *Café* is unique not only because of the manner in which it conforms to the physical space in which it is presented, but also in that each time the exhibit is mounted it introduces new artists to the core group as well as new generic elements. More recent manifestations, for example, have included poetry and fiction readings, performances and original music composed by Cuban and North American musicians, as well as interactive installations and events or activities, which encourage audience participation. The most recent manifestation of the exhibit, *Café VII*, featured a non-Cuban guest artist and included a documentary on Cuban hip-hop titled *The Black Perspective: A Short Radiography of Hip-Hop* by Ricardo Bacallao.[6]

Commenting upon its nontraditional aspects, Leandro Soto points out that *Café* is a show *curated by an artist for artists*. Unlike more traditional methods of curation, which rely on a third party to organize and install the show, Soto takes an active, collaborative role in coordinating each presentation and consequently adapting the various pieces to their environment. Though he is highly selective in regard to whom he invites to participate in the exhibition, Soto generally plays little or no role in actually selecting the works—he leaves this decision to each individual artist. As a result, Soto has no preconceived idea regarding what the show will look like until the artwork arrives at his door. In this sense he approaches each new exhibit as a kind of set designer. Each manifestation, he insists, has its own integrity and represents a different diasporic take on national or cultural identity.

According to Soto, the *larger meaning* of each showing of *Café* depends upon the proximity between the pieces once they are hung or installed, and the consequent manner in which the individual works communicate with one another and interact with the exhibition space. *Café III*, for example, was in a physically small location; yet the space itself was transformed by Soto and his students into an installation, for they painted the walls in the style of a pre-1959 colonial home in Old Havana. The art work was consequently arranged like paintings on the wall of a private home and organized in thematic groupings; and various free-standing sculptures and installations, several of which were interactive in nature, divided up the exhibition space in such a way that one had the sensation of entering various rooms in this house of memory. The exhibition was backlit with a soothing violet light, which made the tropical colors on the walls appear to be luminous; classical piano music composed especially for the exhibition by an Anglo composer played softly in the background as though someone were practicing in another room. At the opening reception, Soto prepared eggs and served *café cubano*. In this manner the exhibit appealed to all five senses.

The hidden links among the works reveal themselves only when they are considered as a whole, Leandro Soto argues. Each exhibition thus operates along a kind of continuum that maintains what he describes as a certain kind of rhythm and tension between integration and implosion. According to the concept of implosion, Soto continues, apparently disconnected elements become connected internally. "At first these meanings are not obvious to me," Soto explains, "but gradually, as I begin the work of installing the various pieces"—which have no preordained or predetermined position—"I begin to see their quantum meaning, their hidden connections."

According to many of those who attended the opening reception, the overall effect of this particular presentation was deeply moving. A number of Cubans present at the event said the exhibition captured the colors and rhythms, the sounds and smells of the island. In general, their response was quite sentimental and nostalgic. In Nelson Garcia Miranda's words, the intimate space not only created a certain *sensual* and *seductive* ambiance, but the atmosphere that Soto created in this particular manifestation of *Café* captured *a certain way of living, a certain way of doing, of being and thinking* that is identifiably Cuban. Those outside the Cuban experience were also deeply affected by the exhibit; many felt as though they had been *welcomed in*.

"*Café*, Soto continues, "is a living entity," which shifts and changes not only according to the physical and geographical context in which it is presented, but also according to the various combinations of works included in each individual manifestation. The inclusion of performances, coupled with the fact that there is no predetermined order regarding the arranging of the works, suggests the postmodern concept that meanings are not static or fixed and can be freely rearranged. Nevertheless, the recurrence of certain insistent elements and motifs, coupled with what Soto refers to as the *sabor* of the atmosphere created at each exhibition, suggests that some aspect of *Café* is quintessentially Cuban. According to Soto and others, each manifestation of *Café* thus becomes a poetic metaphor in which Cuba is both absent and present. Put another way, each presentation simultaneously signifies and collapses geographical distances and thus presents an uncanny *repetition* of the island, which is at once *disjunct and displaced.* This absence and presence mirrors the interstitial or liminal space occupied by the artists themselves. In turn, adapting each show to a new physical space and allowing outsiders to actively participate in the event suggests a manner in which the diasporic subject must adapt to and transform each new environment in which he or she finds their life. These seemingly paradoxical aspects of *Café* invite a dialogue regarding the fundamental nature of diasporic identity formation, transnationalism, and cross-culturation.

In his essay "Cultural Identity and Diaspora," Stuart Hall argues that any fixed notion of ethnic or cultural identity inadvertently imposes an *imaginary coherence* on the ongoing *experience of dispersal and fragmentation* that characterizes the diasporic condition.[7] Hall poses two approaches to cultural identity, which allow for the ambiguities present in each showing of *Café* and the cross-cutting particularities and structural differences or social determinations that differentiate and distinguish its various artists. "There are two ways to think about cultural identity," he observes, "the first position defines 'cultural identity' in terms of one, shared culture, a sort of collective 'one true self,' hiding inside the many other, more superficial or artificially imposed 'selves,' which people with a shared ancestry hold in common" (Morley and Chen 393). This approach emphasizes the aggregate over the individual in that it implicates the very deepest and most fundamental structures and practices that underpin and constitute certain shared cultural codes and modes of interacting. In this sense it confirms the notion of a seemingly stable collective identity, which speaks to the desire for continuity and fixity in the face of what Edward Said terms a *contrapuntal modernity* (Bhabha 140).

The second position complements the first in a harmoniously antithetical manner. According to this approach, the *points of similarity* that bind all diasporic subjects together coexist with points of *deep and significant difference*, which take into account the manner in which time and history have intervened in the process of shaping and reshaping one's identity. Identity formation is thus on a sliding continuum—it is "a matter of 'becoming' as well as of 'being,'" and "belongs to the future as much as to the past," Hall tells us. "It is not something which already exists, transcending place, time, history and culture," for cultural identities "come from somewhere, have histories. But like everything which is historical, they undergo constant transformation" (Morley and Chen 394).

Located within the slippage that exists between the diachronic and the synchronic, *Café* embraces, simultaneously, both theoretical positions without annulling one or the other.[8] And thus, the underlying concept of *café* and its ritual preparation serves as a unifying element that symbolically alludes to the embedded forms of cultural life and practice that bind all Cub*ands*[9] together despite the categorical determinations that distinguish them from one another (such as class, race, gender, ethnicity, generation, geographical location, sexual or religious orientation, and birthplace). In this sense it functions as a fixed referential to homeland in its implication of cultural continuity—a stable signifier that assumes that one can repeat or reproduce some form or aspect of cultural practice in spite of the fact that it has been transplanted.

Although the *Cafeteros* do not represent a unified aesthetic or a single artistic expression, Leandro Soto's intention has consistently been to highlight their common bonds as Cub*ands*, for in his view each individual artist contributes a new component to the collective and shifting idea of what constitutes Cuban identity in diaspora. The first manifestation of *Café*, presented at the University of Massachusetts in 2001, thus focused exclusively upon the dual themes of *café cubano* and cultural identity. In coordinating the exhibition, Soto consciously chose to adopt this thematic framework in order to visually link the artists as opposed to distinguishing among them according to their various generations.

Consequent showings of *Café* have departed from these central themes; nevertheless each presentation has put into relief certain threads of connection that reveal the *Cafeteros'* affinity to one another. In other words, rather than focusing on the binarisms of island and diaspora—a misleading and deceptive dichotomy in the case of Cuba and its political history—each showing of *Café* visibly highlights the artists' points of connection despite their individual social or ideological positions and regardless of where or when they were born or where they reside. In addition to speaking to their collective experience of displacement or loss, their work reveals identifiable continuities with a tradition of Cuban visual art that emerged in the 1920s. "In each new manifestation of *Café*," Soto tells me, "there exists a kind of mystery, which reveals our common ground, our interrelations [in regard to both] the present and the past."

In his catalog essay for the exhibit *Outside Cuba/Fuera de Cuba* (1988), Ricardo Pau-Llosa identifies a certain "set of preoccupations" that loosely define a "collective identity" among contemporary Cuban émigré artists and links them to generations of artists dating back to the beginning of the twentieth century. According to Pau-Llosa, the "transplanting of Cuban life" in diaspora, coupled with the manner in which exile has informed the Cuban imaginary for over two centuries, accounts in part for this continuity, which has in various degrees "survived" the post-1959 exodus. Pau-Llosa proceeds to identify the presence of specific themes and elements, which have traversed several generations and largely originated with the first generation of Cuban modernists shortly after World War I.

Following the establishment of the republic in 1902,[10] Cuba underwent a period of *intense nationalism.*[11] Springing from this sociopolitical milieu, the *vanguardia* artists (many of whom voluntarily relocated to France) forged a set of fundamental motifs and elements that were the result in part of their physical *displacement from* and *reencounter with* a nation struggling to define the essence of its cultural identity though it had officially suppressed its indigenous and African roots and privileged the influence of Europe.[12] These motifs, Pau-Llosa argues, have recurred over generations; they include the trope of historical displacement, which emphasizes the themes of change, violence, alienation, uprooting, and the disruption of space; a search for the origins of cultural identity in its African and European roots; the appearance of the landscape, of regional iconography, the folklore of the island, and the presence of Cuba's peasant population. "The disjunctions of history," Pau-Llosa writes, "have not eliminated [these] certain basic continuities [or structures of visual thinking among] . . . the various generations of artists," which "transcend the hybridness of [multi]-culturalism."[13]

Many of the *Cafeteros* treat a range of themes that fall outside the realm of those outlined above; nevertheless one can discern in their work the presence of these fundamental motifs. For example, a certain kind of metonymic *repetition*[14] of creole cultural forms and practices is evident in the work of a preponderance of the *Café* artists. For many, such as Leandro Soto, Ana María Sarlot, Raul Villarreal, and Laura Luna, the use of Taíno symbols or elements drawn from Afro-Cuban religions such as Palo Monte and Santería are fundamental sources of iconography as well as mediums of artistic expression. In this sense they are linked to a tradition established by Cuban painters such as Wilfredo Lam and Manuel Mendive as well as the anthropologists Lydia Cabrera and Fernando Ortiz. Others, such as Ana Delgado and Nelson Garcia Miranda, draw directly upon Cuban folklore for inspiration, and artists such as Israel León frequently incorporate either overt or implied references to the physical landscape of the island as well as its flora and fauna.[15] Drawing primarily upon a romantic tradition prevalent in the late nineteenth century in Cuba and epitomized by painters such as Leopoldo Romañach, Natalia Perdomo also depicts the lush Cuban *paisaje* (countryside) in her work, yet she has also sought a visual reference in spatial and architectural elements that summon up a pre-revolutionary past and hearken back to the work of the Cuban modernist painter Amelia Peláez. A number of the *Cafeteros,* on the other hand, such as Raul Villareal and Ana Flores, depict iconographic images such as the royal palm or the ever-present sea; while others, such as Armando Tejuca and Baruj Salinas, capture in their paintings the luminescent light and shadows of the island.

Many of the *Cafeteros* also take up more overtly political themes, which are simultaneously universal yet particular to Cuba's turbulent political history. Joaquín González and María Brito, for example, deal overtly with the themes of violence and oppression. González focuses specifically upon the trope of institutional oppression, whereas Brito treats the themes of entrapment and violence especially as they pertain to women's role and position in society. Other *Cafeteros*, such as Yovani Bauta and Jorge Arango, address the dual themes of loss and nostalgia. Bauta utilizes iconic forms such as the coffee pot to express his deep-felt longing for Cuba; whereas Arango's installations, which were featured in *Café II* and *III*, aimed to deconstruct the romanticized vision of Cuba cultivated by certain sectors of the exile community in Miami where he currently resides.

Though their work is visibly rooted in the modernist movement in Cuba, the *Cafeteros* have also integrated new symbolic elements into their work as they explore their evolving sense of self in a new context. Like the *vanguardia* artists, the *Cafeteros* have cultivated a symbolic, visual language that speaks to what many would claim to be an essential component of *Cubanidad* (Cubanness) or *lo cubano;* yet unlike their predecessors, they approach this subject from a diasporic perspective or double consciousness that is at once internal and external. Those who spent their formative years in Cuba express the idea that exile forced them to examine and visually articulate their *Cubanidad.* To put it in other words, the realities of exile prompted them to explore their identities from an external perspective, which they never would have acquired had they remained on the island.

One also finds in the work of the *Cafeteros* a particular form of creative invention that arises out of the diasporic subject's encounter with newness. For some, the diasporic condition endows them with an artistic freedom that calibrates the tensions that exist when one tries to simultaneously resist and integrate new cultural elements. Relying on competing and sometimes conflicting, binary constructions of alterity, this seemingly paradoxical position simultaneously embraces and rejects both cultural *otherness* and Cubanness. Accommodating new cultural elements into their art represents a strategy of survival as they undergo the process of adaptation and explore their changing sense of self in a new context; resistance, on the other hand, ensures cultural continuity and thereby mediates the nostalgic longing for the homeland. Rather than emphasizing loss and displacement, however, many of the *Cafeteros* stress the fertile nature of this dispersion and scattering and celebrate the stratified blending of new cultural elements, in spite of what was for some traumatic rupture. As James Clifford observes, such *relational positioning* is less a *process of othering* and more an *entangled tension* that results from the diasporic subjects' multiple attachments, which are *encoded* with conflicting practices and impulses of cultural preservation, resistance to the host culture, assimilation, and transformation (244–79).

Commenting specifically upon the creative potential that arises as a result of instability or impermanence, Leandro Soto observes:

> Though they yearn to return, Cuban intellectuals and artists leave the Island behind; but they take with them an archetypal island that contains our collective

> memories. As time goes by, Cuban exiles have been forced by reality to give up the idea of recovering the Island, which has been replaced in their memories by a mythical land, a poetic paradise. As hard as this is to believe, this particular attitude encourages Cubans to integrate into the American way of life and, at the same time, allows the historic memory of the Island to remain intact, thus helping them to preserve their cultural identity. As an artist I rely on this poetic condition. It is true for any artist that a certain degree of solitude is desirable. But to be an artist in exile contributes, in my opinion, to the creative process and promotes what Ernest Hemingway called "grace under pressure."[16]

The particular strain of diasporic consciousness to which Soto refers *lives loss and hope* (to borrow Clifford's words once again) *in a defining tension.*

In its total effect *Café* initiates an ongoing dialogue with generations of Cuban artists regarding what defines Cubanness not exclusively in regard to the past or to that which is fixed or stable, but also in regard to the present and the future or to that which is impermanent or yet to be determined. The central metaphor of *café* captures this ambiguity, for each presentation varies according to its unique composition and the physical space in which it is presented, the ritual preparation of *café cubano* changes according to the cultural and geographical contexts in which it is enacted. Considered in this more expansive context, *café* or coffee metaphorically suggests the manner in which the artists participating in the exhibition are transformed by, and have transformed, their experience in a new context at the same time that they have retained their cultural roots and the attendant historical tensions that came in the wake of colonialism and neocolonialism.

The itinerant and organic nature of *Café,* coupled with its radical inclusivity, also points up the instability, indeterminacy, and change that are inherent to the diasporic condition; that Cuba is both absent and present in each manifestation bespeaks the indeterminacy of diasporic space. As Stuart Hall and James Clifford, among others, have noted, any concept of diaspora, including cultural expressions, "exceed[s] a binary structure of representation," "denotes hybridity" and heterogeneity, and connotes "multiple and shifting locations and subject positions" (Hall, "Cultural Identity" 228; Clifford, "Diasporas" 244–77). "Hybridity," Hall argues, "opens diasporic subjectivity to a liminal, dialogic space wherein identity is negotiated" ("Cultural Identity" 5). The diasporic experience is thus defined "not by essence or purity, but by the recognition of a necessary heterogeneity and diversity; by a conception of identity which lives in and through, not despite, difference; by hybridity."

There is no "fixed origin to which we can make some final and absolute Return," Hall continues; as a result, any consideration of the diasporic dictates a discourse that operates on the principle of *positionality* (226). Because one can never truly return to some unchanging point of origin, the diasporic subject inhabits multiple sites that cannot be reduced to the binary here/*aquí* or there/

allí. Rather, s/he is always in a place of transition—wholly belonging neither here nor there. "Given the alienated spatiality of the diaspora," R. Radhakrishnan argues,

> One can both belong to and not belong to either one of two worlds at the same time. To the diasporic sensibility, it is easy to practice a perennial politics of transgression in radical postponement of the politics of constituency. To put it differently, peripatetic transgressions in and by themselves begin to constitute a politics of difference and post-representation . . . [and thus] the diasporic subject may well attempt to proclaim a heterogeneous "elsewhere" as its actual epistemological home. (322)

In its liberal inclusion of Cubans residing on the island and in the diaspora, as well as those born and/or raised on and off the island, *Café* ultimately challenges any exclusively territorial or essentialist notion of cultural identity. Through its conception of a wide continuum of what constitutes Cuban cultures and who qualifies as being Cuban, it stands in direct contrast to, and thereby challenges a binary approach to identity structured around the false dichotomies of *aquí* (here) and *allí* (there), authentic and inauthentic, true and false. On the contrary, *Café* operates on a principle of spatial or geographical indeterminacy and thereby destabilizes identity categories that are rooted in static concepts of national or cultural identity. On the contrary the *Cafeteros'* visual thinking reveals the fundamentally heterogeneous and eclectic aspects of Cuban culture and identity as well as its protean nature. In the act of reconstituting and thereby conserving identifiable elements of Cuban culture, each artist is inevitably reinscribing and ultimately transforming them. In this sense *Café*—when approached literally or metaphorically—defies the notion that a nation can be sovereign and its culture fixed or monolithic. The idea of transnationalism that is implied in each exhibit inadvertently puts into relief the conceptual limits and shortcomings of all overtly politicized, nationalistic, discursive paradigms and practices that rely on territorial claims to authentic national identity. As "an apparatus of symbolic power," Homi Bhabha observes, the "ambivalence of the 'nation' as a narrative strategy . . . produces a continual slippage of categories." "What is displayed in this displacement," Bhabha continues, "is the nation as the liminality of cultural modernity."

In all its diversity *Café* emphasizes the *polyphonic* aspects of Cuban culture, which together constitute an *ensemble*. The fundamental concept that drives *Café* thus pivots upon a creatively unstable definition of cultural identity. "Within this chaos of difference and repetitions, of combinations and permutations" Benítez-Rojo notes, "there are regular dynamics that co-exist" (27–28, 81). The space in which *Café* is exhibited is, therefore, yet another variation of the polyrhythmic, for it also connotes difference and repetition, transformation and continuity in an ever-changing transnational diasporic context.

Approaching the question of Cuban cultural identity from the position of diaspora allows for a more complex and nuanced understanding and continuation of Cuban culture expression outside the island. This open-ended spatiality of the exhibit space and postponement of a fixed meaning acknowledges Cuba's long history of relocation and intermingling, as well as its *seams of continuity*. Working with a more fluid paradigm of national and cultural identity, which acknowledges that *difference resides alongside continuity*,[17] not only allows one to largely bypass ideological concerns and avoid essentialist claims to authenticity, but it also admits the multigenerational transmissions of cultural expression and consciousness that are represented in *Cafe*. A more expansive and inclusive approach, moreover, takes into account the cultural exchanges that arise as a result of the present-day realities of globalization and transnationalism, and admits the discrepant histories and discursive practices that collectively constitute this traveling nation that is Cuba (Hall, "Cultural Identity" 234).

In its transnational, interdisciplinary aspects, the body of work that Leandro Soto has gathered together in various combinations in *Café* simultaneously recaptures the sensation of the island without reducing itself to mimetic reproduction or nostalgic reconstruction. In its various manifestations, *Café* provides evidence of an ongoing tradition in which Cuban diasporic artists and their heirs have redefined and evolved a visual tradition that is at once rooted in the past yet possesses its own organic aesthetic integrity. When I ask Leandro Soto about the future of this exhibit in a post-Castro era, he responds without hesitation, "siempre estoy preparando un buen cafecito" (I'm always preparing a good café).

NOTES

This chapter is excerpted from my forthcoming monograph tentatively titled *"Setting the Tent against the House": Cuban Artists in the Diaspora*. Special thanks go to my dear friend and colleague Jan McVicker for her close reading of this chapter and her insights and suggestions.

1. Though elements of Taíno culture have persisted up to the present day, this aboriginal population was largely eradicated and consequently supplanted by a series of colonial presences beginning with Spain and including Ireland, England, and France. The process of external intervention continued with a series of forced and voluntary migrations from West Africa and China primarily. From the turn of the twentieth century, Cuba was subject to a series of neocolonial influences such as the United States and the former Soviet Union, and she received an influx of immigrants including Ashkenazim and Sephardic Jews and Lebanese to name but a few groups. As a result, Cuban culture and visual thinking are fundamentally eclectic.

2. I am borrowing Antonio Benítez-Rojo's phrasing and terminology here. See *The Repeating Island*.

3. The first manifestation of *Café* was held at the Augusta Sauvage Gallery at the African House at the University of Massachusetts at Amherst (2001); the second, at the gallery of Contemporary Art at the University of Colorado at Colorado Springs (2002); the third was presented at Arizona State University West, Interdisciplinary and Performance Art Gallery, Phoenix (2003); the fourth and fifth manifestations were also in Phoenix at the Art Spaces, Estrella Mountain Community College (2004) and at the Tempe Library Gallery (December 2005–April 2006) respectively. *Café VI* was presented at the Union Gallery at the University of Arizona in Tempe (September 28 October 29, 2007); and *Café VII* was at Arizona State University in Phoenix in October of 2007 and was dedicated to the late Cuban artist Pedro Alvarez, who resided in Phoenix and died in 2004. This latter exhibit was also the first to feature a non-Cuban guest artist (Larry Yañez).

4. All of the artists in *Café* are part of the diasporic population with the exception of Kevin and Kadir López, both of whom reside in Havana. According to Leandro Soto, both artists (who also happen to be brothers) have expressed to him their sense of *insilio* or inner exile despite the fact that they have remained in the island. In Soto's view, their perspective adds yet another dimension to the exhibition.

5. This particular quotation is drawn from Soto's Artist's Statement, composed for the exhibit *Café II* (University of Colorado at Colorado Springs, October 2002).

6. Daniel Lentz's composition "Café Desire" was a permanent feature of *Café III*, which opened at Arizona State University West during the fall of 2003. Lentz is a professor emeritus in the department of interdisciplinary arts at ASU, West. Other musicians and writers who gave readings or participated as musicians in the various manifestations of *Café* are Victor Caldee, Ricardo Pau-Llosa, Armando Fernández, and Andrea O'Reilly Herrera.

7. See "Cultural Identity and Diaspora" in *Identity: Community, Culture, Difference*, 224.

8. The possibility of maintaining a harmonious balance between or among conflicting elements or states of being is what some scholars regard as a quintessentially non-Western concept, which has been developed by Caribbean theoreticians such as Antonio Benítez-Rojo. In its rejection of traditional binary thinking, it purports that one can embrace simultaneously multiple, paradoxical positions. Strict limitations in regard to length prevent me from fully exploring this complex concept; however, a full discussion of this topic appears in the introduction to my forthcoming monograph "*Setting the Tent against the House.*"

9. Cub*ands* is an elastic and all-inclusive term I developed in order to simultaneously take account of the layered *presences* that constitute Cuban cultural and national identity (such as Spain, Africa, Ireland, France, China, the United States, and the former Soviet Union) as well as to allow room for the hybrid identities that are continuously transforming in an ever-changing diasporic context, which is at once global and transnational. See my introduction to O'Reilly Herrera, *ReMembering Cuba: Legacy of a Diaspora*, xxvii–xxx.

10. Following the defeat of Spain, the formal military occupation of Cuba by the United States commenced on January 1, 1899. In 1900, a constituent assembly convened

to prepare a new constitution. In February 1901, the United States enacted the Platt Amendment and required the Cuban constituent assembly to incorporate the statute into the new constitution. In June, the constituent assembly adopted the Platt Amendment by a vote of 16 to 11, with four abstentions; and in national elections in December 1901, Tomás Estrada Palma was elected president. On May 20, 1902, the United States ended the military occupation of Cuba, formally inaugurating the Cuban Republic.

11. The first generation of *vanguardia* artists include Victor Manuel García (1897–1969), Eduardo Abela (1889–1965), Amelia Peláez del Casal (1896–1968), Antonio Gattorno (1904–1980), Carlos Enríquez (1900–1957), Fidelio Ponce de León (1895–1949), and Marcelo Pogolotti (1902–1988).

12. See the introductory essay in Veigas et al.

13. Pau-Llosa actually uses the word "bi-culturalism." In reality, Cuban identity is fundamentally multicultural as a result of the various *presences* of which it is composed. In the same vein, Cuban diasporic identity is multi- or transnational in light of the fact that Cubans have relocated across the globe. ("Identity," 41).

14. My usage of the word "repetition" resembles Antonio Benítez-Rojo's in that it suggests that memories repeat themselves over time and retain some of their essential qualities. However, rather than viewing them as mimetic in any Borgesian sense, they are also *as fugitive as the years* as Proust suggested in *Swann's Way.*

15. Israel León, Leandro Soto, and Raul Villarreal often include Cuba's alligator shape in their paintings or prints.

16. See Soto's testimonial "Cubans in the U.S., An Example of Ethnic Identity in the Making" in O'Reilly Herrera, *ReMembering Cuba*, 245–47.

17. Gilroy uses this phrase throughout *The Black Atlantic: Modernity and Double Consciousness.* I am adapting Stuart Hall's claim that "Difference . . . persists—in and alongside continuity," 228.

WORKS CITED

Benítez-Rojo, Antonio. *The Repeating Island.* Durham, NC: Duke University Press, 1992.

Bhabha, Homi. *The Location of Culture.* London and New York: Routledge, 1994. 140 and 200–04.

Clifford, James. *Routes, Travel and Translation in the Twentieth Century.* Cambridge: Harvard University Press, 1997. 244–79.

Gilroy, Paul. *The Black Atlantic: Modernity and Double Consciousness.* Cambridge: Harvard University Press, 1993.

Hall, Stuart. "Cultural Identity and Diaspora." *Identity: Community, Culture, Difference.* Ed. Jonathan Rutherford. London: Lawrence and Wishart, 1990. 222–37.

Morley, David and Kuan-Hsing Chen, eds. *Stuart Hall: Critical Dialogues in Cultural Studies.* New York: Routledge, 1996. 392–411.

O'Reilly Herrera, Andrea. "Introduction." *ReMembering Cuba: Legacy of a Diaspora.* Austin, TX: University of Texas Press, 2001. xxvii–xxx.

———. *"Setting the Tent against the House": Cuban Artists in the Diaspora.* Texas: University of Texas Press, forthcoming.

Pau-Llosa, R. "Identity and Variations." *Outside Cuba/Fuera de Cuba.* Ed. Ileana Fuentes Pérez et al. New Brunswick, NJ: Rutgers University Press, 1989.

Radhakrishnan, R. "Ethnicity in an Age of Diaspora." *Theorizing Diaspora.* Ed. Jana Evans Braziel and Anita Mannur. Oxford, UK: Blackwell, 2003. 322.

Veigas, José, Cristina Vives, Adolfo Nodal, et al. *Memoria, Cuban Art of the Twentieth Century.* Los Angeles: California/International Arts Foundation, 2002.

ABOUT THE EDITORS

ISABEL ALVAREZ BORLAND is Monsignor Edward G. Murray Professor at the College of the Holy Cross in Worcester, Massachusetts, where she currently serves as Director of the Latin American Studies and Latino Concentration. Alvarez Borland is the author of *Cuban-American Literature of Exile: From Person to Persona* (1998) and of *Discontinuidad y ruptura en Guillermo Cabrera Infante* (1982). She is also coeditor of *Identity, Memory, and Diaspora: Voices of Cuban-American Artists, Writers, and Philosophers* (State University of New York Press, 2008). Her publications are in twentieth-century Latin American literature, Contemporary Spanish American, Caribbean, Latino, and Cuban-American literatures. Her articles have appeared in journals such as *Encuentro, Modern Language Notes, Hispanic Review, Hispania, Revista Iberoamericana,* and *World Literature Today.* She has held visiting professorships at Middlebury College and Amherst College. In 2006, she was codirector of an NEH Summer Seminar for College Teachers on Cuban American Literature, Art, and Philosophy.

LYNETTE M. F. BOSCH is Professor and Coordinator of Art History at Geneseo State College and has been a Bunting Fellow at the Radcliffe Research Institute, Harvard University. Her latest book is *Cuban-American Art in Miami: Exile, Identity and the Neo-Baroque* (2004). In addition she has published *Art, Liturgy and Legend in Renaissance Toledo* (2000), and *Ernesto Barreda: Contemporary Chilean Painter* (1996). She is also coeditor of *Identity, Memory, and Diaspora: Voices of Cuban-American Artists, Writers, and Philosophers* (State University of New York Press, 2008). Her articles have appeared in both scholarly journals and widely accessible magazines. She has curated eleven art exhibitions and edited the ensuing catalogues. In 2006, she was codirector of an NEH Summer Seminar for College Teachers on Cuban American Literature, Art, and Philosophy. In connection with this seminar, she was Curator of *Layers: Collecting Cuban-American Art*, University of Buffalo, July/September 2006.

ABOUT THE CONTRIBUTORS

CAROL DAMIAN received her Ph.D. from the University of Miami. She is a specialist in Latin American and Caribbean Art and teaches classes in Pre-Columbian, Colonial, Spanish, and Contemporary Latin American Art. She lectures frequently on Latin American Art and has curated numerous exhibitions. Her most recent work has been with Latin American women and Cuban exile artists, for whom she has written numerous catalogs and articles. She is the author of *The Virgin of the Andes: Art and Ritual in Colonial Cuzco* (Grassfield, 1995) and is the Miami correspondent for *Art Nexus*.

MARK E. DENACI is Assistant Professor of Contemporary Art History and Critical Theory at St. Lawrence University. He is the author of "The Image of Fetishism: Derrida and the 'Truth' in Art," in *Travelling Concepts III: Memory, Image, Narrative* (ASCA Press, 2003); "Bloodletting," in *Travelling Concepts II: Meaning, Frame and Metaphor* (ASCA Press, 2002). He has curated several exhibitions, among them *Embracing Eatonville* (photographs by Dawoud Bey, Lonnie Graham, Carrie Mae Weems, and Deborah Willis).

JORGE FEBLES is Chair of the Department of World Languages at the University of North Florida (Jacksonville), where he also teaches courses on Spanish American literature and culture. Febles was Professor at Western Michigan University from 1980 to 2006. His publications are on the area of Latin American and Cuban literature and a substantial portion of his research output centers on the works of José Martí, Matías Montes-Huidobro, Alfonso Hernández Catá, and Roberto G. Fernández. Together with Armando González-Pérez (Marquette University), Febles edits the literary journal *Caribe*.

JORGE J. E. GRACIA holds the Samuel P. Capen Chair in Philosophy at the University of Buffalo, and is State University of New York Distinguished Professor. He has been president of several philosophical societies and has held grants and fellowships from the Canada Council, the National Endowment for the Humanities, and the New York Council for the Humanities. Among his recent works are *Images of Thought: Philosophical Interpretations of Carlos Estévez's Art* (2009); *Latinos in America: Philosophy and Social Identity* (2007); *Identity, Memory, and Diaspora: Voices of Cuban-American Artists, Writers, and Philosophers*, coeditor (2008); *Surviving Race, Ethnicity, and Nationality* (2005); *Old Wine in New Skins* (2003); *How Can We Know What God Means?* (2001); and *Hispanic/Latino Identity* (2000). He is the author of more than 250 articles and two dozen edited volumes.

IRAIDA H. LÓPEZ is Associate Professor of Spanish and Convener of Foreign Languages at the School of American and International Studies of Ramapo College of New Jersey, where she teaches Spanish, Latin American Studies, and Spanish American literature. Lopez is the author of *La autobiografía hispana contemporánea en los Estados Unidos: a través del caleidoscopio* (Mellen Press, 2001). The manuscript won the Best Dissertation and Research Award of the Latino Studies Section of the Latin American Studies Association. Iraida's work on Cuban, Cuban-American, and Latino(a) literature and culture has appeared in the *Revista Iberoamericana, Hispanic Review, Letras femeninas, Cuban Studies, Revista Interamericana,* and the *Michigan Quarterly Review*, among other journals.

WILLIAM LUIS is Chancellor's Professor of Spanish at Vanderbilt University. His books include *Juan Francisco Manzano: Autobiografía y otros escritos del esclavo poeta* (2007); *Lunes de Revolución: Literatura y cultura en los primeros años de la Revolución Cubana* (2003); *Culture and Customs of Cuba* (2001); *Dance Between Two Cultures: Latino Caribean Literature Written in the United States* (1997); and, *Literary Bondage: Slavery in Cuban Narrative* (1990). Luis has edited and coedited several works, among them, *Antología: Poesía hispano-caribeña escrita en los Estados Unidos;* with Ann González, *Modern Latin American Fiction Writers*, First Series (1992, 94); with Edmundo Desnoes *Los dispositivos en la flor* (1981). His publications are in nineteenth- and twentieth-century Latin American literature, Contemporary Spanish American, Caribbean, Afro-Hispanic, and Latino literatures. He is the editor of the *Afro-Hispanic Review* (Vanderbilt University).

ADRIANA MÉNDEZ RODENAS is Professor of Spanish and International Studies at the University of Iowa where she currently serves as Director of the Caribbean, Diaspora, and Atlantic Studies Program. Her books include *Severo Sarduy: el neobarroco de la transgresión* (UNAM, 1983); *Cuba en su imagen—Historia e identidad en la literatura cubana* (Verbum, 2002); and *Gender and Nationalism in Colonial Cuba: The Travels of Santa Cruz y Montalvo, Condesa de Merlin* (Vanderbilt University Press, 1998). The latter was also edited as *La Comtesse Merlin: Les esclaves dans les colonies espagnoles, accompagné d'autres textes sur l'esclavage à Cuba* (Editions l'Harmattan, 2006). Her essays on travel narrative and Cuban and Cuban American literature have appeared in *New Literary History, Ciberletras, Estudios, Poligrafías, Encuentro,* and *MLN.*

ANDREA O'REILLY HERRERA is Professor of Literature and Director of Ethnic Studies at the University of Colorado at Colorado Springs. Her publications include *ReMembering Cuba: Legacy of a Diaspora,* an edited collection of testimonials drawn from the Cuban exile community and their children residing in the United States (University of Texas Press, 2001), and her award-winning novel and play *The Pearl of the Antilles* (Bilingual/Review Press, 2001). She has edited a collection of essays entitled *Cuba: Idea of a Nation Displaced* (State University of New York Press, 2007), and coedited a textbook, *The Matrix Reader: Examining the Dynamics of Oppression and Privilege* (McGraw Hill, 2007). Her book *"Setting the Tent against the House": Cuban Artists in Diaspora* (University of Texas Press) is forthcoming.

GUSTAVO PÉREZ FIRMAT is David Feinson Professor of Humanities at Columbia University. His scholarly books include *Literature and Liminality* (1986), *The Cuban Condition* (1989), and *Tongue Ties* (2003). Among his creative works are *Next Year in Cuba* (1997), *Cincuenta Lecciones de exilio y (des)exilio* (2000), a collection of vignettes on language, and a novel, *Anything But Love* (2000). His poetry has appeared in collections such as *Carolina Cuban* (1986), *Equivocaciones* (1989), and *Bilingual Blues* (1995). His 1994 *Life on the Hyphen*, an examination of Cuban culture in the United States during the first half of the twentieth century, served to create what is today the field of Cuban-American studies. He is a member of the American Academy of Arts and Sciences and has been the recipient of fellowships from the NEH, the ACLS, and the Guggenheim Foundation. His latest poetry collection is *Scar Tissue* (2005).

ELIANA RIVERO is Professor of Spanish in the Department of Spanish and Portuguese at the University of Arizona in Tucson. She has authored and/or coedited six scholarly books, and has published numerous chapters in books, review essays, notes, bibliographies, collection entries, and testimonial writings, on topics ranging from Caribbean authors to U.S. Latina identity construction. Rivero is coeditor, with Tey Diana Rebolledo, of *Infinite Divisions: An Anthology of Chicana Literature* (University of Arizona Press, 1993); and *Siete Poetas* with Chicana writer Margarita Cota Cárdenas. More recently, she coedited *Telling To Live: Latina Feminist Testimonios* (Duke University Press, 2001). Her latest book is a bilingual collection of her essays on Cuban-American topics, *Discursos desde la diáspora* (Aduana Vieja, 2005).

INDEX

Q

R